THE GENDER DIVISION
OF WELFARE

The Impact of the British
and German Welfare States

differentiation and social inequality. The book traces
the consequences of different welfare state and social
policy arrangements for women and men and the
households in which they live. Mary Daly examines the
British and German welfare states showing that both
countries differ markedly in the measures they have
instituted in various areas. These include the support
of families with children, as well as policies established
for the provision of care for the ill and aged. The
author investigates how each of these hugely influential
welfare state models affects financial relations between
women and men and the extent to which women and
men can participate in the labour market and the
family.

Mary Daly is Professor of Sociology at the Queen's
University of Belfast. Previously, she worked at the
Georg-August Universität, Göttingen, Germany, and
the European University Institute, Florence, Italy. Mary
Daly has completed a number of projects for the
European Commission and is a member of a number of
international networks on gender and the welfare state.
Her many publications include *Women and Poverty*
(1989), and *European Homelessness: The Rising Tide*
(1992).

D1340590

THE GENDER DIVISION OF WELFARE

The Impact of the British and German Welfare States

MARY DALY

The Queen's University of Belfast

CAMBRIDGE
UNIVERSITY PRESS

PUBLISHED BY THE PRESS SYNDICATE OF THE UNIVERSITY OF CAMBRIDGE
The Pitt Building, Trumpington Street, Cambridge, United Kingdom

CAMBRIDGE UNIVERSITY PRESS
The Edinburgh Building, Cambridge CB2 2RU, UK   http://www.cup.cam.ac.uk
40 West 20th Street, New York, ny 10011–4211, USA   http://www.cup.org
10 Stamford Road, Oakleigh, 3166, Australia   http://www.cup.edu.au
Ruiz de Alarcón 13, 28014, Madrid, Spain

© Mary Daly 2000

First published 2000

Printed in Singapore by Green Giant Press Pte Ltd

Typeface Baskerville (*Adobe*) 10/12 pt.   *System* QuarkXPress®   [RM]

A catalogue record for this book is available from the British Library

National Library of Australia Cataloguing in Publication data
Daly, Mary
The gender division of welfare: the impact of the British
and German welfare states
Bibliography
Includes index
ISBN 0 521 62331 6.
ISBN 0 521 62621 8 (pb.).
1. Welfare state. 2. Public welfare – Germany – Sex
differences. 3. Public welfare – Great Britain – Sex
differences. 4. Social policy. 5. Equality. I. Title.

Library of Congress Cataloguing in Publication data
Daly, Mary
The gender division of welfare: the impact of the British
and German welfare states / Mary Daly.
        p.   cm.
Includes bibliographical references and index.
ISBN 0-521-62331-6 (Hardbound: alk. Paper). – ISBN 0-521-62621-8
(pbk.: alk. Paper)
1. Public welfare – Great Britain. 2. Public welfare – Germany.
3. Women – Great Britain – Economic conditions. 4. Women –
Germany – Economic conditions. 5. Income distribution – Great Britain.
6. Income distribution – Germany. 7. Welfare state. I. Title.
HV245.D27   2000
361.941—dc21   99–41039

ISBN 0 521 62331 6 hardback
ISBN 0 521 62621 8 paperback

Contents

Tables

Figures

Acknowledgements

In terms of data sources and related assistance, I should first like to thank Hans Peter Blossfeld and Götz Rohwer, who were invaluable in gaining access to the German Socio-economic Panel while I was a researcher at the European University Institute in Florence. For access to the Family Expenditure Survey, I acknowledge the assistance of the Data Archive at the University of Essex and thank them and the Deutsches Institut für Wirtschaft for permission to use their data.

During the course of my writing this book, part of which was spent at the European University Institute, I benefited from discussions with many people and from participation in many seminars. I especially thank Colin Crouch and Yossi Shavit for their constructive responses to my work. The book was completed while I was a staff member of the Georg-August Universität in Göttingen. I would like to thank my colleagues at both the Institut für Sozialpolitik and ZENS for their responses to the various papers that I presented at seminars and for their friendly welcome to Germany. Among these I wish to make special mention of Jens Borchert. This would have been a much more difficult task without the intellectual and personal support of friends and colleagues like Johan DeDeken, Bernhard Ebbinghaus, Pauline Ginnety, Barbara Maclennan, Axel West Pedersen, Carmen Sarasua Garcia, Kirsten Scheiwe and Anne Sinnott.

Many other people made a valuable contribution to the work by reading drafts and generously sharing their ideas and knowledge. Jane Lewis deserves special mention in this regard. Other people who helped and whom I thank include Dorothea Herreiner, Stephen Jenkins and Katherine Rake.

I also acknowledge the helpful comments of the anonymous reader for Cambridge University Press and the assistance there of Phillipa McGuinness and Paul Watt.

Introduction

Postwar Europe did not have a great variety of welfare state models available. The choice essentially ranged between the Beveridgean vision of universal but low-paying state support on the one hand and the model of meritocratic social insurance on the other. These two poles encompass more or less the main postwar settlements around the welfare state in Europe. Great Britain and the Scandinavian countries embody versions of the Beveridgean ideal, whereas (West) Germany is the classic social insurance welfare state. Looked at in their historical context, the postwar welfare states were remarkable by virtue of the degree to which they institutionalized broad-ranging state intervention. Over the course of time welfare institutions carved out for themselves a niche between the market and the family. Among other processes, the definition of what constitutes family and 'private' social relations came more and more to be influenced by welfare state and other public policies. It is no exaggeration to say, therefore, that in the late twentieth century what it means to be a woman or a man, married or single, young or old, is crucially influenced by the welfare state.

Although contemporary debates may lead one to believe otherwise, the postwar models have proved enduring. For the struggles that are being played out around the welfare state in our time are essentially contests over the viability of the seasoned social policy institutions. As the old settlements begin to give way, some assessment of the outcomes associated with the postwar European welfare arrangements is overdue. The British and (West) German welfare state models are put under the spotlight in this work.[1] Not only are these two of the most important social policy formations historically but they are also perceived to define more or less the range of choices available for the future. In identifying important constituents of and outcomes associated with these two classic

1

state/society models, this book goes in search of a key aspect of European contemporary history. The point of time at which to undertake an appraisal exercise merits careful deliberation. History is extremely important in this context: welfare state models require one or two generations to come to fruition. There is also the consideration that the 1980s represents a watershed for both of these, as well as other welfare states. In the British case Margaret Thatcher initiated in the early 1980s a series of reforms which would over the course of time pull the rug from under the Beveridgean postwar welfare state model. In Germany the catalyst for significant welfare state change would be the fall of the Berlin wall in 1989 and the subsequent reunification process. For these reasons, the mid-1980s suggests itself as an appropriate period from which to take stock of these postwar welfare state models, and it is in this period that the empirical parts of the present work are set. But from which vantage point should the models be considered?

The class-related settlements accompanying different European welfare states are by now familiar. What is less often appreciated is that other integrating mechanisms are as instrumental in sustaining advanced welfare societies as those deriving from interests around capital. Gender relations, embracing not just the relations between women and men but also the series of accommodations between the state, the family and the market, form a core such mechanism. As much as the welfare state involves a settlement with markets and politics, so too does it set about securing particular types of arrangements pertaining to the family and relations between women and men. In its location between the market and the family, the one 'public', the other 'private', the welfare state is ideally placed to mediate relations among individuals whose lives are woven in a continuous interplay of home, work and society. By granting access to its 'own' resources and through its influence on other channels of distribution and participation, it can ameliorate or exacerbate inequalities. The welfare state is, therefore, a powerful agent in shaping all forms of social stratification, not least that between women and men. There are of course variations, and it is these that fire the imagination of this work. For European societies do not simply line up along a one-dimensional continuum of more or less public welfare and, relatedly, more or less inequality. The situation is more interesting than this. Interweaving and competing sets of influences lead not only to relatively complex (and sometimes, indeed, contradictory) policies but to multi-layered outcomes also. A comparative, empirical enquiry is therefore called for.

Feminists have made many claims about the welfare state. It has been accused of being the embodiment of male interests and a vehicle for male exploitation of women, just as it has been hailed as exercising a liberating function in freeing women from dependence on male incomes. Much of this debate has taken place without the benefit of concrete knowledge of how welfare states actually affect resource distribution and opportunities for participation between women and men. The present work places itself firmly within this knowledge gap. Two sets of questions drive the book. The first is conceptual, relating to how welfare states can be understood and theorized as an arena of gender stratification. What is it about the make-up of social programs and their relations to other aspects of social structure that may embody differential treatment of women and men, and how can this be accounted for theoretically? Posing this kind of question leads to a conceptualization of the welfare state as one of the most important mechanisms structuring social inequalities, in its own right and by virtue of its relations with other social structures. The second question is empirical, pertaining to the identifiable gender-relevant outcomes of welfare state programs and taxation. These are approached in this work as issues to be observed through an examination of women and men's relations to the main institutions of production and consumption. The focus here is on how particular types of welfare state arrangement affect the distribution of resources and opportunities between women and men. Using two survey data sets – for (West) Germany the third wave of the German Socio-economic Panel and for the United Kingdom the Family Expenditure Survey, both pertaining to 1985/86 – I examine how men and women are linked to the state, the family and the market for income and participation purposes. I am especially interested in identifying processes, seeking to decipher not only the relevant effects of certain types of policies but the very conditions under which such policies operate and are themselves sustained.

Theoretical Origins and Orientation

The disciplinary 'home' of this work is the comparative welfare state literature. This body of scholarship is to be valued for both its focus on the institutional properties of welfare states and its cross-national comparative frameworks of analysis. Scholarship here has spoken to the stages through which Western welfare states have travelled on the road to their current distributional order, the class struggles that have attended these orders, the structural webs connecting states and markets, and the influence of a range of political and economic institutions across societies. In recent years welfare state research has strongly favoured a comparative approach. Contemporary scholarship is dominated by efforts to typologize welfare states on the basis of both their programmatic distinctiveness and the nature of their insertion into national political and institutional structures (Esping-Andersen 1990; Leibfried 1990). Comparison of policy regimes now looms large in a literature that models national policy logics by means of ideal types.

The literature on the welfare state is distinguished by a number of emphases. One of the most long-standing fields of study has sought the shaping influences of social policies and located them especially in the political engagements that accompanied the foundation and development of welfare states. Argument and counter-argument have been vigorous – debate bouncing back and forth between structural factors (often conceived as general background conditions or stages of economic development) and political agency (which treats of a gamut of actors from organized labour through employers, state bureaucracy and political parties). Second, and partly as a consequence, the market and the politics associated with it have been privileged among contingent institutional domains. In essence, the policy dynamic is seen to lie on the state–market intersection, just as the interests animated by social policies are located primarily in struggles over production and associated political identities. Third, the welfare state has tended to be viewed relatively narrowly. Not only is it normally treated as the dependent variable but it has been conceptualized and operationalized most often as social expenditures or the institutional elements of social policy. Together these spell a particular approach to the welfare state: a product of organized economic interest groups, to be understood in monetary or institutional terms, the main significance of which lies in its capacity to either uphold or modify relations of class or economic power. As always, imbalances and even outright neglect of certain issues provide the impulse to further study.

One characteristic of existing work is a set of approaches that all too easily relegate the family and non-market relations to the margins of analysis. We know that certain types of family policies tend to coexist with particular welfare state forms. The origins and development paths of many of these family policies are also familiar. But much of existing work appears content to treat family-related policies, and family forms themselves, as derivatives, by-products of other processes. To the extent that the family has been kept on the sidelines of comparative welfare state analysis, intra- and inter-familial relations as well as relations between the family and welfare state remain an unelaborated domain of scholarship. This is a pity, for such linkages can introduce a number of new dimensions to the discussion of welfare state and societal forms. They serve, for instance, to reveal how the activities and outcomes of both family and welfare state, which have key functions in common, intersect. This in turn provides a route to a better understanding of how the well-being of individuals and families is secured. Furthermore, the family-related dimensions of policies reveal some of the more hidden effects of public policy. If we are to understand public systems of economic and social welfare, we need to trace their effects beyond the front door, as it were. A third insight concerns variations. With social policy regimes generally conceived of as the systematic set of arrangements governing the relations between politics and markets, the literature is fairly silent about the kinds of variation we might expect in the family-related components of social policies. This conceals vital aspects of the public/private divide in society and hides the extent to which welfare states foster and rely upon private solidarity. A key goal of the present work is to identify in its own right the policy stance taken by these two welfare states in relation to the family or household and to problematize any variation found in the context of how different models of social policy affect gender relations.

While women's relationship to the welfare state has become a popular field of study, a comparative perspective on gender has been the trademark of a fairly small, if growing, group of scholars (Lewis and Ostner 1991; Leira 1992; Lewis 1992; Orloff 1994; Sainsbury 1996). Uncovering the fact that women and the welfare state have something of a special relationship, this work has pinpointed an inferior position for women as an apparent regularity of the welfare state. It has demonstrated that the conventional understanding of the welfare state falters when confronted by the complexity of welfare systems that differentiate between women and men, and that in reality arrangements for public welfare tend to be secured by a combination of, largely female, paid and unpaid work. Feminist scholarship has also, if somewhat selectively, investigated the sets of male–female relations that are implied by different welfare-related arrangements. However, even if the earlier neglect of this aspect of cross-national variation has been overcome, we still lack models of how particular effects occur and theoretical terms with which to imagine them. To the extent that work on gendering the welfare state has not produced theoretical explanations, the interconnections of state and market remain the cradle of theory-building. As a result, gender-based processes, either in their own right or in association with other interests, still play an insignificant role in theoretical understanding of the welfare state.

These observations serve as the rationale for the present work, which advances a particular line of analysis towards the gender dimension of contemporary welfare states. Three features characterize its approach. The first point of reference is how welfare states embody principles of differentiation between women and men in the manner in which claims to public resources are established, managed and treated. This pertains to what we might call the content of welfare and invites us to analyse the existing institutional structures and normative design underpinning welfare and taxation provisions in the two states to be compared. While I shall isolate out the welfare state for analytic purposes, the second feature of my approach is a focus on state–family interrelations. Here I am not so much interested in challenging the old argument of the family as handmaiden to the state but rather in investigating how the interaction between the state and the family is organized around processes of differentiation, between individuals within households and among households themselves. The third element of my approach holds that welfare states have outcomes that are gender-stratificational in nature. Relevant outcomes, I argue, are to be uncovered in how welfare states affect relations of inequality between women and men, both directly in terms of how they distribute their own resources and indirectly in the manner in which they respond to inequalities arising elsewhere in the social system.

A Gender Paradigm

This work is set in the tradition of studying gender relations at the level of historically specific and concrete institutional structures and practices. As a form of middle-range theorizing this is less abstract, resting upon investigation of the gendered processes inhering in specific domains. Such an approach is part of a trend away from very general or abstract theorizing that seeks to elaborate patriarchy as a property of social systems. It is today the predominant idiom in gender studies. Macro-theoretical work is more or less seen to have reached an impasse, and therefore a shift of emphasis has taken place from patriarchy to the more middle-range concept of gender. The kind of shift involved is well described by Acker: 'from asking about how the subordination of women is produced, maintained and changed we move to questions about how gender is involved in structures and processes that previously have been conceived as having nothing to do with gender' (1989: 238). In other words, probing the embeddedness of gender relations in particular domains is perceived as the best way of discovering how relevant structures and practices reproduce differences and inequalities between women and men.

With 'gender' so central to this work, it begs a clear definition. Now very widely used, the term lacks sharpness, resembling more a label than a concept. Treated as a category of sociological analysis, gender refers to inequality processes and relations that create, sustain and change systems of social organization (Anderson 1996: 733). Such practices of inequality are embedded in social structures and find an expression in social, political and economic aspects of relations between women and men. To clarify these it is first helpful to differentiate sex from gender. Sex as a biological distinction provides a basic building-block from which social processes act to mould socio-economic and other differences between women and men.[2] But sex by itself is an insufficient guide to socially constructed differences. This leads to the identification of a second building-block for gender in sex-differentiated family statuses and roles. This is not to claim that gender is limited to the family but rather that the assignment of differing family statuses and activities to women and men is one of the main roots of gender differentiation and one of the main practices reproducing gender relations. Third, gender is distinctive in involving a particular ranking of characteristics and activities so that those associated with men are normally given greater value (Benería and Roldán 1987: 11–12). Consideration of ranking evokes hierarchy and behoves us to make an analytical distinction between difference and inequality.[3] Men and women may well differ from each other in relation to a particular resource or social situation, but whether this amounts to gender inequality or not in any given social context is a separate question.

Empirical work demands precise definitions and at the same time sets clear limits to the analysis. This book investigates inequalities and differences between women and men associated with their family status and relations. As it proceeds I shall turn the empirical lens on gender-related processes as they are to be observed in economic relations and risks associated with family roles and relations (for both women and men). Some empirical questions will be asked to identify these aspects of gender in practice: What patterns of economic and social relations are associated with male and female marital statuses? Which obligations attend motherhood and fatherhood and how are these affected by welfare state provisions? How do welfare and taxation policies interconnect with women and men's familial ties to affect their general economic and social roles and opportunities?

The way gender is here conceived has a number of merits. For a start, it offers a relatively clear guide to the empirical investigation of gender-related processes in terms of a three-level model: first in relation to *sex*; second in relation to *male and female family statuses*; and third at the *level and type of economic activity* in terms of how family-related roles are associated with income procurement and financial relations. Second, this schema can embrace in a comprehensive way key aspects of the lives of men as well as of women. Third, it is an embedded perspective, conceiving of women and men in the context of their social relations. The emphasis throughout will be on situating individuals and families within their broader relational setting, observing exchanges and trade-offs imposed by the interaction of state, family and market. The empirical analyses will focus, therefore, not just on individuals but also on the households and families of which they are a part. Fourth, the perspective devotes attention to the welfare state–family relation as a crucial filter through which gendered effects occur. To the extent that this relation varies, gender-related outcomes can be expected to vary. For all its merits, this way of conceiving of gender also imposes some constraints. In particular, in leading us in the direction of prioritizing economic relations around family-related roles and relations as either sources or manifestations of gender-related inequalities, it diverts us from differences among classes of women and men. This is a trade-off that I make but reluctantly, and mainly in the interests of going somewhere new. Investigating the economic structures and processes that underpin welfare states' relations with different family forms and the associated relations of women and men over the life course can, I believe, reveal important and hitherto under-explored aspects of how gender relations operate and are reproduced.

Conceptual Focus: the Relations between Gender and the Welfare State

As Korpi (1980: 297), rightly observes, the analysis of how state measures affect distributive processes requires a theoretical conception of what these processes are and how they function. Here the welfare state is approached as an agent shaping gender relations. This is not meant to imply either that women and men respond or react to welfare provisions in a uniform way or that the welfare state is the only agent shaping gender relations. But it is to accord the welfare state its rightful role as a, if not the, key social agent mediating the relation between home and market. It will become obvious that the present work sets the welfare state in a broader nexus of its relations with the family/household and the market. These are seen as spheres that interact in key ways to the extent that individual life courses and well-being are constituted at the intersection of state, family and labour market. The interrelations can be graphically represented as in Figure 0.1.

The interface between the state, family and market can be conceptualized in terms of the nature of social policies and services. That is, the three domains are connected by the structure and content of social policies and programs. The substance identified in the shaded parts of Figure 0.1 is those areas of social policies that define the interface in each case. The connections between state policies and each of the other two institutions on their own are fairly obvious. Family policies, usually defined as measures oriented to the support of families with children, connect the state and the family, while the labour- and economy-related aspects of policies configure the linkages between the state and the

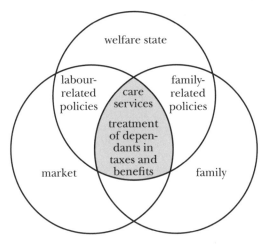

Figure 0.1 Interrelations between welfare state, family and market

market. The conjunction between state, family and market is perhaps the most complex. In this regard, I identify as crucial the extent of service provision and income compensation provisions for work- and caring-related activities and the construction of male–female relations that inheres in cash transfers, taxation and social services. These lead to the heart of welfare states' objectives, variation in benefit generosity, program type and general organization allowing us to judge the relative priority given to poverty alleviation, income security and income redistribution. There is probably no better way to uncover how the state stacks individuals and groups vis-à-vis each other on the resources' hierarchy.

It should be clear from Figure 0.1 that the three institutional spheres are treated as interactive. Among other things, this enables us to conceive of welfare state provisions as both 'classed' and 'gendered'. Provisions are 'classed' to the extent that they articulate income security with labour market position and political relations deriving from employment (Shaver 1991: 149). Welfare provisions are 'gendered' in the manner in which they connect income security to family status and relations between women and men. But this separation between policies – their nature, sphere of operation and effects – has limits. The most important aspects of Figure 0.1 for our purpose are those in the domain where state, family and labour market intersect. This is where class and gender interact. Here nest the policy constituents and processes through which the three institutional spheres affect the distribution of resources and opportunities in general and between women and men in particular. An overriding objective of this work is to thematize these relations by substantiating the processes that bring them to life and the structural impacts they engender. Since the class-related components and outcomes of welfare ring the more familiar chime, this study gives analytic priority to gender. But it treats gender neither in isolation nor as an independent structure. Welfare states are not neutral economically, and indeed by focusing on the material aspects and outcomes of the welfare state, I have made, an essential, if background, feature of the present work how gender and class are enmeshed in practice.

The Comparative Framework

The first promise of comparison in this book is the discovery of how the relationship between gender and the welfare state proceeds under different institutional and ideological conditions. The comparative framework pits against each other two welfare systems that are typically represented as hailing from very different welfare state 'families'. Germany's is a model which, through a reliance on a particularistic form of social insurance, rewards a lifetime's employment and ties benefit entitlement closely to labour market status and earnings. For Schmidt (1989), Germany's is a policy of the middle way, having a unique market-oriented and étatist complexion. The German welfare state is strongly biased towards compensation and security, wherein entitlement to social insurance benefits is something akin to a property right. Social rights in Germany are embedded in a hierarchical order that mirrors the divisions and differentials prevailing in the market and civil society. The British welfare state, in contrast, commits itself only to a low level of security through a set of flat-rate and generally meagre benefits. Needs-based provision dominates but in a fashion which over time has made for a complex amalgam of programs and services. Its universal health service and a relatively wide array of publicly provided social services lend Britain a certain 'social democratic' character, but in its approach to income support and compensation, this welfare state increasingly follows a neo-liberal line. The long reach of the market is reflected in policies that encourage employment participation for all. The state is, however, prepared to ameliorate the consequences of market and family failure, guaranteeing low-level payments under fairly strict conditions. Britain's particular combination of policies frustrates classification: for some it is 'institutional collective' (Jones 1985), for others 'liberal' (Esping-Andersen 1990), for still others 'liberal collective' (Ginsburg 1992).

So, a first axis of comparison is the differing models of public welfare that prevail in the two national settings. But, this is not a comparison of two totally different cases, for the contrast between the guiding logics of how the German and British welfare systems relate to the market and their treatment of familial well-being is far from complete. In fact, given their strong market orientation, the two welfare states share a problem in how to secure the well-being of those who lack the necessary productive career, the majority of whom are women with family commitments. A second shared problem is how the family can be integrated into the national distributional order. In some respects, there is a strong similarity in how each resolves these problems. Both tend to interact with the family through the persona of the productive worker, who is treated also as a (potential) head of household. Moreover, both welfare states are marked by an emphasis on the independence of the family. Public provision of family-related services is low in both, and neither could be said to take an interventionist stance in relation to the family.

Comparison of these social policy models also promises dimensions of variation and ambiguity, however. Characterizing Germany's policy stance on the family as 'conservative' and Britain's as 'liberal' is little more than description. Competing undercurrents make for a more complex representation of policies within and a more elaborated comparison between these two welfare states. In Germany, an emphasis on the state as a guarantor of security established through the market is paralleled by a set of commitments around the support of families. Social programs there are guided by the principle of subsidiarity whereby priority is accorded to the smaller unit over the wider community or state. Demarcating lines of responsibility and boundaries between spheres, the subsidiarity principle places the family as the first unit of social and economic support and circumscribes the degree to which the state and public organizations in general are to intervene in it. Upholding these commitments makes for a complex interaction, and considerable tension, between different elements of social provision and between individual and collective well-being. The treatment of women and men and of gender relations in Germany, therefore, flows from the inherent tensions between status maintenance and subsidiarity, the protection of the individual and collective good, and the necessity to manage carefully their realization in practice.

As the birthplace of the social citizenship ideals that came to fruition elsewhere (Scandinavia), Britain's welfare state is something of a hybrid, having no clear position or formulaic impact on the family or gender relations. At the centre of this model stands the contractual individual, who is increasingly expected to be responsible for his or her own welfare. The British welfare state encourages provision through the market and other private channels as the main means to security. Moreover, there is no formal commitment to the protection of the family as in Germany. Britain's configuration of law and practice, especially its marital property law, operates to quite a strict principle of individual rights, with marriage less privileged as an institution of private maintenance for adults as compared with Germany. However, the British welfare state does underpin its 'social contract' with a commitment to alleviating need or want, and it is from this that its treatment of the family, and of its individual members who cannot achieve welfare through the market, largely flows. Women's welfare and gender relations are therefore constituted by another type of tension in Britain: between basic provision from the state according to a logic of poverty alleviation, and the encouragement of more substantial provision through market and private channels.

The current fashion in comparative work on the welfare state is typology-building. My objective is not in any way to 'complete' existing typologies by adding in gender considerations. If anything, this book continues the trend away from large typologies and binary matrices in favour of research less concerned with neatness of fit and more with the messy and stubborn practices encountered in social reality. In the light of contemporary developments, the merits of a two-country framework deserve emphasis. Comparison of a large number of countries risks superficiality, tending to compress dimensions of variation into universal categories. Working with a small set of units allows us to examine national patterns in greater detail and to focus attention on the complexities of small-scale as well as large-scale variations. In the context of research on the welfare state, studying two models in detail releases us from the constraints of 'ideal types' which have been over-relied on, in recent work especially. It is, in addition, timely to (re)focus on micro-level outcomes, for practically all of the recent welfare state typologizing has not only rested on macro characteristics but has failed to integrate micro-level outcomes systematically into the framework. A two-country comparison has other more general merits. The categories of comparison can be as detailed as preferred and, at the same time, we retain the advantages of a cross-national focus. This adds a certain degree of rigour by forcing concepts to travel across national frontiers, and compels us to develop a more complex argumentation.

Organization of Chapters

The book is organized in three parts. The first sets out the theoretical background and outlines the guiding conceptual framework. The second part examines the two welfare state policy models in detail, while the third empirically identifies their outcomes.

Part I has two chapters. The first reviews different theoretical approaches to the welfare state. Designed in part as an introduction to how the welfare state has been treated in sociological and political science thought, it offers a concise overview of where the main approaches within the literature have placed explanatory emphasis and how they have conceptualized the political settlements around welfare. Having identified some general strengths and shortcomings, I argue that the literature has, in a particular and problematic way, marginalized the family and gender as analytical categories. Following a discussion of the main implications of this, the remainder of the chapter considers some conceptual issues that arise by bringing both the family and gender into the picture. This critical scrutiny leads to an outline of a theoretical framework that guides us into the next chapter.

Chapter 2 undertakes to put flesh on this theoretical skeleton. The accent here is on the empirical side of existing work. To open, I examine which characteristics have been employed to assay the welfare state by some of the more empirically oriented literature. Existing indicators and concepts are reviewed and critiqued, especially for their capacity to reveal those components of welfare state provision that connote a gendered imprint in policy and in turn lead to gendered outcomes. A more detailed discussion follows on two issues seen to require clarification: the utility of a regime-based approach, and the links between welfare state structures and outcomes. The final section of the chapter develops the study's conceptual framework.

Chapters 3 and 4 apply this framework and together form the second part of the book. After a brief historical overview, Chapter 3 carries out a review of policies and provisions relevant to gender in each national setting. Built around the question of which type of family- and gender-relevant policies characterize the two welfare states, it aims at laying bare both the policy configuration in each and the nature of the cross-national comparison. Axes of comparison in the first part of the chapter include the degree of support provided for family care activities through service provision, cash transfers and taxation. The particular institutional and normative imprint of cash transfer and taxation policies is then put under the spotlight, on the basis of the approach taken to male and female risks, the construction of entitlement implicit in income maintenance and tax programs, and the treatment of different types of household. To end, the chapter sets out some propositions about likely sex- and gender-related outcomes in the context of structural and normative variations in social provision in the two welfare states.

Chapter 4 investigates how the two cash transfer systems operate in practice. It begins the empirical analysis proper and its main goal is to ascertain how the social policy models described in Chapter 3 actually function in real life. In particular, it tests the degree to which the two sets of cash transfer arrangements embody systematic differentiations between women and men as individuals and as heads of families or households. For the purpose of such analyses the 'transfer relation' is decomposed into three elements: access to benefits; the structuring of claims; and transfer size. As the chapter proceeds, I shall elaborate the conditions under which transfer programs can be depicted as gender-differentiated or stratified. I begin with individuals, tracing the reach of the two transfer mechanisms and identifying the factors that significantly predict both transfer access and level. A similar line of analysis is then undertaken for households.

Having clarified how the two transfer systems work, in the remainder of the empirical analyses, consisting of three subsequent chapters, I consider outcomes in one form or another.

The main focus of Chapter 5 is on income inequalities and how these are affected by both the state and the family or household. After investigating the composition of women and men's income packages, I identify the extent of horizontal redistribution effected by public policies. In the context of transfer-related and other differences in how the two welfare states are organized, I examine economic inequalities between women and men and identify the degree to which the welfare state is implicated in the redistribution of income. A central interest is how individual well-being and financial relations within families or households are affected by income maintenance and taxation provisions. In the context of a comparison between income secured oneself and that ideally available through other members of one's household, I then move on to consider the degree to which the family or household can make up financial gaps between women and men. The final part of the chapter considers the situation of households, investigating especially if and how transfer and taxation arrangements affect the comparative level of living of women and men's households.

Chapter 6 turns to another vital matter for welfare states – poverty. Searching for the sex- and gender-based structure of poverty across a range of measures, it compares household and individual poverty rates. It also investigates how the incidence of poverty, and its sex- and gender-based distribution, is affected by the transfer and taxation provisions of the welfare state. One of the main themes of the chapter is the specific effect of different types of welfare state program on women and men's risk of poverty. The chapter also undertakes to identify, through regression and other modes of analyses, how sex and gender among other factors are implicated in the distribution of individual and household poverty. The final part of the chapter compares the roles of both the state and the family in ameliorating the risk of poverty.

Chapter 7 occupies itself with the welfare state's effect on the set of opportunities available to women and men around marriage, the family and the labour market. In the process it seeks to uncover some of the conditions sustaining and the constraints surrounding each model of welfare, for women especially. The first part of the chapter examines what might be called the financial interior of the family. In essence, the focus is on the patterns of income reliance and intra-familial dependencies that co-exist with various types of welfare state model. The nature of support obligations and dependency relations characterizing a range of family situations in each national setting is examined. The financial costs and benefits associated with marriage are next subjected to analysis. The ensuing part of the chapter considers how, in the context of their current circumstances, women could be expected to fare in certain risk situations. Through a series of hypothetical exercises, it examines especially the income risk associated with lone motherhood and marital breakdown for women and men. In an effort to further uncover the extent to which women can or could live without access to male incomes, and hence outside conventional family life, it then goes on to estimate how much of the income loss women can expect to be made up by public and private sources. The situation of existing lone-mother families provides a complement to these analyses.

The concluding chapter develops some of the issues raised by both the theoretical and conceptual discussions and the empirical findings. Moving beyond the detail of the results and of the two countries studied, the discussion in this chapter centres on the impact of welfare state models in general, and these two in particular, on gender relations, the conditions and constraints attaching to each model, and the relevance of gender as a category for sociological analysis, with particular reference to scholarship on the welfare state.

The list of references and two appendices follow. The first appendix describes the two data sources, the missing cases and the main transformations made to the data for the purposes of the analyses. (The copyright holders, the original data producers, the relevant funding agencies and the Data Archive bear no responsibility for the further analysis or interpretation of the data.) The second relates to Chapter 6, detailing the procedures followed for conceptualizing and measuring poverty.

PART I

*Conceptualizing the Relations
between Gender and the
Welfare State*

CHAPTER 1

Theory on the Welfare State: The Place of Gender?

The welfare state embraces all of the major themes in the sociological tradition: the interrelations between social action and social structure, macro- and micro-oriented analyses, wealth and poverty, power and inequality, social stratification, class, status and gender. Little wonder, then, that it has been studied from many points of departure, nourishing a formidable literature in sociology, political science and economics. It is to this broad body of work that we turn in this chapter. As well as providing an overview of theoretical thought on the welfare state, the chapter seeks to answer one main question: how in the light of existing work is it possible to account theoretically for differences in the position of women and men vis-à-vis the welfare state? The ultimate objective is to elaborate a theoretical framework that is capable of defining the nature of distributional politics of welfare states in such a way that one can identify and account for the possibility of systematic differences in outcome between women and men.

Two basic tasks structure the chapter, dividing it more or less in half. The first is to investigate how the welfare state has been explained; the second is to explore the treatment of women in scholarship and the role that has been attributed to gender in theoretical approaches to the welfare state. Limitations of space dictate a parsimonious approach, placing beyond reach the breadth and richness of all the scholarship on the welfare state. The relevant literature will be outlined only in broad strokes. The first part of the chapter focuses on what one might call the conventional approaches to the welfare state. It sketches each in brief and considers the configuration of distributional politics that each employs to explain the welfare state. The feminist literature[1] has provided a critique of many of the conventional approaches, although it has not itself produced a counter theory of the welfare state. Rather than

19

setting up a head-to-head contest between the two sets of literature, I proceed in the vein of a dialogue, discussing in the second part of the chapter important theoretical issues raised by inserting the family, women and gender into the welfare state picture. This leads me on to developing the skeleton of a theoretical framework. The main themes will be further developed in the next chapter, which specifies the empirical criteria through which we can explore the gender dimension of contemporary welfare states in a comparative context.

Conventional Approaches to the Welfare State

As a macro-sociological institution, the welfare state is a post–Second World War phenomenon. This state form is set apart not only by the degree to which brute market force is tamed but by the institutionalization of a set of social and economic policies to alter the distribution of power, income and life chances. The contract it embodies between citizen and nation-state is far more broad-ranging than that inscribed in earlier social policies, whether those given life by poor-law provision or the earlier versions of social insurance. The nation-state makes a double and binding commitment through the welfare state: it grants citizens social rights and claims on government, and guarantees to uphold the welfare of the social community (Esping-Andersen 1994: 712). In a narrow sense then, the welfare state may be taken to refer to state measures to protect and enhance citizens' welfare but, more broadly, it represents a particular form of the state itself.

Theoretical developments reflect the emergence of an increasingly broad-ranging conceptualization of the welfare state. In terms of its disciplinary roots, the welfare state was once the province of a group of specialists, mostly drawn from the fields of social policy and social administration, whose concern was to enhance its functioning. Pride of place was held here by the British social administration camp, which in its purest form studied welfare within a pragmatic, empirical and particularizing idiom (Lee and Raban 1988: 3). This branch of study focuses on the substance of social policies and holds the view that social policies are as interesting for how they represent particular responses to needs or social problems as for their outcomes or effects. In the last two or three decades, however, welfare state scholarship has broadened as the field of study was colonized by students of social and political theory (Pierson 1991: 2). This approach is mainly interested in how welfare policies alter the distribution of power, income and life chances. In other words, welfare-related policies and institutions are situated within their broader social, political and economic context(s). This body of work places great emphasis on politics – both formal and informal – as explaining the content and form of the welfare state within and across national settings. It has been the cradle of theory on the welfare state.

Certain modes of theoretical explanation have reigned in different periods. In this (as in virtually every field of enquiry) there has been a procession of competing traditions. But, over time, dominant theoretical frameworks have tended to be overshadowed, albeit sometimes incompletely, by the heir aspirant(s). I recognize three sovereign currents of welfare state theorizing: *structural-functionalist*, *neo-marxist* and the *social interpretation*.[2] No single orthodoxy currently prevails and each has been subject to fairly critical scrutiny from existing and emerging approaches.

Structural-functionalist Approaches

Focusing on the emergence of welfare states, structural-functionalism has yielded two related perspectives: the *logic of industrialism* thesis (Wilensky and Lebaux 1965; Rimlinger 1971; Kerr et al. 1973; Wilensky 1975), and the *political development* approach, which has emerged out of modernization theory (Marshall 1964; Flora and Heidenheimer 1981; Flora 1986; Alber 1988).

In the first, industrialization is seen to lead to a changing social order generating new problems or needs and new responses. A demand for public welfare is created because, as industrialization proceeds, the functional capacity of the traditional institutions, especially the family and community, is diminished. At the same time the expansion of industrial society furnishes a new form of security – the welfare state – which is treated as a more or less automatic response to economic growth and surplus. The emergence of the welfare state is to be explained in terms of the needs it fulfils and the new resources generated by the process of industrialization that simultaneously create a need for it and make it possible. This thesis postulates that industrializing nations are on a convergent course. An evolutionary process shaped by economic and technological growth is rendering societies more similar. This approach construes the welfare state largely in a twofold sense: social security effort (conceptualized in terms of program coverage or relative expenditure levels) and the bureaucratic structure through which social programs are organized. Concepts of state and class, and the tensions between them, are submerged (Quadagno 1987: 112). Neither is there much place here for the market – the significance of the welfare state lying in its functional relationship to the community rather than the economy. Its functionalist underpinnings apart, the *logic of industrialism* thesis proved a poor predictor of causal processes once scholars began to inquire into the origins of specific kinds of social policies and once they focused on the long-run experiences of a large number of industrial nations. What ultimately wreaked greatest havoc on the approach was the destruction of its empirical base, occasioned by the economic changes of the early 1970s that signalled the end of the halcyon years of Keynesian consensus (ibid: 113). No longer could a thesis postulating a symbiotic relationship between industrialization and welfare state growth be sustained.

What then of modernization and the political forces it unleashes? These are the concerns of the *political development* approach formulated initially by Lipset (1969) and Bendix (1970). In what has been called a 'politicized version of the industrialism thesis' (Pierson 1991: 21), the welfare state is seen as a response to two crucial development problems arising in the course of the differentiation process that attends modernization: increasing demands for socio-economic security and demands for socio-economic equality (Alber 1988: 456). The essence of the welfare state for scholars of this persuasion lies in governmental responsibility for security and equality. T. H. Marshall's (1964) work is in key respects sympathetic to a modernization approach, especially his charting of a three-stage development path for citizenship (from civil to political to social). The modernization approach also confers considerable importance on political mobilization and especially that of the emerging working class. Ultimately, though, the welfare state is an integrative mechanism, a response to functional requirements, through its institutionalization of social reform diffusing the demand for further class-based, political action. The typical focus of empirical interest here is the timing and different stages involved in the early life course of welfare legislation. In empirical fact, though, this approach is troubled by its failure to recognize fully whether and how politics makes a difference. No explanatory mechanism exists for how needs are translated into the welfare state as an outcome. Relatedly, critics ask how variations in quality or character among welfare states can be problematized given the assumption of a normal course of development involving several stages (van Kersbergen 1990: 8).

Neo-marxist Explanations of the Welfare State

While society is characterized in the structural-functional perspective by a broad social consensus in which state action is an adjusting mechanism, neo-marxist approaches furnish an account rooted in societal conflict and contradiction. Such dissensus derives ultimately from a fundamental difference of interest between a dominating ruling class or elite and a subordinate or working class. Through an analysis that is at times highly abstract, the welfare state, and in particular the crises that confront it, is depicted as a fundamental flaw in the capitalist heaven. Different views of the role of the welfare state are yielded by the *system-determinist* marxists on the one hand and those who accord a *greater autonomy* to the state on the other.

For *system-determinists* the state and the economy are inextricably intertwined, with the state in the role of handmaiden to the interests of both capitalism and a dominant ruling class or elite. The welfare state furthers these interests either through actions aimed at creating the conditions for optimum capital accumulation or through interventions aimed at legitimizing the capitalist process (O'Connor 1973). The social control functions of the welfare state are emphasized: welfare regulates the labour force and the poor and its emergence is linked to the instabilities generated by capitalism. The social security system, in this view, serves capitalism by reproducing a reserve army of labour, bolstering the patriarchal family and disciplining the labour force (Ginsburg 1979). The benefits that may result for workers become little more than by-products of institutions that operate to achieve other ends.

An attempt to break free of the functionalist reasoning involved in this kind of approach has led some neo-marxists to allow for a greater degree of *autonomy* on the part of the state and some agency on the part of the working class. Favoured theoretical hinges here have been the contradictions inherent in the welfare state itself and the apparent crises that surround it. The welfare state 'simultaneously embodies tendencies to enhance social welfare, to develop the powers of individuals, to exert social control over the blind play of market forces; and tendencies to repress and control people, to adapt them to the requirements of the capitalist economy' (Gough 1979: 12). So it may not be straightforwardly functional for capital. Lenhardt and Offe's work (1984) advances a case for agency: their interesting hypothesis is that social policy is the state's manner of effecting the lasting transformation of non-wage labourers into wage labourers. As such it is part of the construction of the working class rather than just a response to it. Offe (1984) himself arguably presents the most developed account of the welfare state as a contradictory and contested domain. He regards it as a crisis response to save capitalism from its central contradiction between social forces and private relations of production. The welfare state is, however, subject to a crisis logic of its own that has its most significant manifestations in the fiscal crisis, the administrative shortfall and the legitimation shortfall. The future of the welfare state is rendered increasingly insecure by new economic, social and political pressures associated with the emergent disorganized capitalism (Offe 1985).

The neo-marxist approaches represent an advance to the extent that they provide a critical analysis. Moreover their claims for the effects of the welfare state are, *prima vista*, plausible. It is quite probable that social policies effect social control and legitimation, for example. However, these possible effects of welfare need to be differentiated from the functions that welfare performs (van Kersbergen 1991: 129). In any case, these approaches still lack a capacity to countenance centrally the agency of political forces. The structures of capitalist societies remain determinant, with the result that the potential effect of political action and political institutions is underdeveloped. Therefore, problems encountered, such as for example the inadequacy of social insurance in times of high unemployment, are attributed to the contradictions inherent in capitalism rather than reflecting a political struggle as yet unresolved (Sullivan 1987: 55).

The Social Interpretation

Interest in the transformation potential of class politics, and the mobilization of workers politically and organizationally, has spawned an impressive body of work that proffers what is called the '*social interpretation*'[3] of the welfare state. This work has had theoretical aspirations as well as being strongly empirically grounded. Focusing on the study of rich capitalist economies, the Scandinavian countries in particular, the welfare state is analysed as both an arena and outcome of class politics by largely quantitative methodology.

The leading claim is that the bulk of the observable variation in the emergence and growth of welfare states can be accounted for by the strength of social democratic–oriented labour movements (Shalev 1983: 316). Put at its simplest, workers organized in the marketplace significantly influence if not capture the state apparatus through electoral strength and use it as a vehicle to modify distributional outcomes.[4] The more successful are the political forces of the working class, organized especially in social democratic parties, the more entrenched and institutionalized will the welfare state become (Shalev 1983; Esping-Andersen 1985; Korpi 1989). Yet outcomes are not guaranteed, and the process whereby structural contradictions are transformed through political contests is problematized. The *social interpretation* is dynamic to the extent that it displays an openness to the possible outcomes of democratic politics and allows for feedback from the consequences to the potential for mobilizing political classes. A more refined version, the *power resources* model, emphasizes the distinction and inherent tensions between economic or market-based power and political power and the resources that can be mobilized for each (Korpi 1980, 1985). The conditions under which power can be mobilized are de-commodification of labour power (in the sense of a loosening of individuals' dependence on the market), the institutionalization of solidarity, the inclusion of allied classes and the formation of class alliances (Esping-Andersen 1985). A second core (but not universal) claim of the social interpretation is that the welfare state represents a first step towards socialism (Stephens 1979: 72). Sustained social democratic governance can counteract the dominance of capital and reinforce the effective solidarity of organized labour. This process is seen to be at its most advanced in Sweden.

Empirically, these theses have been tested, with considerable support, by quantitative cross-national analyses of the relationship among union mobilization, leftist governments and levels and types of welfare intervention (Cameron 1978; Stephens 1979; Castles 1982). Conflicting evidence also exists, however, as well as considerable criticism. In particular, both the specific nature of politics and their effects on welfare need to be further differentiated. Welfare states other than those of social democratic persuasion display high levels of equality, for example the Netherlands and Germany, leading to the conclusion that dominance of a social democratic party is not a necessary condition for welfare state development (Castles 1978; van Kersbergen 1991). Moreover the effects of social democratic parties may be mediated by the strength or weakness of other parties (Castles 1982).[5] Esping-Andersen, for instance, shows that political forces, rather than the level of welfare expenditure itself, are crucial in determining the policy regime under which welfare is organized (1990: 35–54). Furthermore there are good grounds for doubting several of the assumptions underlying the *social interpretation*: those relating to the uniformity of workers' interests, the equation of the power mobilization of the working class with social democratic mobilization, and the weakening of the powers of capitalism in the face of collective action by workers (Baldwin 1990; van Kersbergen 1990: 12–18; Pierson 1991: 32–9).

Challenges of Recent Work

In recent years, work on the welfare state has tended to be less tightly bound to existing theoretical frameworks, at the same time critically developing them. While not denying the contribution of the other theoretical positions, newer work draws attention to the influence of factors previously taken to be quiescent or remaining underdeveloped. An underlying if not always stated concern is to explicate agency as well as structure in the politics of welfare states.

With the emergence of what came to be known as the *state-centred* approach, the state's capacity, in the form of its institutional structures, traditions and/or personnel, for independent effect has been conceptually exploited in a number of ways. The resulting body of work tends to emphasize the historically unique and contingent nature of developments within nations. Approaches here do not so much offer a new theory as add a new dimension to existing theories, to the *social interpretation* in particular. One strand brings the state bureaucracy to life as an important component of the policy formation process. The role of civil servants in the innovation of policies is emphasized (Heclo 1974), as is the influence of bureaucratic capacity on the inauguration of welfare programs (Flora and Alber 1981). A second thrust highlights institutional learning, emphasizing the importance of existing institutional arrangements for shaping current policies and the impact of policy legacies. Policy-making is therefore regarded as an inherently historical process in which actors consciously build upon or react against previous policy efforts. A third variant of the *state-centred* approach asserts that historical variations in state structures shape the content and timing of policy initiatives (Skocpol 1980). The late development of the American welfare state in comparison to the British, for instance, has been linked to the prior existence in Britain of a centralized bureaucracy and professional civil service (Orloff and Skocpol 1984). Overall, while the approach is a welcome corrective to the view of the welfare state as a product of either economics or politics, it gives relatively little to bite on in terms of the active political character of welfare. In a recent work, however, Skocpol (1992) makes a significant theoretical and empirical departure to a polity-centred model in which the state remains important but now, in explaining US social policy between the 1870s and the 1920s, she argues for a complex interaction among state structures, policy legacies, political identities and the organization and tactics of social actors.

The nature of political agency in relation to the welfare state has also been to the fore in some recent work. Esping-Andersen (1990) explores the links between the development of certain types of social policy regime and the social movements that promoted them. Within his framework, class mobilization, class coalitions and the historical legacy of regime institutionalization are the forces making for divergence in social policy configurations. The dominance of class agents in the inauguration of social policy to the exclusion of other social forces is also being revisited. Baldwin's (1990) work questions whether classes were the contestants in the redistributive game at all. He prefers to use the concept of 'risk categories', by which he means actors whose common interests rest on their relations both to the means of security and the redistribution of risks promised or threatened by social insurance. The growth of 'new' social movements, especially the feminist movement but also the 'anti-racist' and green critiques, has highlighted how divisions other than those based on class are constitutive of public systems of welfare. The shaping influence of interest-group politics is another important recent current. Scholars here do not represent this as the definitive guiding principle of welfare, but they insist that the prevailing accounts accord too little attention to non-class ascriptive groups, such as the retired and the aged, and other social groupings, for example professional associations (Ashford 1986; Pampel and Williamson 1989). According to Pierson (1991: 97), the essential point of this discourse is procedural or methodological rather than substantive: it calls for 'a clear interrogation of the historical record to be used to discipline the rather grander generalizations of some other approaches'.

Critical Overview of Conventional Work

Needless to say, the foregoing has presented a somewhat simplified and stylized view of the main theoretical orientations. Yet the whirlwind nature of the tour should not be allowed to shroud the merits of each of the competing approaches. The *industrialism* thesis sensitizes us to how economic growth makes possible the spread of structures for redistribution and security, and it has elaborated some of the long historical processes through which welfare states are shaped. Moreover, it leaves little doubt that economic development and industrialization are preconditions for welfare state development. The integrative mechanisms of welfare are clarified by the *modernization* approach, which has also helped to demonstrate how the welfare state is an outcome of increasing social and political differentiation. In elaborating a more critical perspective on the welfare state, *neo-marxists* have produced a valuable analysis of the operation of social policy under conditions of capitalist social relations. They have, moreover, opened for debate the future of the welfare state and been foremost in exploring the different dimensions of the 'crisis' that is seen to confront it. The *social interpretation* also has its book of virtues. The jewels in its crown are its focus on the processes and outcomes of working-class power mobilization and its advancement of a view of the welfare state as the embodiment of different forms of power resources. Other recent work has also taught us important lessons. Attention has been drawn especially to how variations among welfare states require approaches sensitive to history and to the effects of other interests along with class within the national context.

A key commonality in the *explanans* of the theories is, however, their heavy reliance on class factors as the mainspring of social provision. Theories differ in how they attribute a causal role to capital, labour and the state in forging political identities around issues pertaining to welfare provision. Generally, however, they assume that class politics provided the template for social policy innovation, just as they imply that the resulting redistribution is significant only or mainly in class terms (Mink 1990: 92). While the agency of interest-group politics is allowed for in some cases, this too is often reduced to class politics. Save for Skocpol's (1992) work, the possibility of gender politics did not seriously exercise the minds of mainstream welfare state analysts, or if it did it never saw the light of day in their work. As a consequence, central gaps are identifiable in the existing theories.

Let us remind the *industrialism* and *modernization* perspectives that the 'lost' or changed functions of the traditional institutions were mainly those performed by women. And, as Gordon (1990a: 178) points out, modern welfare systems do not replace them with anything except differently organized female labour. Nowhere has welfare state expansion taken place without a significant engagement with female labour, whether paid or unpaid. Integrating gender, then, emphasizes the nature of female labour as one common thread in the growth of welfare states. The social-control view of welfare, central for some *neo-marxist* theorists, is also rendered incomplete by an exclusion of women. In fact welfare can have important empowering potential for women and therefore affects both the distribution of resources between women and men and the processes whereby such redistribution takes place. An independent income from public sources can, for instance, enable women to reduce their financial reliance on men. At a more macro level, the marxist view of the hegemony of capitalism is challenged by feminists, who place patriarchal dominance as either superior to or co-determinative with capitalism. The nature of the 'crisis' in welfare may also be better understood by linking it with issues of care and the effects of existing policies on gender equality. In any case, the *neo-marxist* theories are considerably weakened by their failure to account for how the family operates as a key mechanism through which capitalism is reproduced. Finally, with regard to the *social interpretation*, the now (re)discovered agency of women and feminist activists in campaigning for welfare clearly indicates that organized workers' interests were not alone in shaping the welfare state (see esp. Koven and Michel 1990; Skocpol 1992; Pedersen 1993; Lewis 1994). A further point to be made in regard to this approach is that the interests aroused by social policies are complex and that some, such as family policies for example, are not reducible to a contest among class interests.

It should be clear that the theoretical literature has tended to define the territory around the welfare state in ways that exclude both women's experience and gender-related politics and processes. While they have made their way onto the pages of some welfare state scholarship, women have been given no more than a 'walk-on' part, appearing either as mothers in analyses of family policy or as paid workers when they have become visible in the labour market. Furthermore, gender, either as a stratifier of interests and resources or as a source of political identity and mobilization, has been given little if any space in theoretical argumentation.

Significance of the Marginalization of Gender and Women

I suggest that this has serious implications. The omission of gender touches on issues relating to the political engagement around redistribution, the institutional nexus within which the welfare state is situated, the role of the state in the construction of labour as waged or unwaged, and the outcomes of welfare state provision. More precisely:

- *gender as a source or constituent of political identity*, either in its own right or in conjunction with other interests, has not received due consideration. As a consequence, the possibility has been largely overlooked that the distribution of power and resources between women and men may have been an important wellspring of political struggles around the welfare state itself, as well as influencing the content of social policies. This has also meant a neglect of the possibility that the classical collective actors could have been motivated by concerns rooted in gender interests. Recent work, for example Skocpol (1992) and Pedersen (1993), has helped to reveal that the construction of interest was more complex than just around class alone and that issues concerning redistribution between women and men and the rightful role of each sex were engraved in the early struggles around welfare in the USA and in some parts of Europe.[6]
- Nor has *female political agency* received sufficient space in mainstream theorizing about the origins of welfare states. In Skocpol and Ritter's (1991: 74) words, ' "Public" life is typically presumed to have been an exclusively male sphere, with women regarded as "private" actors confined to homes and charitable associations'. Yet we now know that women were politically active – albeit often in social spaces removed from the male political landscape – in civic, confessional, feminist and voluntary arenas. Not only did women play a part in the struggles, especially early ones, around welfare but they were influential in shaping social policies in a number of welfare states (Zaretsky 1982; Koven and Michel 1990; Pedersen 1990, 1993; Skocpol and Ritter 1991; Skocpol 1992; Lewis 1994).
- The main currents of scholarship on the welfare state have largely neglected *the family as an institutional domain* centrally affected by welfare developments and in turn shaping them. If family policies are considered at all they tend to be consigned to a separate box, often in a tray marked 'horizontal redistribution'. One can identify a tacit

division of labour whereby study of the welfare state is market- and employment-biased while family research sticks to its own narrow terrain. Neither seems to question the borderline. As a result, the family is most often relegated to the status of subsidiary institution rather than, as Pedersen (1993: 12) puts it, 'a changing set of relationships that interact in crucial ways with many labor and social policies'. Esping-Andersen (1990) suggests that different types of policy regime coexist with different roles for the family; yet his work gives no more than a taste of such interrelations because the family is not integrated systematically into his analysis of welfare state variations.

- The *role and place of unpaid labour* as influenced by and in helping to sustain welfare state forms has also been neglected. Because the crucial influence has been seen to be the market–state relation, if labour is brought into the analysis it is only paid labour that tends to be considered. The role of the welfare state in shaping the form of labour as paid or unpaid is therefore ignored, as is the degree of reliance of particular welfare states on unpaid labour. As a consequence of this neglect, the state's contribution to a gendered division of labour is overlooked. This leaves a number of unanswered questions. First, are particular kinds of paid and unpaid labour arrangement associated with different models of welfare? And second, what role does the state play in designating caring as a public (paid) or private (unpaid) responsibility?

- The neglect of gender has also left its mark on *which welfare state programs are studied.* In the recent rush to study the programmatic content of welfare states, policies targeted on old age and absence from work through illness have been favoured, to a general neglect of the more complicated unemployment and safety-net assistance programs as well as policies oriented to the family and dependence (Pedersen 1993). Social policies targeted on women specifically, whether as mothers and/or workers, and the dependant-relevant aspects of social provision have especially tended to be obscured in a scholarship that has mainly been preoccupied with the search for the state's imprint on relations between collective interests, conceived in class, and to a lesser extent generational, terms.

- The fact that welfare can be *gendered in outcome,* either consolidating existing differences or leading to a change in the balance of resource distribution between women and men, has not received due attention either. Again most interest has been expressed in how states redistribute burdens and resources among collectivities. Yet welfare states play quite a large part in the construction of (inter-) dependency relationships among individuals, especially women and men.

Some of these omissions are more significant for the present purpose than others. The outcomes of women's political activism are more relevant to work that seeks the shaping influences on welfare states rather than the present endeavour to understand the relationship between the form and outcomes of contemporary welfare states. In a similar fashion, that (large) part of the theoretical literature on the welfare state that has focused on the historical concomitants of and struggles around welfare development has to be regarded as background. In any case, some of the above omissions have not only been recognized but have led to a rapidly growing body of work that takes as its *raison d'être* the exclusion of women from scholarship. Mirroring the trajectory of events in other fields, it was only with the advent of this scholarship that women's relationship to the state and other structures of power came to be studied in its own right. Most but not all of this work has been feminist in orientation.[7]

Feminist Scholarship and the Welfare State

Feminist work on the welfare state is impossible to understand apart from its historical context. This means seeing it as a critical response to either the downgrading of women and gender in mainstream work or their outright exclusion from it. Looking at the body of feminist work on the welfare state as a whole, it could be said to have proceeded along two lines. Either scholars felt that they must develop new theories, concepts and approaches or, implicitly or explicitly, they reworked existing frameworks so as to render them more 'gender-friendly'. The latter approach comprises the greater bulk of the recent work, although the former would probably have been the more desired end. It would be wrong, though, to characterize feminist scholarship on the welfare state as solely reactionary. While it may have self-consciously measured itself against the accounts of mainstream work in its early years, feminist work has for a considerable time now sought to explore in their own right the components, immediate objectives and effects of state policies on women, on their relationship to men, and on the more general institutional and ideological configurations within which such relations are set.[8]

The feminist work on the welfare state has not followed the same trajectory as the conventional scholarship. It is of a different order. Whereas the conventional work sought to theorize the welfare state itself, feminist work aimed, in the early days especially, to produce a general theory to explain 'women's oppression'. Naturally the state was identified as a key locus of (male) power, but feminist theorizing has tended to train its sights above the level of particular institutions, locating itself at the most abstract of levels – that of societal systems.

Among other things, this means that feminism has no fully elaborated theory of gender in relation to either the state or the welfare state. It is useful to consider, if only briefly, the general orientation of feminist theorizing.

The Main Theoretical Orientations of Feminist Work

A dual-systems approach has dominated the most influential theoretical works. These works posit the existence of two systems, capitalism and patriarchy, which are represented as related social structures. Although united in their rejection of earlier single-system positions as too extreme, theorists vary in their view of the exact relations between the two systems and indeed in the degree of effort they devote to the connections. There have been three main streams in this work.

Hartmann (1979) and Walby (1986), for example, devote considerable attention to elaborating the characteristics of patriarchy and establishing it as an analytically independent system from capitalism. Their work emphasizes dualism rather than seeing patriarchy and capitalism as a duality. This approach encountered huge problems, many of which are as yet unresolved. The theory and concept of patriarchy have been accused of being inherently descriptive, imprecise, essentialist, ahistorical and structuralist (Acker 1989; Bradley 1989; Pollert 1996). Walby (1990) attempted to develop the theory further by specifying lower levels of abstraction, in particular differentiating between specific social structures of patriarchy (the household, paid work, the state, sexuality, male violence, culture) and the sets of patriarchal practices associated with each structure. Even if this work went some distance in routing her critics, the imprecise relationship between patriarchy and capitalism remains problematic. In fact in this and other variants of the dual-systems approach, either patriarchy or capitalism appears to bear the predominant explanatory burden. Gender is either ultimately explained as deriving from capitalism or patriarchy is posited as an independent system.

As Connell (1987: 46) comments, it is not immediately clear what makes the patriarchal 'system' systematic and in what sense capitalism and patriarchy are the same kind of phenomenon. His own work, which represents the second theoretical approach to be introduced here, offers a social theory of gender. Seeking to interweave personal life and social structure, gender is for Connell a property of collectivities, institutions and processes, extending into a gender order at the societal level. Connell's work did much to represent gender relations as present in all types of institutions and practices. The gender order of societies is in his view made up of a number of gender regimes that are essentially structures of relations between women and men. Such gender regimes exist in each of the following substructures: labour, power, and cathexis (the patterns of emotional and sexual attachment and antagonism). Within each domain, gender is structured in a different way and the relations between the gender regimes are constantly in flux. This is how change comes about. The domain of labour, which embraces the social organization of production and the sexual division of labour in paid and unpaid activity, Connell sees as being organized according to both a gendered logic of accumulation and a political economy of masculinity. Authority, control and coercion, the constituents of the domain of power, are gendered first by virtue of the connection between authority and masculinity and second by hierarchies of power within gender. Cathexis is gendered by virtue of heterosexuality and the organization of social practices in couple relationships. Connell allows for variation and contradiction and emphasizes that the regimes themselves and their relationship in the gender order may not always be coherent. Change is generated by the relationship between regimes, which can take either a complementary, conflictual or parallel form, and the constitution of social interest. Connell's work is helpful in conceptualizing the state as a process in which gender is embedded. He emphasizes the need to understand the institutional apparatus of the state, a goal that lies close to the heart of the present book. Overall, however, Connell leaves the relationship between gender and class unspecified. Furthermore, as Pollert (1996: 350) points out, his theory is based on a diffuse Foucauldian notion of 'power' relations that can be detached from class relations. This has the result of rupturing the synthesis between class and gender.

The third theoretical paradigm, that of Swede Yvonne Hirdman (1994), seeks to add agency to the dual-systems theory. Gender rather than class is uppermost in her work and she is more interested in charting gender-related developments in specific historical periods than in elaborating the nature of the relationship between patriarchy and capitalism in general. She posits that three systems or structures govern the relationship between women and men: capitalism, democracy and gender. Contradictions and tensions at the intersection of the three are the motors of social change. The gender system operates to two general rules: gender segregation in all areas, and priority of the male norm. As a system it is maintained by the cultural superstructure, social integration in institutions, and socialization practices. As Duncan (1994: 1186) describes her focus, Hirdman is most interested in the gender contract, which she postulates as the social form that operationalizes the gender system in particular societies at particular points in time. Hirdman analyses the recent history of public policy in Sweden by virtue of this heuristic device and offers a number of variants of this contract. One is a housewife contract that reigned between the 1930s and the 1960s. Men were promised full employment, and the home-making role of women was valued by granting them as mothers, enti-tlement to the benefits of the welfare state. This was followed by a transitional phase after which an equality contract was put in place. Guaranteeing all adults economic independence and a place in the labour market, the latter kind of contract is in the process of being replaced by an equal-status contract that is driven by a push towards an equalization of roles for women and men. The advantage of this formu-lation of a gender system is that it can encompass agency as well as structure. But, two doubts about Hirdman's approach linger. First, it is developed in relation to only one country, Sweden, and while it can easily account for events in that country, its application in less corpo-ratist countries remains in some doubt.[9] Second, the origins and roots of gender-related activity are not clearly theorized, nor indeed is the relationship between gender and the other two 'systems' of democracy and capitalism.

Considering the trends in the literature at this stage, it would be true by way of summarizing to say that the main thrust of current work appears to be to more or less abandon the search for a 'grand theory' in favour of more modest theoretical endeavours. It is in this body of work that the concept of gender has matured: a product of a more middle-range schol-arship that has quietly pieced together the concrete processes in partic-ular sociological and historical settings whereby differentiation and inequalities between women and men are generated, reproduced and institutionalized. This literature leans towards the concrete rather than the abstract and is, of late anyway, especially intrigued by variation. Sharp dichotomies are no longer in vogue, the relational nature of gender is emphasized and inequalities between women and men are problema-tized rather than assumed. This literature has flourished and has given rise to a large volume of work on the welfare state. Attempts have been made to rework existing analytical frameworks so that gender can be incorporated (Shaver 1990; Skocpol 1992; Orloff 1993) and to explore hitherto underdeveloped elements and consequences of welfare provi-sions relevant from the standpoint of gender (Hobson 1990; Shaver 1991; Leira 1992; Anttonen and Sipilä 1996; Sainsbury 1996). It is probably the comparative dimensions of welfare states, however, that have most exer-cised the feminist imagination, especially in recent years. Comparison proceeds apace in a climate where the most interesting aspects of welfare states are seen to reside in how they compare with each other. This, still new, focus has acted to transform the feminist approach to the welfare state – from a perspective focusing on the complexity of particular welfare states to one interested in variation. The result has been to subject existing regime typologies to scrutiny or to develop new regimes on the basis of gender-related factors (Lewis and Ostner 1991; Lewis 1992; Sainsbury 1994a; Siaroff 1994; Mósesdóttir 1995; Ostner 1995; Daly 1996)

I have found this latter body of work especially perceptive in a number of ways. For a start, the scope of the domain of welfare is broadened beyond the formal economy to encompass the domestic sphere. Social reproduction, which embraces not only the process of bearing children but the physical, emotional, ideological and material exchanges involved in caring for and sustaining others (Williams 1989: 41–2), is drawn to the centre of analysis. Linking the public and domestic spheres in this way also illuminates the dualism characterizing much of the classical analyses that separate social from economic policy, reproduction from production, and private from public. Second, this body of work draws attention to other divisions in welfare states apart from those based on class, and in this regard has helped to expand existing understanding. Concepts that act as central planks in mainstream theories have been seen to necessitate clarification and refinement. Third, one of the greatest insights of the women-centred scholarship in my view has been its consideration of the individual–state relation. The welfare state has been brought to life as a presence and an actor structuring the everyday lives and choices of women and men. In the process, this work has raised for debate the ideologies embodied in welfare and has put on the table for our consideration the degree to which social citizenship is sex- and gender-differentiated.

Neither set of scholarship, however, provides a blueprint for theorizing how the welfare state and gender are interrelated, although from each certain insights can be retained and developed. The remainder of the chapter is devoted not to a head-to-head contest between each body of work but rather to a consideration of the important theoretical issues relevant to gender that span both.

Towards a Theoretical Framework

The key theoretical issues surrounding the conceptualization of the relations between gender and welfare states may be appreciated through consideration of the dichotomies that have sundered existing scholarship.

On the structural side, for instance, one can identify the tendency to divorce the family from the state–market nexus and paid work from unpaid work. Among the fissures to be found in the literature on outcomes are the separation of de-commodification from commodification and independence from dependence. If we follow the definition of gender given in the Introduction – a set of practices founded at least in part on family-related statuses and roles that acts to generate and institutionalize systematic differences and inequalities between women and men – the intellectual exercise of conceptualizing gender in relation to the welfare state can be said to involve two tasks: integrating the family; and taking account of the life situation of women, in its own right and as it compares to that of men.

Finding a Place for the Family

At issue here is the most appropriate conceptual framework for linking the state and the family. To date the family has been Cinderella to the labour market in welfare state theory, relegated to the sidelines by a primary if not exclusive focus on the state–market relation. Only under two conditions is such a confined analysis justifiable. The first is if welfare state programs were targeted only at risks arising from waged work and treated these as risks of the individual; the second is if class relations were accepted as the only significant form of politics in which welfare states are engaged (Orloff 1994). The first is true of no known welfare state that would aspire to be described as such. All developed welfare states are centrally concerned with the support of families, targeting transfers on individuals as (implicit or explicit) members of families and instituting policies specifically designed to support certain types of families. The second condition is also unmet because, as the analyses in this book will demonstrate, viewing the welfare state in terms of class divisions captures only a part of the activities and politics in which it is engaged. Bringing gender into the analysis casts serious doubt on whether a class framework can by itself account for how women as well as men experience the welfare state.

To be fair, some mainstream theorists have sought to integrate the family. For example, Ringen and Uusitalo (1992: 70–1) suggest a frame of reference that includes the family. Work inspired by the French regulation school ascribes to the family a more central role. Setting the welfare state firmly within the Fordist model of industrial mass production and consumption, some work (e.g. Myles 1990) has provided an account of how welfare state programs came to mirror the life-cycle profile of the prototypical mass worker. Embedded in the Fordist model was support for a particular form of family – the breadwinner/housewife model. One of its outcomes, then, was the reproduction of a traditional family structure and pattern of gender relations. While it is weak on explaining variation, Myles's analysis of the changes, and choices, attendant on the transition to a 'post-Fordist social order' contains at least one point worth retaining: the welfare state has generally been slow to respond to the changing nature of household structure and female labour force and life patterns. In a word, it promotes a family form that has become outmoded.

In these and other works, however, the theoretical status of the family is underdeveloped. In the Fordist literature, for instance, family form is treated more or less as a by-product of industrial organization. Furthermore, while existing scholarship demonstrates that particular family arrangements coexist with certain types of approach to economic security, it devotes little attention to the mechanisms and processes whereby welfare policies promote particular kinds of family and family relations.

With mainstream theorizing cool towards the family, most of the work that has sought to theorize the family–welfare state relation directly has originated from (early) feminist theorists. McIntosh (1978) approached the question from the standpoint of how state intervention acts to maintain the family household and waged labour – the two institutions she saw as oppressing women. Her analysis represents the state as a capitalist animal, working through the allocation of its welfare benefits, the degree of its intervention in certain arenas, and the ideologies that colour its practice to facilitate the accumulation of capital. The means through which the state acts is its support for a particular form of household in which women provide unpaid domestic services. Capitalism ultimately benefits from this through the cheap reproduction of labour power.[10]

While McIntosh's general argument has to be criticized for its functionalist overtones, there is considerable evidence to suggest that the welfare state has historically exerted an important shaping influence on the form assumed by households and families (Zaretsky 1982). Even further, analysis of the ideologies embedded in welfare offers substantial support for the thesis that the welfare state has operated with and helped to sustain a particular model of the family. Variously conceptualized, this argument dovetails with that of many feminists as well as Myles (1990) in suggesting the maintenance of a traditional family form of breadwinner husband–dependent wife as one of the long-term organizing principles of welfare. The family wage, as ideology and practice, is one of the main theoretical hinges here. As an attempt to theorize the welfare state, the family wage poses a challenge to the work ethic as the main or only organizing principle of welfare.

A focus on the system of a family wage, with its associated constructions of male and female roles and power relations, may be useful in a number of ways. First, it alerts us to the possibility of a systematic source of variation in the treatment of different categories of women and of women and men for welfare purposes: their marital and/or familial status. Second, it provides a framework for conceptualizing the relationship between state, family and market and does so in a manner that is sensitive to gender. There is, however, a large (theoretical) gap between identifying a family wage ideology as a common organizing principle of welfare and claiming that the welfare state maintains a particular form of the family or household for capitalist purposes. In particular, the approach falters in the face of variations and changes in the relationship between the state and the family. Different states support the family to different degrees (Gauthier 1991; Lewis 1992), with at one extreme the Swedish and Danish welfare states, which have pursued a conscious policy of socializing important parts of human reproduction normally carried out by women, and at the other extreme the USA, where little explicit state support for the family has been institutionalized. So, positing a universally predominant family form for welfare purposes does not appear to hold water empirically. Rather, energies may be more usefully applied to investigating how family forms vary according to how welfare states have institutionalized different models and types of social policy and to developing theoretical devices to capture the relations involved.

The family has an important place in all societies, and the welfare state, while it has altered and affected family forms, has nowhere dispensed with the family. Conceptual attention must therefore be directed to variations in the kinds of accommodations that are possible between the family and the welfare state. Towards this end I suggest a conceptual framework that distinguishes between the *family as an institution* that performs certain functions, and *families as sets of relations.* These two levels are essential if we are to clearly conceptualize the relation between state and family. In regard to the first aspect, a useful way of capturing the connection between the family and the state, and in some ways also the market, is in terms of the division of labour that exists between them as regards the performance of work related to providing welfare. The concept of care, in defining as it does the labour aspects of both institutional spheres, provides a central hinge here. Long conceived of in relation to the unpaid domestic and personal services provided by women through the social relations of marriage and kinship, the application of the concept has been broadened over time to embrace the activities of providing for the welfare of others in a variety of settings and social relations (Ungerson 1990, 1997; Graham 1991, 1993; Leira 1992). Concerned to draw out the political economy aspects of the concept, Daly and Lewis (1998) link care more explicitly with social policy and variations therein. Their definition of care reflects this concern with embeddedness: care is defined as the activities involved in meeting the physical and emotional needs of dependent adults and children, and the normative, economic and social frameworks within which such activities are assigned and carried out. In other words, care as a set of activities cannot be conceived of independently of the normative, economic and social context within which it is carried out. Taking care as one central hinge in the state–family connection directs analytical attention to the boundaries between the state and the family as regards the construction (which work is paid and unpaid?) and performance of this 'welfare work' (where are both types of work performed and by whom?).

With regard to the family as a set of relations, the central issue is how to conceptualize welfare policies' effects on both interpersonal relations within families and relations among families. How far do public policies extend the reach of the state? In my view positing a family wage model is too crude to grasp the myriad ways in which public policies contribute to the definition of intra-familial relations and resource distribution. Skocpol (1992: 34) also criticizes the concept for obscuring important differences between 'paternalist' and 'maternalist' versions of family wage policies. The former, she argues, attempt to shore up the working conditions of all workers in ways that reinforce male trade unions, and channel public benefits to women and children through male wage-earning capacities. Maternalist policies, typical of the early USA, dealt directly with women regardless of the previous wage-earning capacities of their dead or departed husbands. While I am not convinced that Skocpol's is a satisfactory differentiation between policies (being especially unhappy about the absence of a theoretical term or concept to link the two types of policy), I agree with the general point that the family wage concept is too blunt a conceptual instrument to capture variations in the relation between policies and different types of roles and relations within and among families. Therefore, I adopt a more open approach and suggest, as the most appropriate focus of attention, first, the norms and practices that are embedded in welfare state policies and, second, a consideration of these for the kind of familial relations they envisage. Two specific elements of social policies are relevant here: those pertaining to appropriate relations within families and those that reach out to shape relations among families. Their significance in revealing the connection between the welfare state and the family lies in the sets of power relations and idealized views about the legitimate scale and direction of familial resource flows that they embody.

The family and the state are therefore linked by the practice of care and how the ideologies and practices in one sphere shape processes and relations in the other. In the latter regard I am most interested in the influence exerted by the welfare state. This is not meant to imply that the relationship between the state and the family is one way but rather that it is a focus dictated by the orientation of work that takes the welfare state as its departure point.

Integrating the Situation of Women

When the life profiles of women and men are explicitly compared, a broad mosaic of factors sets them apart. To cut a path through the undergrowth to those differences of most significance in the present context, the following question is strategic: how can women's relationship to the welfare state be different to that of men? The nature of (social) citizenship provides a vantage point from which to begin to answer this question.

Citizenship, as the bundle of rights to which people are entitled by virtue of their membership of the nation, is given an expression in the services and benefits provided by the welfare state. The citizenship paradigm has provided rich fruit for the analysis of welfare state variations. The *social interpretation* especially has broken new ground by differentiating policy regimes on the basis of the citizenship packages that underpin them. This approach has tended to take an unproblematic view of citizenship, however, following Marshall's (1964) model of a progression from civil to political to social citizenship. Yet, as Pierson (1991: 36) points out in relation to this unilinear model of expanding citizenship, 'the question of who counts as a citizen, whether full citizenship is gender-specific, what is to count as a citizen's entitlement and under what circumstances welfare rights will be granted and by whom continue to be daily concerns of contemporary political life'. Feminists have invaded the space that is opened up by this kind of question and have fashioned a broad critique of what they regard as the false universalism of the language of abstract citizenship. They have, in a word, drawn attention to citizenship as a (gender-) differentiated concept (Pateman 1988; Lister 1990, 1997a, 1997b; O'Connor 1992). The present work foregrounds the state–citizen relation as, first, a social relation and, second, one that is not undifferentiated but conditioned by several factors, some of which are related to gender.

Today the citizenship paradigm is in fact a predominant approach in the feminist literature on the welfare state (sharing the limelight with the concept of care and that of the male breadwinner). The two different historical traditions of citizenship – the liberal notion of rights that construes citizenship as status and right and the civic republican that emphasizes practice and participation – have each received critical attention, and some scholars have seen a better future to lie in a synthesis of the two (Lister 1997a). Pateman (1988) has traced the emergence of social citizenship, showing that social rights have historically attached to those who are 'independent'.[11] In contemporary societies, independence is achieved through integration into the labour market, employment having replaced military service as the key to modern citizenship. There are, then, two potential barriers to citizenship: non–labour market participation and non-independence. Both are crucial for women. For a start, women are much less likely than men to participate in the labour market, especially on a full-time, continuous basis, and when they do such participation does not automatically confer financial independence. Furthermore, female citizenship status was for long defined by the marital relationship: women were denied legal personhood; as 'minors', control of their financial and other activities was vested in their husbands. In this perspective lies both a particular analysis of the relation between women and the (welfare) state and a set of analytic categories for understanding that relation. In regard to the welfare state the perspective of citizenship has facilitated consideration of who is included and who excluded from social rights and has allowed the feminist literature to contribute to a significant broadening of the analytic categories associated with the concept.

The association of citizenship rights (as embodied in welfare state provisions) with freedom or autonomy is an important current in contemporary research. Some work (e.g. Esping-Andersen 1990), invites us to regard freedom from the dictates of the market, conceptualized as de-commodification, as one of the main factors by which welfare states can be clustered. While this is a valuable category of analysis, it is too limited to capture the freedom-enhancing or freedom-delimiting character of the welfare state for most women. Although couched in formally gender-neutral terms, the concept's capacity to embrace the relationship of the welfare state to the citizenship of women is questionable. For at the end of the day, the most important 'source' of income for many women is the men with whom they are having intimate relations and, given this, the most significant aspect of the welfare state may be the manner in which it influences these sets of relations. In effect, women's life chances are conditioned by their relations and status within the family in a manner that sets them apart from most men. A second complication is revealed when we consider the social relations surrounding women's labour patterns, and the role of the welfare state in this regard. The fact is that, in contrast to men, women may be as likely to be commodified by public provisions as to be de-commodified by them. This effect can occur in two ways, one direct, the other indirect. The welfare state can be directly commodifying in its role as employer: witness the large numbers of women in the social welfare labour market and female predominance over men in this arena (Rein 1985). Second, through public provision of caring services – institutional or other care for the ill or elderly, child-care services – the state substitutes for women's private (that is, unpaid) labour, thereby releasing them for other activities. So the implicit market–state relation, whereby the former is the commodifier and the latter the de-commodifier, is not so neat when women are brought into the picture.

It should be clear from this discussion that I do not consider the de-commodification concept by itself as sufficiently revelatory of the relation between women and the welfare state. At the minimum, the role of the state in commodifying labour, never more than implicit in existing frameworks, has to be factored in. But lying in the background here is a much larger issue about the welfare state as a social agent. A fundamental advance of the de-commodification concept is that it can be used to bridge macro social processes and outcomes for individuals. In the latter regard it behoves us to ponder how the welfare state might be liberating for individuals while at the same time institutionalizing certain forms of accommodation between class and other interests. Including both sexes in this thought exercise suggests the additional possibility that the family or domestic sphere, while sometimes a choice by women, can and does also act to curtail freedom. The insight that follows is that the welfare state may, therefore, have a role in loosening or tightening individuals' economic reliance on the family.

Many women scholars are now trying to theorize social citizenship rights in terms of the degree to which they promote the autonomy and economic independence of women, especially those with caring responsibilities. Different end-points and conceptual hinges are deployed for this purpose. O'Connor (1992) speaks of personal autonomy or insulation from dependence; Hobson (1990) views the options in terms of exit (from a bad marriage or unsatisfactory relationship, for instance); Orloff (1993) takes one step back and speaks in terms of the freedom from compulsion to enter into potentially oppressive relations; while Lister (1994) and McLaughlin and Glendinning (1994) use a concept of 'defamilization'. The latter embraces the terms and conditions under which 'people engage in families and the extent to which they can uphold an acceptable standard of living independently of (patriarchal) "family" participation'(ibid: 65). While each of the concepts has its distinct merits, the concept of defamilization seems most promising, not least because it has the broadest frame of reference – the state–family–individual nexus of relationships. Among other advantages of defamilization are its capacity to problematize women's family-related roles, and hence intra- and extra-familial power relations, in the context of the complexion of welfare state policies.

Where this leads us essentially is to the broader sociological referent of stratification and the role of the welfare state in ordering and reordering social relations. This is a rather different view of stratification, though, for it augments the conventional view by treating the family as an arena in which public processes also effect social divisions.

Analytically, this raises the possibility that the welfare state either constructs new divisions between women and men, inside and outside the family, and/or mirrors gender-stratification processes originating elsewhere in the social system. To ponder if and how the welfare state engages in these kinds of relations is to ask the broadest of questions: whether the welfare state's pattern of resource redistribution is such that it (directly or indirectly) leads to or mitigates inequalities between women and men, regardless of where such inequalities originate.

Overview

The argument of this chapter can be summarized as follows. Focusing on wage labour and class dynamics captures only a part of the inequalities and power relations that shape welfare states and condition their social effects. I take issue not with a focus on class – there is no doubt that welfare provisions are 'classed' – but rather with the elevation within scholarship of class as the only significant form of politics with which welfare states are engaged. I submit that the sovereignty of class renders mainstream theorizing incomplete. The brunt of my argument here rests on demonstrating that welfare states are centrally implicated in gender relations, both directly in the form of the orientations of their policies and indirectly in terms of the norms that they embody and the processes they set in train as regards resource distribution among, and the appropriate roles of, women and men. For a conceptualization of the welfare state I shall in this book think of it in terms of a set of institutional and normative arrangements. We know from mainstream work that such arrangements engage with the economic sphere and with individuals as wage-earners. What remains to be established is how and the degree to which the welfare state across national settings engages with the family and women and men as gendered actors. Towards this end, I have argued that developing a gendered conceptualization of the welfare state can proceed on the basis of two exercises: formulating a conceptual apparatus that embraces the trilogy of institutions within which the family–state relation has a central place; and integrating the experience and life situations of women alongside those of men.

To conceptualize the family–state relation I suggest a twofold approach. I first believe that the two are connected by virtue of the labour content and labour-related goals of their activities. More precisely, with the welfare state as my departure point I am suggesting that it sets in train certain processes that serve to shape the activity of care within and outside families. A second aspect of the state–family relation is how intra- and inter-familial relations are envisaged by social policies. On the second step in developing a gendered conceptualization of the welfare state – integrating the life experience of both women and men – my understanding of the welfare state is as an agent of stratification. Welfare states act as channels of redistribution: they redistribute key resources and opportunities across different 'risk' categories or groups and in the process affect the distribution of inequality and poverty. These processes may be located inside and/or outside the family.

CHAPTER 2

A Framework for Analysing the Gender Dimension of Welfare States

To develop the theoretical framework sketched so far, this chapter turns the lens on the more empirical welfare state scholarship. Three areas of existing work are especially pertinent: the conceptualization and definition of the welfare state; the methodologies employed to study welfare states; and the links that have been established between the structure of welfare state arrangements and associated outcomes. The guiding analytic question is how best to ascertain the particular patterning of gender relations that is encoded in social policies. A first step towards answering this question is to identify which of its components tap the gender-salient dimensions of the welfare state. From this angle the broad institutional architecture of welfare state provision and the content of specific policies are drawn to the centre of attention. A second essential exercise is to identify how social policies and programs can lead to gender differences and inequalities. Making sense of outcomes requires, first, some consideration of what has been identified as social patterning resulting from the welfare state. Second, it requires the development of a model of how welfare state provisions could affect resource distribution and relations between women and men and the households in which they live, as well as the wider opportunities available to each gender group.

In focusing first on how the welfare state has been conceptualized and studied, I examine the criteria used by existing research to differentiate welfare states, stopping a while with work that has sought to typologize welfare regimes. This work is helpful in a number of ways. For one, it gives a good idea of the range of variation characterizing the welfare state universe as a whole, something that is important even when one is focusing on a small number of welfare states. In fact the distinctive features of the cases being studied reveal themselves more fully in the larger context. Another reason for taking a larger purview is that the most recent round of comparative research on the welfare state has developed an impressive set of criteria to capture the quality of welfare state provision, while at the same time linking welfare states to the wider political economies within which they operate. As we shall observe, though, there are limits to this scholarship, from both a conceptual and methodological viewpoint. The second part of the chapter engages in a discussion of how the gender dimension of welfare states, in terms of the constituents of policies and their outcomes, are best identified. Some of the criteria for studying the welfare state need to be considerably modified if gender processes are to be identified and accounted for. This leads to the final section, which elucidates a model for the comparative analysis of the extent to which welfare states are gendered in content and outcome.

How have Welfare States been Conceptualized and Studied?

Two aspects of the existing literature are especially pertinent to this part of the discussion: the conception of the welfare state that has informed research and the kinds of methodology that have been employed to study welfare states.

Conceptualizations and Definitions of the Welfare State in Early Work

Until recently, a relatively narrow conceptualization of the welfare state prevailed. One could say that, for many research exercises, the welfare state was reduced to a mere fraction of its sum. Some studies, for example, were content with no more than a series of historical landmarks regarding the timing of the introduction of social policies. If not in this guise, the welfare state most often came to life as social expenditures, 'welfare effort'. Such reliance on timing or fairly crude financial indicators could perhaps be justified if they were found to be discriminating predictors. But they are not. It is now being demonstrated increasingly that social expenditures are a poor guide either to nations' commitment to welfare or to the quality of social rights obtaining in societies. Countries sporting similar levels of social expenditure have been shown to share divergent understandings of solidarity, to confer quite different types of social rights and to assign varying roles to the state and the market in the provision of welfare and income (Korpi 1989; Esping-Andersen 1990; van Kersbergen 1991). Hence the view of one set of commentators: 'Levels of social expenditure not only provide a poor basis for welfare state comparison but they also mask decisive institutional differences'(Rein et al. 1987: 7). This kind of judgement links into a body of work that has taken as its departure point variations of an institutional character.

Alber's work (1988) offers a good example of this approach. He identifies five basic dimensions of institutional variation. The first concerns the target groups or scope of public welfare programs. The variation here ranges from selective schemes catering for the most needy to universal programs that cover all citizens. Alber's second parameter embraces the range of state activities and countenances the diversity of services and benefits provided by the public authorities. The quality of benefits and services, ranging from minimal to optimal, comprises the third dimension. Fourth there is the mix of instruments used to realize the tasks of public welfare. This embodies the differential extent to which the taxation system, direct income transfers, public goods and public subsidies effect redistribution. Finally the method of financing public provision varies, with differing emphases given to general revenues and earmarked fees.

While these represent important dimensions of welfare states, they can be taken as significant in a cross-national perspective only if they can distinguish the organizational logics differentiating systems of welfare. In effect, comparative welfare state analysis has moved on, elaborating dimensions of variation that tap the wider political economy of the welfare state. In some cases this has involved institutional comparisons, but recent work is especially marked by an emphasis on the welfare state as a configuration of policies embedded in a particular economic and political order. There has occurred an associated shift in research emphasis, away from charting welfare state convergence (a leading thesis of the *logic of industrialism and modernization* approaches) towards a greater recognition of diversity. The last decade especially has seen the growth of a particular 'school' of welfare state research: work which has sought to model variations and to group or categorize welfare states on the basis of the configurations of social, and economic, policies that underpin them (Furniss and Tilton 1977; Korpi 1980; Schmidt 1982; Jones 1985; Castles and Mitchell 1990; Esping-Andersen 1990; Leibfried 1990; Lewis and Ostner 1991; Mitchell 1991; Lewis 1992). This work has spawned a distinctive way of comparing welfare states as well as a remarkable degree of reliance on ideal types.

Types of Welfare State

According to Sainsbury (1991), two particular approaches have figured prominently in discussions on welfare state variations. The first is deductive in nature, constructing analytical models based on contrasting ideal types (Titmuss 1974; Wilensky 1975; Korpi 1980; Jones 1985). Titmuss sketched three models on the basis of the tasks or functions attributed to social policy: the *residual* model, the *industrial performance achievement* model and the *institutional redistributive* model. Although under-developed by Titmuss, the models themselves, and the analytical task of modelling welfare state variations, were to prove influential. Korpi, for example, usefully distinguished between *marginal* and *institutional* welfare states, each an ideal type epitomizing extremes in possible welfare state forms. The marginal represents a minimal welfare commitment, the institutional state undertaking a wider range of welfare responsibilities. The distinction rests on a number of criteria among which are: the proportion of the national income spent on welfare programs; the proportion of the population receiving some welfare state benefits; the universality or selectivity of welfare policies; the progressivity of the taxation system; and the importance of full employment. In another variant of this approach, Jones used the concept of welfare capitalism to classify states, obtaining a continuum from *welfare* capitalist states to those which are welfare *capitalist*. In the former, social policy is focused on the welfare of individuals or families, whereas welfare *capitalist* social policies are intended to support and reinforce a capitalist system. Jones derived her continuum on the basis of three criteria: the funding of social policies and in particular the degree of reliance on revenues from income tax and social security contributions; the types of social provision that exist; and the effects of such provisions on social inequalities and life opportunities.

A second approach to typology-building has been more inductive, starting with a particular country or set of countries and seeking to pinpoint the distinctive features of the welfare state(s) in question. Furniss and Tilton (1977) decipher three models on the basis of linkages between the extent, form, aims and beneficiaries of state intervention. They distinguish between the *positive state*, the *social security state* and the *social welfare state*. This approach to model-building has some shortcomings, however. In the case of Furniss and Tilton's work, Sainsbury points out that the dimensions of variation underlying the three models remain implicit and that the approach's emphasis on the most salient features in each case can easily obscure the fact that the same features characterize the other two types, although they are less prominent (1991: 5). Also, given that the models are derived from three specific countries, the USA, Britain and Sweden, their broader application to other systems remains in some doubt.

Esping-Andersen (1990) has overcome many of the shortcomings of earlier attempts to model welfare states, developing and applying a more systematic set of indicators to a greater number (eighteen) of welfare states. His focus embraces qualitative variations across states, not just in terms of the organizational features of welfare programs but also in the context of their relations with surrounding institutions and political configurations. He begins with a number of convictions, some of them promising from a gender perspective. In particular, the manner in which he links welfare state and labour market is useful, not least for his recognition of the potential of welfare states to affect the (labour market) position of women as well as that of men. With a close eye to their historical development, he selects the following as the key criteria differentiating modern welfare states: their logic of organization (especially their capacity to de-commodify individuals by loosening dependence on the market), their social-stratification effects, and their configuration of state–market relations (see Table 2.1). His work has made it common to speak in terms of 'social policy regimes' – a concept generally taken to refer to nations' configurations of institutional arrangements around work and welfare.

Evaluated on such characteristics, eighteen advanced capitalist welfare states are judged by Esping-Andersen to cluster into the now familiar three types of regime. There is, first, the world of the selectivist *residual welfare state*, where means-tested benefits and a liberal stratification system prevail. This type of state pays modest benefits directed mainly to low-income groups, subsidizes private welfare, and limits social reform by a strong work ethic. The USA, Canada, New Zealand, Australia, and, less comfortably so, Britain are countries with, according to Esping-Andersen, liberal welfare state regimes. The second world, labelled *conservative*, embraces Germany, Austria, France and Italy, among others. Here rights are linked to work performance, being founded on the principle of earnings-related social insurance. Given its status-maintenance character, the stratification system is typically conservative and corporatist. Finally, there is the *social democratic* world of welfare capitalism in which social citizenship rights are well established and the welfare system is universalist in orientation and aspires towards a high level of benefit equality. In these societies, mainly the Scandinavian states, the stratification principle is depicted as socialist.

Esping-Andersen's work was greeted with acclaim in most quarters but strident critique in a few. Without doubt his perspective moved the comparative welfare state scholarship a considerable distance. While people had spoken before about regimes of welfare, Esping-Andersen offered the most systematic, and broad-ranging, conception of regime types yet. Perhaps his greatest contribution to scholarship, though, lies in the elaboration as axes of variation of the qualitative dimensions of welfare state provision together with their stratificational outcomes. When his work has provoked criticism, two themes have formed its heart: that he neglects crucial aspects of the welfare state, and that he misclassifies or leaves no place in his schema for particular national

Table 2.1 Conceptual and empirical focuses of some recent work on welfare state variation

Author	Conceptual Focus in Relation to the Welfare State	Empirical Indicators
Esping-Andersen 1990	Degree of de-commodification	Wage replacement rates; length of contribution periods; method of financing of transfers; degree of transfer equality
	Principles of stratification	Degree of corporatism; etatism; significance of means-tested poor relief; private pensions; private health spending; average universalism; average benefit equality; range of entitlements
	State–market relations	State/market mix in pension provision; conditions under which individuals exit from and enter the labour market
Castles and Mitchell 1990	The redistribution process	Distribution of market incomes; final distribution of incomes; extent of net redistribution
	Linkages between welfare effort, instruments and outcomes	Degree of transfer equality; household transfers as a percentage of GDP; income and profit taxes as a percentage of GDP
Lewis 1992	The strength of the male breadwinner model crossnationally	Extent and form of female labour force participation; bases of women's entitlements; treatment of mothers and other carers; primacy of family policy; treatment of and outcomes for lone mothers
Scheiwe 1994	How institutional arrangements in labour market, welfare state, family and marital law construct poverty risks for mothers	Form, conditions and levels of child support payments; childcare service provision; conditions of transfer entitlement as they relate to family situation; treatment of marriage as against parenthood; tax allowances; ideology underlying transfers

Table 2.1 (Cont.)

Shaver and Bradshaw 1993	Degree of support for domestic labour in tax benefit package	Comparison of net disposable income of one-earner couples to single person; support for a dependent wife compared to that for children; comparison of lone parents to one-earner couples
Orloff 1994	The institutional division of labour among states, markets and families in providing welfare	Resources provided by each to different types of household, men and women; levels of adequacy of such resources
	The gender stratification structures and effects of income maintenance provision	The level of differentiation of programmes directed at ameliorating the consequences of market vs. family failure; the proportions of men and women making claims based on workforce participation, citizenship, need and family or marital status
	The bases of social rights	The relative treatment of men and women, workers and caregivers; conditions of access to transfers; the degree of leverage given to workers vis-à-vis the market; women's capacities to form and maintain autonomous households
Sainsbury 1996	The elaboration of models of social policy as they impact upon women	Familial ideology; basis of entitlement; recipient and unit for transfers; unit of contribution; taxation, employment and wage policy; state involvement in the sphere of care
	Outcomes of gender equality reforms	Women's access to transfers; location of women in insurance- and assistance-based programs; equality of transfers received

welfare systems. Feminists have been heavily represented among both types of critic, although they accepted in the main the orthodoxy of his approach. Indeed, it is somewhat ironic that Esping-Andersen's work aroused such feminist fire since it not only provided the springboard for a major growth in feminist writing on the welfare state but provoked one of the most meaningful engagements yet between the feminist and conventional perspectives (O'Connor 1996).

Part of this engagement has been around alternative, women-friendly welfare state typologies. The wish to develop a gender-specific typology led Lewis (1992) and Lewis and Ostner (1991) to examine the organizing logics of welfare states from a gender perspective. These works have highlighted especially the assumptions regarding the role of women that lie embedded in welfare policies and some of their consequences (see Table 2.1). More precisely, a number of European welfare states are compared on the basis of whether they recognize and cater for women solely as wives and mothers and/or also as workers. In large part, Lewis represents this as a dichotomous choice, and the general tendency, she says, has been to treat women as mothers. Put simply, this means that women's relations to welfare systems are defined in terms of their family role rather than on the basis of their status as individuals. From this framework, Lewis derives a threefold categorization of several contemporary European welfare states: those with *strong, moderate* and *weak breadwinner* models. This leads to a some-what different clustering of countries to Esping-Andersen. Britain and Ireland are categorized as *strong male breadwinner* countries. They are marked by their tendency to draw a firm dividing line between public and private responsibility and to treat married women as dependent wives for the purposes of social entitlements. France is categorized as a *moderate male breadwinner* state because women there have gained en-titlements as both citizen mothers and citizen workers. Female labour market participation is encouraged, but at the same time the policy framework is strongly supportive of families. Motherhood is treated as a social function rather than a private matter by family-centred, pro-natalist-inspired social policies. Post-1970 Sweden and Denmark consti-tute the third variant in the typology, being *weak male breadwinner* states. Swedish social democratic governments took conscious steps to bring all women into the labour force and to make the 'two-breadwinner family' the norm. The basis of women's social entitlements was trans-formed: they have been treated as workers and have been compen-sated for their unpaid work as mothers at rates that they could command as members of the labour force (Lewis 1992: 169). Lewis's work remains the most influential typology in the gender-focused wel-fare state literature.[1]

Looking at the field overall, the trajectory of work can be charted on an axis of increasing complexity in the conceptualization of the welfare state. We have travelled from an almost total reliance on expenditures through a predominant interest in institutional features to a view of the welfare state as one of a number of interacting social structures. However, as conceptions of the welfare state become increasingly comparative, there is a possibility that the uniqueness and specificity of welfare state institutions will be lost in the web of more diffuse state–society ties. While it may be correct to claim as Kolberg and Uusitalo (1992: 84) do that the demarcation lines between the welfare state and other institutions are becoming increasingly blurred, we still need a clear conception of the welfare state for empirical research purposes. To reap the benefits of recent work, it seems important to retain a concern with both institutional make-up *and* the broader embeddedness of welfare states. These two criteria will therefore provide the frame for the development of gender-sensitive concepts in relation to the welfare state in later sections of this chapter.

Issues of Methodology

There is no one way of comparing, although observers of developments in the comparative welfare state field in recent years would be forgiven for thinking so. The many countries–few variables approach has dominated, with ideal types as the favoured comparative device. It is a scholarship that is for the most part preoccupied with typologies. Such a research approach is not uncontroversial. The nature of the typologizing methodology, the coherence of the regime clusters identified and the appropriate characterization of particular countries are each problematic. Esping-Andersen's work, as mentioned earlier, has provoked criticism both for its regime types and for how it classifies individual countries. Indeed, judging from the spate of objections by scholars, Sweden and the USA appear to be the only uncontroversially placed countries. There are in my view two points in this entire debate worth retaining. First, some country cases are definitely problematic for the purposes of regime clustering. Failing to emerge clearly from his empirical work, they had to be dragged by Esping-Andersen into particular clusters. Australia, France, Germany, Ireland, Italy, the Netherlands and the UK are the most obvious outliers. Of course, with so many problem cases the legitimacy of clustering itself comes into question, not least because the regimes are left with fewer and fewer exemplar countries and so serve an ever more compromised heuristic function. Second, there is a valid critique to be made about the completeness of Esping-Andersen's clusters. Castles and Mitchell (1990), for example, suggest that greater attention to how welfare states vary as regards (the extent and means of) redistribution serves to reveal a further regime type – the 'radical' – with Australia, Canada and the UK as the constituent countries.

Similar problems bedevil the contributions of Lewis and Lewis and Ostner. This work is in fact less secure empirically than some of the conventional work on typologies. To all intents and purposes, the bread-winner model awaits a proper empirical application, for it appears that the country cases described are those that best fit the model. In any case only a handful of countries are covered and there are real doubts about the wider application of the breadwinner model, in particular its ability to differentiate further among countries. Where, one might ask, do the southern European welfare states fit in – are they not also strong male breadwinner models? And what about the welfare models of New Zealand and Australia as well as those of Canada and the USA? Cursory consideration of these countries and others suggests that they are all versions of the strong male breadwinner model. This leaves the frame-work overweighted at one end and hence unable to satisfy a basic crite-rion regarding the discriminatory properties of typologies. As I shall show in the next section, these problems stem partly from a failure to elaborate the conceptual properties of the model as well as from short-comings in regard to its operationalization.

Apart from matters of empirical application, some more general doubts persist about typologizing as method. Legitimate questions can be raised about an approach which assumes that the complexity of indi-vidual welfare systems can be meaningfully categorized on the basis of a small number of general criteria. In relation to the, admittedly more primitive, dualistic institutional/residual framework, for example, Sainsbury (1991:17) finds that just four countries – the Netherlands, Sweden, the UK and the USA – represent hybrids uniquely combining various attributes of each dimension. But more tellingly in terms of the models' analytical utility, she found no coherent pattern in the interre-lationships between dimensions conforming to the logic of the ideal types. Second, the dualistic nature of the schema led to difficulties in forcing characteristics to be reduced to two discrete categories (re pro-grams into selective versus universal; re funding into contributions versus taxation). The dualistic logic is also incapable of differentiating the ideologies underlying welfare states and the role of private organi-zations in welfare provision (ibid.). It is little surprise, therefore, that no sooner had Esping-Andersen's work been published than other research began to appear that had the effect, if not the intention, of destabilizing his regime clusters (Castles and Mitchell 1990; van Kers-bergen 1991; Ragin 1994). The underlying point here speaks not only to the act of selecting a small number of criteria to represent national policy configurations but also to the degree of constraint and generality that is acceptable. The lesson, perhaps a somewhat obvious one in the context of a two-country study, is that typologizing has high costs, forcing one to forfeit especially the richness and complexity of welfare state provision within and across national contexts.

By way of overview, one can say that enabling concepts and explanations to travel has yielded substantial fruit. It has enriched scholarship by forcing us to think in larger categories and by bringing together types of welfare state models that were formerly treated in isolation. However, the scale of its contribution to the methodological development of welfare state scholarship and the extent to which it should detain us further can be questioned. I am of the view that typologizing should be set aside in favour of few countries–many factors type of work. Comparative energies, especially in periods of transformation, are best concentrated on developing concepts and modes of analysis that do justice to the rich detail of welfare state provisions considered in their context. Given the general methodological underdevelopment of much of the new feminist work on the welfare state as adverted to by Adams (1998), work that advances a bold line of interpretation and causality is especially beneficial.

In turning in the next section to elaborating my approach to the gender dimension of welfare states, I foreground the search for concepts that are not only comparative but can pick up the important institutional finer points as well as the broader embeddedness of welfare states.

Conceptualizing Welfare States from a Gender-sensitive Perspective

From a gender viewpoint, some of the current trends are undoubtedly helpful. Contemporary work is strongly relational in the sense that types are identified by virtue of welfare states' ties to surrounding institutions in the wider political economy. Significant progress has been made in linking welfare state forms to the economic and political nexus within which they develop and operate. Second, for the purpose of trying to discern general patterning, it is useful to be able to group welfare states, and the criteria used by the 'new typologists' for doing so are undoubtedly more discriminating than the aggregate social expenditures so favoured in the past. At a macro level the ordering principles linking the welfare state and the economy, and to a lesser extent the family, have been elucidated through an investigation of how welfare states are differentially embedded in national political and economic structures. At the micro level, which it must be admitted has received less attention than the macro, what becomes of importance is the nature of the individual's ties to state, family and market, and in particular the terms and conditions under which claims can be made on public resources. Finally, the focus on more qualitative characteristics is helpful. Clarifying their distributive mechanisms and empirically tracing the features of welfare states on the basis of whether rights hinge on citizenship, performance or need is a welcome advance. All in all, current work delivers a message of substantial divergence as well as complexity among contemporary welfare states. This, as Kolberg and Uusitalo (1991: 92) rightly point out, should serve as a definite warning against monocausal theories or simplistic quantitative research designs.

Issues relating to the constituent elements of policies and their outcomes must be considered separately.

Pinpointing a Gender Dimension in the Constituents of Policies

An outstanding question is how capable are the existing concepts and frameworks of capturing the gender dimension in welfare states and of doing so in a manner that is sensitive to both variation and embeddedness within the national context. Existing work shows promise as well as problems in these regards. Beginning with the conventional work, the de-commodification criterion, which bears the heaviest analytic burden of Esping-Andersen's three indicators, is problematic in a gender context. Its sovereignty as the indicator of the quality of social rights is especially troubling, for it is incapable of accounting for key aspects of women's experience of the welfare state and insufficiently embracive of the main functions or achievements of welfare states (Daly 1994).[2] As outlined in the last chapter, de-commodification presumes commodification, and welfare states play an important role in commodifying people as well, women especially. To the extent that welfare states help to secure the livelihood of women, they do so by a more complex set of functions than those oriented to de-commodification alone. Hence while de-commodification may be posited as the cutting edge of the relation between men and the welfare state, it is only partially indicative of how welfare states influence women's lives. These and other points undermine the degree of reliance that can be placed on de-commodification as the indicator *par excellence* of the character and orientation of welfare state benefits and services. Esping-Andersen's second indicator – the welfare state's labour market-related stratifying effects – usefully draws attention to welfare as an instrument or means of social stratification. While his focus on the labour market reeks of mainstream analysts' proclivity to treat class divisions as the only significant line of social cleavage, there is, as Orloff (1993) points out, no reason why the understanding of the welfare state's stratifying effects cannot be expanded to incorporate inequalities between women and men and stratification along gender lines. There is some gender potential also in Esping-Andersen's third criterion – the state–family–market nexus. But much of this potential remains to be realized in his own work since the family is the poor relation of the trilogy. The key analytical relation for Esping-Andersen is that between state and market. The crucial question here is whether the family- and gender-related policies of welfare states fit neatly into classifications deriving from a narrow understanding of political economy. This is a question that pervades the present book.

Feminist work provides a counterpoint to this way of thinking. Never satisfied with expenditure and other quantitative indicators, it has over the long run tended to lay more emphasis than conventional approaches on the details of social programs and how they condition people's experience of welfare. This kind of orientation has conferred on feminist work a certain edge when it comes to identifying the qualitative dimensions of welfare states. In a scholarship that has tended to relish the complexity of public provision, issues such as social expenditure and the administrative landscape of policy had less appeal than the ideologies underlying social programs and how welfare-related processes police access to public largesse. Much of this work has sought to unpack the assumptions and norms, especially those pertaining to gender relations, that are encoded in welfare policies. A second focus of feminist analysis has been the organizational dimensions of welfare states. The institutional components of welfare systems and the detailed conditions of access have been the focus here. Scholars have, for example, differentiated between the units of contribution, entitlement and benefit (Roll 1991). This type of work reflects a long-standing concern among feminist scholars about how systems of public provision function in practice and how they are experienced at the receiver end. The resultant scholarship has demonstrated not only that welfare states relate to different units – sometimes the individual, sometimes the married couple, sometimes the family, sometimes the household – but that the particular arrangement of benefits affects the distribution of financial resources and power among family members (Sainsbury 1993).

While feminists may have been to the fore in elaborating the significance of social policy's institutional and ideological complexity, their work tended to focus on the details of provision without embedding them in the wider political economy of the welfare state. There was too little bold conceptualizing. This tendency has been overtaken, however, in the last years by a feminist scholarship that has deliberately employed larger concepts. Work on care and the male breadwinner model has been to the fore here. To what extent is each useful in capturing gender dimensions in social policy and variations therein?

Care, one of the truly original concepts to emerge from feminist scholarship and arguably one of the most widely used in analyses of welfare states today, has its origins in an attempt to define the work that makes up caring for others and to analyse how that work reinforced the disadvantaged position of women. Care has matured into both a complex concept – it does not dovetail for example in any simplistic way with the paid/unpaid work differentiation – and one with considerable analytic potential in relation to the welfare state (Knijn and Kremer 1997). Part of its beauty is that it is enlightening about the content and context of a defining element of women's life situation and how welfare states relate to that. This is a strength, indeed a considerable one. But the question also has to be posed of how well care as a concept captures the gender dimension of welfare states. Here it is useful, especially in the present context, to register the difference for analytic purposes between the content or structure of welfare states, the processes that policies and practices engender and the outcomes that they bring about. These have tended to be elided in the literature. Although there have been some intimations of welfare states as caring regimes, and Jenson (1997) even goes so far as to suggest that the development of welfare states can be understood as being primarily about (the avoidance of dependency on) care, it seems to me that the concept speaks more readily to the processes and outcomes of welfare states than to their content. My main point here is that it may be misleading, especially in a comparative context, to ascribe comprehensive care policies to welfare states, for in many there is relatively little congruence between policies on caring for children and those on the elderly and other adults who may be in need of care. Hence I propose to integrate care into my analyses as a key element of the processes set in train by welfare states. All of this leads me to conclude that, while its capacity to embrace a defining feature of women's lives makes care an essential component of any gender framework, it is on its own insufficient as an indicator of the gender dimension of the content of welfare states.

The male breadwinner concept, another main axis of recent feminist scholarship on the welfare state, speaks more directly to the content of welfare state provision. In seeking to make the concept travel, Lewis (1992) has transcended a simplistic application and demonstrated that, while common, the family wage is by no means uniform. Another strength of the male breadwinner model is its inherent dynamic and implicit trajectory of change. Although Lewis does not develop a change-related analysis – indeed her characterization seems to be set some time around the 1970s – the male breadwinner typology has the potential to generate hypotheses about welfare state change and transformation. But for what we require of it here –

that it pick up the characteristics most indicative of a gender design in welfare – Lewis's formulation of the model requires further development. If earlier feminist scholarship was too specific, this is too general. While it may be a casualty of the degree of generality inherent in a typologizing methodology, too little attention has been devoted to specifying the attributes of the male breadwinner model. In particular, a specification of the terms of the model as it pertains to all women and to men is missing. This is problematic in a number of respects. For one, the dichotomous treatment of women as mothers or workers is an unacceptable oversimplification of welfare states' gender dimension. The treatment of mothers is unlikely to serve as the template for the experience of all women at the hands of welfare states. Other work suggests the benefits of differentiating between the subsidization of marriage as against parenthood (Scheiwe 1994), as well as showing that different models of motherhood are envisaged in and sustained by public policies (Leira 1992) and that states may and do support a wifely as well as a motherly role for women (Shaver and Bradshaw 1993). A second problem with the dichotomy mother/worker is that the treatment of mothers has no unidimensional interpretation: it could reveal a societal or state position on mothering, on marriage, on the family or on a combination of all three. Third, in regard to men it is undoubtedly important to note that high male wages, especially for men with families, are a condition of the male breadwinner model. After all, to differentiate among women, welfare states must also differentiate among men. These points call for a much more careful interpretation of where countries cluster together on their treatment of women and men and whether in fact such treatment approximates a male breadwinner model. This is especially true of the continental European welfare states, which have tended to be lumped together as 'male breadwinner countries' even though they vary widely on the generosity of male wages.

The framework nevertheless has potential, the breadwinner model offering a powerful way of conceptualizing welfare state variation. The integration of men and of a more differentiated set of female roles could, I suggest, render the model more discriminating and give it an empirical applicability beyond a few states. The work of Diane Sainsbury (1996) is helpful when thinking about elaborating the model. Through a consideration of the bases of entitlement to welfare benefits and services in the Netherlands, Sweden, the UK and the USA, she shows that the principle of supporting motherhood is only one of a number of principles underlying welfare state provision. Sainsbury's work leaves no doubt that a simplistic version of either the 'breadwinner' or 'de-commodification' approaches fails to do justice to the complexity of how welfare states govern access to their resources and how they have developed programs over time. Revealing the universe of variation represented by just these four welfare states, Sainsbury proves the need to differentiate between the support of women as wives (which, translated into social policy terms, means a principle of maintenance) and as providers of care (whereby mothers and other carers do or do not get benefits in their own right independent of their marital status). Sainsbury suggests that the four welfare states she studied are a mix of these two principles together with benefits provided on the basis of citizenship, need or want, and labour market status. Searching for the broad distributive principles that underpin welfare state provision is therefore a very important indicator of how welfare state benefits are organized. The underlying point speaks to the complexity of welfare states: they can, and most do, operate to a number of principles simultaneously.

Summarizing, while it is clear that none of the existing concepts is sufficient on its own to capture the gender dimension of welfare states, each of the main focuses of existing work has something to contribute to a more comprehensive perspective. The de-commodification approach is useful in identifying some of the key qualitative features of welfare states in a comparative context. The work on care highlights how variations in the processes initiated by welfare states in regard to this sphere of activity serve to reinforce or weaken inequalities between women and men. Third, the breadwinner model is helpful in encapsulating gender variations in the principles underpinning welfare state organization and provision. These emphases will be further discussed and developed in a later section. I now turn to a different aspect of the welfare state: the connections between policy and outcomes.

Conceptions of the Welfare State and the Links to Outcomes

Concrete outcomes of individual policy instruments and of welfare state configurations as a whole remain less developed than the input side. Until quite recently, knowledge about outcomes was limited largely to hypothesizing about the impact of policy instruments on the basis of implications drawn from ideal-typical characterizations and expenditure data. As Castles and Mitchell (1990: 6) describe it: 'The debate about the linkages between the extent and type of government intervention and social justice became a matter of demonstrating what nations for whatever reasons spent most on social objectives and of devising a quasi-moral calculus by which it could be shown that some types of instruments for achieving those objectives were more welfare-conferring than others'.

As a result, today's scholarship on the welfare state is more assured in exploring the interconnections of a range of institutional elements than in linking these to outcomes, at both macro and micro levels. Castles and Mitchell's own work highlights an important consequence of Esping-Andersen's relative neglect of the links between the specific character of welfare instruments and their redistributive outcomes. In effect, they suggest that a further regime type – the *radical*, whose constituent countries (Australia, Canada and the UK) are to be uncovered by greater attention to the means and extent of redistribution – lay undetected by Esping-Andersen's approach to regimes.[3] The underlying point here speaks to the need to problematize the link between the character of welfare institutions, the process of redistribution to which they give rise, and their outcomes in terms of the ordering of economic and social relations.

A lack of clear links between particular policy configurations and outcomes is also true of the micro level. To some extent this has been a question of the availability of data, a problem that has been alleviated in the last decade by the development of the Luxembourg Income Study database.[4] The growing availability of micro income data has led to a qualitative change in the investigation of welfare state impact. In particular, the availability of synchronized cross-national data sets enables poverty and economic welfare in general to be linked to both welfare effort and welfare state configurations in a comparative context (e.g. Smeeding et al. 1990; Mitchell 1991; Sørensen 1994; Korpi and Palme 1998). But the neglect of outcomes cannot be solely attributed to data scarcity. Welfare state research has shown a distinct preference for macro processes over those that are micro in nature. Thus, for example, citizenship is considered mainly as an indicator of social structure and de-commodification as a macro characteristic of regime types, to the relative neglect of the large purchase of both on individual quality of life and social relations. As of now then, it is still the case that what Ringen and Uusitalo (1992: 70) call 'the long road from the formation of market income to economic welfare, a road twisting through the arenas of politics and the family', remains under-explored.

Each of these points is reinforced if existing approaches to the welfare state are appraised from a gender perspective. While work is beginning to elaborate how welfare structures are systematically implicated in different patterns of redistribution, the effects of specific welfare programs on the distribution of resources between women and men are hardly known. This is true even if one takes account of the fact that feminist work has devoted considerable attention to welfare state–related outcomes. For feminist work too suffers from the shortcoming of leaving under-developed the links between policy and outcomes. Only in the recent past has variation entered its research grammar. For the present comparative purposes, work that has focused on women's relationship to the welfare state has two particular weaknesses: the conceptualization of outcomes is insufficiently elaborated, and the systematic links between outcomes and particular social policy configurations are too little explored.

In feminist conceptualizations outcomes tend to be viewed either very narrowly or very broadly. At the narrow end, there is some evidence of a *cui bono* approach, in which not only is the contest viewed as a binary one between women and men as two distinct and opposing camps but the outcomes are conceived as absolutist in the sense that if men are 'winners' then women must be 'losers'. Such polarities are unhelpful. For a start, they allow little or no space for the possibility of significant differences within gender groups, thereby denying a role to other stratifiers such as class, race or age. Second, while it may be valid to portray the welfare state as a battleground, attributing to it over-arching political motives conceives of it as some kind of unitary whole with coherent policies and consistent goals.[5] Welfare states are not like this. They are, above all, political constructions, subject therefore to strong contestation about individual components and to change over time. Gordon (1990a: 186) frames it aptly: 'most welfare policies represent the jerry-built compromises which are the artefacts of political and social conflict.' So while welfare policies may be clearly patterned and favour some groups over others, this is a long way from proving that they are the embodiment of the political will of a ruling capitalist elite or men writ large. At the minimum, uncovering the interests served by different domains of welfare policies, especially as they relate to gender, remains a task requiring further work in different national contexts.

An alternative tendency in feminist work is to define outcomes very broadly. Dependency – a current running through many evaluations of the relation of women to the welfare state – provides a good example of the complexities involved. O'Connor (1992) has suggested personal autonomy as an appropriate measure of the gender dimension of welfare states. Apart from the fact that they are often left undefined, there are a number of problems in setting up concepts such as independence or personal autonomy as measurement devices in relation to welfare states. The greatest problem that I recognize here is associated with cross-cultural variation. Independence has neither the same meaning nor the same place across cultures. It is mainly in societies of a liberal provenance that independence is a strong societal value, independence and individualism tending to go together. Both are relatively foreign in continental European societies where ideas of social embeddedness and interdependence predominate. Kolberg captures the ambivalent nature of independence when he sums up his evaluation of Scandinavian welfare states for women: 'What some scholars term control and dependence, we are inclined to call improvements, independence, emancipation, and empowerment'(1991: 144). Second, evaluating welfare state outcomes on the basis of dependency is of limited use if it does not discriminate between the effects on women as against those on men. After all, men too are involved in interactions which could be labelled 'dependent'. Third, it is also arguable whether it is helpful to use the same concept to capture an interpersonal relationship (between men and women) and a structural relationship (with the state) (Dahlerup 1987: 121–2). So if one wishes to employ a concept like dependency, a more refined conceptualization is needed to take account of the different types of relations in which people are embedded and how the welfare state affects them.

The task now is to build the insights from existing work and the critique that I have made of it into a comprehensive framework for the study of how welfare states are implicated in gender relations and inequalities.

A Gender Framework on the Welfare State

On the basis of the discussion so far, a gender-friendly approach to the welfare state must capture the material resources provided by the state to women and men, as individuals and as members of families, the conditions under which redistribution is effected between them, and the outcomes in terms of gender-based processes of stratification. Three analytical directions follow from this: conceptualizing the relevant dimensions of welfare state provision; imagining the processes that are set in train by welfare state arrangements; and modelling the outcomes that follow from these provisions. My overall approach to each of these questions can be graphically represented, as in Figure 2.1.

This kind of approach implies a particular conceptualization of the welfare state. Mine is notable in a number of respects. For one, I differentiate between the structures of welfare states, the processes they set in train, and their outcomes. For another, my approach directs attention to the scope of welfare provisions, in which services rank alongside income maintenance and taxation programs. Third, it leads to a search for differentiations among welfare states as regards both the extent (how much) and nature (which kind of services and benefits are provided? whose caring labour is substituted?) of their engagement in services and financial support. The definition of the welfare state that follows from these is the body of publicly funded and/or provided services and income maintenance programs designed to affect the distribution of resources among individuals and households.

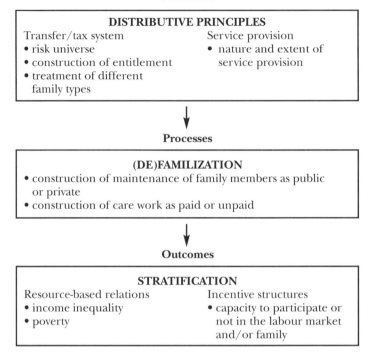

Figure 2.1   The welfare state as a gendered domain: conceptual and empirical framework

The Relevant Dimensions of Welfare State Policies and Provision

Linking both service provision and cash transfers is a wider notion of the *distributive principles* whereby public resources are allocated. Such principles embody both institutional elements as well as normative prescriptions about making claims on public resources. Conventional scholarship on the welfare state has helped to elucidate these principles, identifying citizenship, desert and need as the overarching distributive mechanisms that differentiate the range of public measures directed towards security and redistribution. To these Sainsbury (1996), with an eye to how welfare states treat women and gender relations, has added the principles of maintenance and care. Where do we search for the defining principles of welfare state provisions?

Programmatic structure and the conditions underpinning receipt of cash benefits, relevant social services and tax allowances are at the empirical coal face. Although considerable debate surrounds the selection of parameters of welfare state variation, existing work provides some useful guidelines. Figure 2.1 above has summarized the most relevant work, outlining a selection of the empirical indicators employed in some recent analyses of welfare states which are useful for the present purpose. Building upon but at the same time ranging beyond existing work, I suggest that three indicators capture the distributive principles of welfare as they affect gender relations: the '*risk universe*'; the *construction of entitlement*; and the *treatment of different family types*. Individually they isolate key structuring mechanisms of welfare state provision; collectively they identify the extant norms and principles with regard to, *inter alia*, families and gender roles.

The idea of the risk universe serves to identify the contingencies covered for social protection purposes. As I conceive of it, the '*risk universe*' has three dimensions: the range of risks covered; the location and conditions under which risks are covered; and the hierarchical relationship between risks. A defining feature of welfare states is their collectivization of some income risks. Men and women, while they have some risks in common, also experience different risks for the purpose of income maintenance (Holtmaat 1992). For men, income level and security are mainly endangered by the possibility of interruption or loss of earned income through illness, accident, unemployment or old age. While women share such risks, they are also subject to a set of risks that are but indirectly related to market-induced insecurity. Unique income risks for women are defined by the female biological constitution (giving birth) and the social construction of caring as primarily a woman's role. Women, therefore, experience three additional risks: loss of a male income (through widowhood, divorce and separation); loss of personal income through pregnancy; and loss of personal income through the need to care for others (either adults and/or children), that is, through having to engage in 'private' work.

A first empirical parameter of the risk universe is, then, the range of risks collectivized by welfare states.

A further revealing characteristic of the risk universe is the conditions under which different risks are covered by welfare states. Very few services and transfers are available as a general right for all, certainly in the two welfare states under consideration here. It is much more often the case that the public authorities carefully delimit access, demarcating 'insiders' from 'outsiders', the 'deserving' from the 'undeserving'. Almost all income maintenance systems are internally stratified, a common dichotomy being the insurance/means-tested divide. These and other differentiations connote systematic variations in access, amount, nature of the right and the conditions under which the service or benefit is granted.[6] Of signal importance is the relationship between one set of benefits and another. Behind the insurance/means-tested dichotomy, for example, may lie traces of a more complicated 'claims hierarchy'. If we conceptualize individuals or collectivities' claims on the state as emanating from three possible sources – paid employment, financial need, and family (either family activities or family relationships) – we may well find differentiation on these grounds. Among the empirical issues that flow from the risk universe are the coverage and location of female income risks as against those more typical of male lifestyles, the conditions under which each type of risk is integrated into welfare state provision, and whether a gender, or indeed other, faultline can be discerned in existing risk hierarchies.

The *construction of entitlement* defines the framework within which individuals and/or collective units are granted access to state support. It is to be differentiated from the risk universe in that, whereas the latter envisions the relationship between the individual applicant and the state, the construction of entitlement speaks to the status of the applicant within the context of his or her family and market circumstances. There are two related elements here: the unit of entitlement and the treatment of 'dependants'. Social rights are usually thought of as individual-based. Across national settings the basis of entitlement varies, however. One source of variation, especially important from a gender perspective, is the individual/collective unit divide. In the former case, benefits are granted independently of the consumption needs or resources of the recipient's domestic unit. When a collectivity such as household or family is the unit of entitlement, the transfer system usually interacts with one member on behalf of the collectivity, making certain assumptions about relations between members and the appropriate flow of resources among them. In selecting one member to represent the household, welfare states are in effect helping to construct or reinforce relations of power between members of the collective unit. The degree to which access to benefits, services and tax allowances is individualized or collectivized is, therefore, an important gauge not only of access to public support but also of the intra-family and gender-based practices embedded in public support systems.

Constructions of 'dependants' form the other side of this coin. All welfare states contain norms in regard to 'dependants' and relations of dependency. In some cases the very right to a benefit or service itself stems from public legitimation of dependency responsibilities. Payments and tax allowances for survivors, for example, embody public assumption of responsibility for spousal maintenance. For the women involved – survivors are mainly female – the right is a derived one, secured through a relationship to a 'covered' individual. At one time, welfare states, in their attempt to mirror and even reinforce traditional spousal relationships, directly discriminated against women. With the most blatant sex discriminations eliminated, the pertinent question is now whether public provisions operate on the basis of gendered norms by, for example, constructing one individual as the secondary partner in marriage for public support and taxation purposes. The significance of such differentiations is that they not only dictate the size of the transfer but their influence may also extend to determining the economic behaviour of partners and spouses. Receipt of social security and tax allowances sometimes directly stipulates conditions with regard to both partners' labour market involvement. Welfare states may also indirectly affect the labour market role of the female partner in that the level of payment or the conditions attaching to it may make it a rational decision for only one or both partners to be employed.

Finally, it may be that welfare states systematically vary in their *treatment of different family types*. It is not unknown for states to encode desired norms about population policy in cash and tax transfers, nor is it uncommon for norms about social propriety to underlie state support. Of relevance, therefore, is the extent to which particular family types are favoured by transfer and tax systems. Such patterns can be uncovered by juxtaposing the treatment of families with children as against other families, and that of one-parent with two-parent families. Other differentiations may also be operating: the encouragement of one-earner as against two-earner couples; perhaps larger families with children are favoured in comparison to those with just one or two children. Among the relevant empirical indicators are the extent to which specific provision is made for different types of families, how provision compares across family types, and what kind of incentives are contained within policies towards particular family types and forms.

The Processes Set in Train by Welfare State Practice and Provision

These components lead in turn to a number of processes that span the gulf between provision and outcomes. Such processes may be generally described as '(de)familization'. Two aspects of this are crucial for our purposes: the definition of family maintenance obligations as public or private (or as located at some point on a continuum between public and private); and the construction of caring labour as paid or unpaid and as located inside or outside family relations. Such processes allow us to explore how welfare states serve to set up roles and circuits of redistribution for women and men individually and as members of families.

Family maintenance obligations are of value here because they reveal the type of female and male roles envisaged in and, at least partly, shaped by welfare states. To the extent that marriage and family are constructed by legal and welfare provisions as institutions of maintenance, the range of female and male roles will vary. The ultimate reference point here is the extent to which welfare states envisage and support a range of roles for women and men.

Care-related activity and norms are a second key focus. The management of caring, defined to refer to the tasks involved in caring for the personal needs of others, especially the young, the ill and the elderly, is, along with the provision of income security, one of the main functions of contemporary welfare states.[7] While it is not by any means the only determinant, the welfare state is a key actor constructing the boundaries whereby caring is considered a public responsibility, a market option or a private obligation. Welfare states vary empirically in this regard and a continuum, ranging from public to private, exists as regards caring work. Such a continuum has two specific referents: it defines the location of the activity and specifies the nature of the labour input as either supported by the state or not. Consideration of the labour input brings us to the micro level. The risk of requiring care or having to give care are two major life contingencies for individuals. Both are especially important in the lives of women. The concept of care, in providing an *entrée* to the construction of work as paid or unpaid, is therefore one key to uncovering the distribution of resources, roles and life opportunities between women and men. A very important set of empirical questions, then, centres on to what extent the welfare state in any given context contributes to the construction of paid and unpaid labour for women and men.

Gender-relevant Outcomes of Welfare States

Great things are expected of the welfare state (Jallade 1992: 40). While varying national trajectories and diffuse political aspirations around the welfare state call for caution in identifying a clear set of policy goals, it does seem reasonable to identify contemporary welfare states with a number of broad policy objectives. The first relates to the distribution of income, and in particular less inequality in income distribution. A second associated policy objective is the reduction of poverty. Third, welfare states have a principal concern with ordering relations to the means of security, whether that resides in the market or the family or both.

At their core, welfare systems are designed as redistributive processes. While the association of welfare states with equality is problematic, it can be reasonably assumed that: 1) income (re)distributed through the state will be less unequal than that distributed by market forces; and 2) through its income redistribution functions the state effects some reduction in income inequality overall. While we can make no far-reaching assumptions about states' gender-redistributive goals, it is important to trace the consequences of particular welfare state configurations not only as they affect the financial situation of women and men individually but also in terms of how they structure resource distribution between them. On the outcome side, it is not such a long journey from conventional stratification analysis to that based on gender: the same processes, such as access to resources and the extent of income inequalities, are at the empirical cutting edge. This has two empirical referents: the extent and nature of income redistribution achieved and the scale of and redistribution of the risk of poverty.

To capture the more qualitative effects of state provisions on gender relations, the idea of 'incentive structures' is helpful. This concept is intended to plumb the kinds of role options that are available to each sex group in regard to economic activity and the state's role in influencing the relevant choice environment. Incentive structures as used here are close to Dahrendorf's concept of life chances: 'Life chances are opportunities for individual development, provided by social structure, "moulds" as we have called them. As such they provide an important bridge between an understanding of society which emphasises the structural quality of things social ... and a normative theory of society which emphasises individual liberty' (1979: 61–2). For Dahrendorf 'chances' are a function of two structural elements: options and ligatures. The former embraces the choice or alternatives of action given in social structure, whereas ligatures represent allegiances or bonds that he likens to 'railings to which people can cling as they walk into the mist of their social lives just as they can be barriers which they can encounter in this mist' (ibid.: 32). In the present context, options can be defined as opportunities for economic activity and gender roles may be considered among the most pertinent aspects of ligatures. One empirical expression of these is the degree to which the welfare state can be said to have a broader stratificational role by structuring the environment within which life choices and conditions are determined. Empirically, then, I investigate how economic activity patterns vary according to gender role and marital status and the significance of state policies in expanding or contracting opportunities for economic activity and economic independence.

But incentives in relation to which spheres? Here I focus on both the labour market and the family. The empirical issues in relation to the former are fairly clear. We know from existing work that different welfare regimes are associated with different patterns of, especially female, employment. Therefore, in the exercise of comparing welfare states, the nature of the labour market involvement of men and women is likely to be closely associated with particular configurations of benefit and taxation provision. But following up on the points made in the last chapter, we have to ponder other domains that might be liberating or constraining for individuals and collectivities. Especially important here is the welfare state's role in loosening or tightening individuals' economic reliance on the family. Does the state's guarantee of autonomy from the labour market also embrace autonomy from the family? To bring in the family in this way is a necessary clarification because it may be that the state provides resources in a manner and form which, while they enable individuals to exit from the labour market, presume the availability of income and services from other family members. So the other side of the coin is the degree of freedom in relation to the family, what Lister (1994) and McLaughlin and Glendinning (1994) call familization/defamilization. It is also pertinent to inquire, therefore, into the extent to which states enable individuals to be autonomous of the family. What exit options exist here, in the sense of 'freedom' to participate in the labour market and to enter or exit marriage itself?

To summarize, the model of welfare state outcomes that is being advanced here conceives of the state's agency in the direction of gender stratification. Such a conceptualization renders questions about whether women lose or win from the welfare state too simple. Stratification as conceptualized here focuses attention on two types of outcome. The first relates to welfare states' effect on resource-based relations between women and men. Here income redistribution and poverty are placed at the centre of empirical enquiry. The second type of outcome captures the extent to which welfare states shape incentives for different types of life choices and opportunities on the part of women and men. In regard to such incentive structures, I refer especially to the opportunity to participate, or not, in the labour market and to be independent, or not, of the family.

PART II

Key Characteristics of the British and German Welfare States

CHAPTER 3

The British and German Welfare States and the Support of Family and Gender Relations

Two themes have run like a watermark through this work so far: the sparsity of theoretical attention given to institutional arrangements connecting welfare states and patterns of social stratification, and the relative under-analysis of how social policies are constitutive of gender relations. This chapter turns to the two welfare states themselves, seeking their relevant institutional and normative architecture for the purpose of elucidating the comparative framework. The approach taken by public policies to the support of individuals and families and their treatment of family activities and attendant gender roles and relations are the focus of enquiry. At the macro level, the linchpin of the analysis is the distribution of care work and related obligations among family, market and state; the analysis of the organization of family life and related activities serves as a point of reference for the scope and limits of public support of the family. At the micro level, the focus is on the distributive principles of welfare as they shape patterns of income, family, work and relations between women and men. The existing literature emphasizes the differences between the two welfare states, but it will be interesting to observe whether extant classifications retain their import when parameters deriving from gender and family are applied.

A brief historical reflection on the development and some general features of the British and German welfare states in a comparative context sets the backdrop. The chapter then moves on to a systematic comparison of relevant policies as they were around the mid-1980s, the period to which the empirical material in the rest of the chapters refers. This periodization should be noted, not least because it forces us to exclude the many changes made to the transfer and taxation programs in the intervening period. These will, however, be integrated into the discussion of the final chapter. For the purposes of the comparison here, I focus first on programs that could be classically labelled 'family policies'.[1] Measures for the support of families with children and the degree of public support for the care of ill, elderly and disabled people will be reviewed in turn. The field of inquiry will then be broadened to include all income maintenance and personal taxation policies. This second part of the chapter seeks to lay bare the underlying policy models as they pertain to gender roles and female–male life profiles. In line with the framework developed in the last chapter, the following guide the investigative agenda:

- the scope, range and significant features of policies to support families with caring-related work;
- the normative referents of these policies and their links to other welfare state provisions as well as to wider societal configurations;
- the institutional architecture in terms of male and female risk coverage, the rules of entitlement governing transfers to individuals and families and the treatment of different family types.

The chapter's ultimate goal is to highlight key cross-national differences and similarities in provision so as to develop a set of propositions about the likely effects of cash transfers and social services in Britain and Germany. Needless to say, this is a big agenda and, since the objective is to specify the cross-national comparative picture, many of the finer points of provision in both systems fall by the wayside.

A Backward Glance: A Brief Historical Overview of the British and German Welfare States

Germany led the European way in instituting social insurance as a means of dealing with the costs and consequences of industrialization. Its long-term preference has been for an income and status maintenance model of social security. A succession of acts was passed there in the 1880s, some ten years after unification, introducing compulsory social insurance against sickness (1883), industrial accidents (1884), and invalidity and old age (1889). These programs embody the basic principles of German social protection today (Alber 1986: 6). Insurance is compulsory by law and is self-administered by a plurality of autonomous bodies; benefits, founded on a legally codified entitlement, are based on past contributions rather than need; contributions and benefits are graduated according to earnings; financing is on a bi- or tripartite basis; there is a high degree of institutional separation by occupational status and by 'branch' (pensions, sickness, accident, unemployment and, since 1995, need for long-term care). Although benefits were initially low in value, especially for old age and invalidity pensions, they had a number of important effects: inaugurating the principle of a legal claim to protection; introducing predictability through a guarantee of protection against the worst excesses of paid work; giving workers a financial stake in the system (Rosenhaft 1994: 29). In the light of his belief in the potential for class conflict, a key trigger for Bismarck's introduction of social insurance was to secure loyalty to the constitutional monarchy by tying workers' interests closely to state provision (Rimlinger 1971: 90). However, the unfolding of what was to turn out a very particularistic form of social insurance owes much to the maintenance and reproduction of status and other differences (Alber 1989).

Once introduced, the next forty years marked efforts to consolidate and improve access to social insurance in Germany. In 1927 unemployment was incorporated as a risk for social insurance purposes. When they got round to catering for salaried employees, the German authorities did so in a manner that reflected and substantially maintained the separateness, and relative privilege, of this sector of the population. Distinct and more lucrative schemes were created for them, thereby further consolidating differences among programs and status groups. Dealing with poverty was of secondary priority. A program of social assistance was established by the Social Democrat–governed Weimar Republic in 1924, instituting a system of locally based social provision. This was, according to Rosenhaft (1994: 34), family-focused and associated with disciplinary intervention. The structure of today's German benefit system was then in place, to be interrupted for a time by the National Socialists' accession to power and subsequent postwar superpower haggling over the reconstruction of Germany. Allied proposals for reform sought to assist the needy by creating a common risk pool that would include both the affluent and the unfortunate in a unified system of social insurance. These failed (except for the Soviet Zone), however, and the traditional structure of the German social security system was almost completely reinstated, consolidating the stratification of social insurance funds and the principles of social insurance, equivalence and self-administration. Moreover, one of the defining characteristics of the German social order was reaffirmed: an obligation on private associations and groups, families and individuals to be self-supporting, complemented by the state's commitment to a role of guarantor of income and employment security. Such an attachment to the principle of subsidiarity is telling in three respects: the state's role in redistribution is limited; public assistance is subsidiary to individual and familial self-help; and the state intervenes but reluctantly in intra-familial processes.

British welfare state history emphasizes a contrasting dynamic. It is dominated by the long shadow of needs-based provision – up to the beginning of this century in the form of the poor law (first the Elizabethan Poor Law and then the New Poor Law of 1834) and thereafter in the shape of means-tested assistance (variously titled but always growing over the years). When Britain was forced to deal with similar social problems for which Germany had created an elaborate new social machinery, it did so by retaining elements of ideology and institutions reminiscent of the New Poor Law. Britain was a good twenty years after Germany in instituting a social insurance scheme. Its tardiness in this regard can be attributed to a widespread ideology of self-help (as exemplified by the Friendly Societies and trade union benefit funds), of *laissez-faire* liberalism together with the absence of a powerful political workers' movement and of an effective large-scale state bureaucracy. In a further contrast with Germany, the impetus for the policy innovations that flooded the five years between 1906 and 1911 stemmed more from the need to solve the problem of mass poverty, perceived to be sapping national efficiency, than from the fear of an angry working class.[2]

Among the spate of policies introduced by the Liberals in the first decade of this century were non-contributory (but means-tested) old-age pensions (1908), a network of labour exchanges (1909), and a national insurance system (1911). The last, inaugurating accident, unemployment and combined compulsory sickness and disablement insurance, was organized on the basis of flat-rate contributions and benefits, no test of means, and significant state funding. From the outset, then, Britain showed a fondness for the flat-rate principle and general revenue financing. With the expansion of social insurance over the second and third decades of the century, the British pattern for the future was established: social insurance covering the main causes of earnings loss, conferring flat-rate survival benefits on those who could earn them, with social assistance as the recourse of people outside the pale of labour market protection. Beveridge in his report of 1942 cemented such foundations. Affirming the primacy but minimalist character of social insurance, a system of tripartite financed, comprehensive, compulsory social insurance on a flat-rate basis – one payment, one benefit irrespective of earnings and status – was the centrepiece of his proposals. Acknowledging a continued, but lessened, need for social assistance, he proposed a second tier of means-tested, non-contributory payments that he saw, wrongly as it turned out, as being residual. Given the perceived incentive effects of subsistence-level benefits, the Beveridge arrangement was in essence a plan for compulsory self-help, organized and funded by government at a national level.

In contrast to that of Germany, the British social insurance system has consistently offered low replacement rates, poor coverage of risks and relatively tough eligibility conditions in return for modest contributions

(Ginsburg 1992: 144). For a short time (between the 1960s and the early 1980s), Britain experimented with earnings-related components in social insurance, but these, along with many other provisions, fell under the axe of Thatcherite revision in the last two decades.[3] The insurance principle has been continually downgraded. As a result, means-tested benefits, tightly targeted at particular categories of people officially defined to be in need, came to challenge social insurance as the main plank of income maintenance in Britain. By 1986, 8.29 million people were dependent on the catch-all safety-net program (then Supplementary Benefit, now Income Support) (Ogus et al. 1988: 409). Throughout the 1980s Conservative policy sought to replace Beveridge's call for the abolition of poverty and benefits as of right with the idea of a new partnership between the individual and the state. The new arrangements would amount to 'a system built on twin pillars', with stronger emphasis on individual provision than formerly (Smart 1991: 158). In the process, the reliance individuals can place on the state for support in certain contingencies has been considerably undermined.

As this took place in Britain, the German welfare state more or less held its place and form in a pattern marked by consolidation – a gradual and consensual adaptation to changing economic and social circumstances generally within the confines of the traditional structures, institutions and principles. A major reform of retirement pensions in 1957 tightened the earnings link and transformed pensions from a supplement to a substitute for earnings. This, together with other reforms in the 1950s and 1960s, removed the basic security elements from German social insurance and replaced the more static income orientation of the system by a dynamic one. The provision of a social minimum became the function of *Sozialhilfe*, which in 1961 introduced a safety net against poverty – instituting a general right for all citizens to a locally financed and administered system of public assistance. Although some alterations followed in the course of the financial pressures of the 1970s and 1980s, Germany has retained a welfare state model that grants strong rights to income replacement (once these have been earned through participation in the labour market) while guarding the 'independence' of the family and other non-statutory institutions.

Comparison on the axes of ideology and institutions emphasizes strong divergence between the British and German welfare states. Ideologically the German *Sozialstaat* represents a conceptual fusion of bourgeois constitutional liberalism, mutual solidarity, and the idea of subsidiarity as articulated in Catholic social thought (Freeman and Clasen 1994: 9; Daly 1999). Hierarchy is the watchword for Germany, epitomized by the differentials between the principles of *Versicherung* (insurance), *Versorgung* (a privilege whereby certain categories of citizens, such as civil servants and victims of war, enjoy a right to public benefits without contributing) and *Fürsorge* (social relief – the basis for the safety-net scheme *Sozialhilfe*). It has been characterized as 'a system of social insurance with welfare elements' (Hentschel 1983, cited by Rosenhaft 1994: 40). The British system, in contrast, could be said to be one of 'welfare with some insurance elements'. Comprising low-level, flat-rate and delimited social insurance and a set of basic but ever-widening means-tested provision, the lines of demarcation between social insurance and means-tested benefits are more fuzzy and the degree of stratification among benefit recipients lower. The perpetuation of labour market status differences and the maintenance of living standards throughout the life cycle have never held sway there as first principles to the extent that they did in Germany. The British welfare state, rather, provides a minimum floor, funded in large part from general revenues, that is designed to provide a stop-gap during periods of market or family failure.

But what kind of family and caring policies follow from these principles and how are relations between women and men 'managed'? For the two welfare states as just described, making provision for families and care-related activities raised quite fundamental dilemmas. For Germany the key question historically was how non-labour market-related concerns, such as the need for private as well as public care and the promotion of family solidarity, can be catered for by a social security system in which *Sozialpolitik* is essentially *Sozialversicherung*. The situation in Britain had a rather different complexion, given the country's contrasting, hybrid system of flat-rate insurance and needs-based social assistance. There, the crucial question troubling public provision was how families could be subsidized and the encroach of poverty stemmed without undermining employment incentives.

Policies in Support of the Family and Caring Activities

The following two areas of public provision best define the relationship between the welfare state and the family: policies for the support of families with children, and provisions for other forms of caring. Each relates in key ways to labour market considerations, general and gender equity issues, population levels and the quality of life enjoyed by individuals and families. They also engage with the social definition of the family.

Support of Families with Children

Welfare states have at their disposal a variety of policies through which they can provide support for child-rearing activities. In the context of the availability of a broad range of measures – Kamerman and Kahn (1981), for instance, list nineteen possible policy interventions, ranging through cash allowances, different types of paid and unpaid leaves, social security credits, services – both countries have limited provision. Of the two, Germany follows the more diversified path (see below). The two countries differ therefore in their overall range of policies directed towards assisting families with children. To ascertain the cross-national variation, some features of national policies are more telling than others. The range and nature of policies is a first important considera-tion. The policy objectives provide a second clue. An especially revealing characteristic here is the socio-economic group targeted for policy purposes, itself an indicator of the extent to which policies pursue hori-zontal and/or vertical redistribution. A further dimension is the relative generosity of payments to families with children. The identity of the benefit recipient within the family is also helpful in laying bare the vision of intra-familial relations that underlies particular provisions. The final aspect to be considered is the extent to which the state substitutes for or assists with familial activities by involving itself in the provision of child-care services. Table 3.1 shows how the two countries compare on these criteria.

Britain and Germany differ markedly in the measures they have insti-tuted for the support of families with children. Germany has followed the more diversified policy path, providing, along with cash transfers, tax relief, paid and unpaid parental leaves, and public child-care services. Britain limits its support for families more or less to cash trans-fers; no parental (as distinct from maternal) leave or child-related tax allowances exist, and public child-care facilities are to all intents and purposes non-existent. The British practice of paying supplements to transfer recipients in recognition of their child and partner support obligations and of targeting special cash assistance on low-earning fami-lies with children draws on an anti-poverty logic, with the addition in the case of the latter program of a desire to maintain work incentives. To the extent that it adjusts for non-market factors, the British welfare state breaks with a strict insurance principle, introducing elements of need into social insurance. The German social security arrangements much more faithfully reproduce the wage and therefore income inequalities. They take child support obligations into account only in transfers to the unemployed. In terms of the income orientation of policies, Britain's approach could be said to be both general and targeted on the low-income sectors. Germany also offers support with child-related costs on a general basis (through *Kindergeld*) but employs tax allowances as the main conduit of such financial support.[4] This renders Germany distinc-tive – one of only five countries in a recent fifteen-country study to

Table 3.1 Configuration and characteristics of policies for the support of families with children in Britain and Germany in the mid-1980s

Policy configuration	UK	Germany
Range of policies	Targeted and general cash transfers Support for low-earner families with children	General cash transfers Paid and unpaid parental leaves Tax allowances Child care for children over three
Primary policy objective(s)	Alleviation of child poverty	Horizontal redistribution Support of the traditional family
Socio-economic group targeted by tax and transfers	Low-income families	Middle- and higher-income families
Level of financial support provided[a]	Lower	Higher
Whom family support is directed towards	Mother	Father
Provision of child care	No public child care except for children considered to be 'at risk'	Widespread *Kindergarten* for children over 3 but mainly part-time; although funded by the state they are provided by non-statutory organizations and groups

Note: [a] This evaluation is based on a comparison of the average level of benefits (cash transfers and income tax) for families with children in the two countries.

distribute more than half of its child support through the tax system (Bradshaw et al. 1993).[5] Progressive tax allowances as in Germany benefit higher-income earners, although they are also horizontally redistributive. The widespread use and legitimacy of the concept of *Familienlastenausgleich* (compensation for family-related burdens) in German social policy speaks to its commitment to horizontal redistribution. In considerable contrast, the relatively low value of child benefits and the absence of tax relief for children have the effect in Britain of limiting the degree of horizontal redistribution towards families with children.

In an additional contrast, Germany introduced in 1986 both paid and unpaid parental leaves. The former, *Erziehungsgeld*, offers a flat-rate allowance for up to two years to each parent (mother or father) who acts as primary caregiver for a child aged under three.[6] With no provision for paid parental leave, Britain is, along with Ireland and Luxembourg, unique among European Union countries. But there is no unambiguous gender interpretation of the kind of paid parental leave that was introduced in Germany. For while it does represent a recognition of the need to compensate the caring parent for forgone earnings, the low level of the payment, in rendering it uneconomical for the higher-earning parent to take the leave, also has the effect of reinforcing traditional gender roles. Introduced in a period when the christian democratic–led government sought to bolster traditional family caring patterns for young children, its effect is likely to confirm the woman as the provider of care and to encourage mothers to exit from the labour market for this purpose. In addition, one has to look closely at the gender and family implications of Germany's extensive network of *Kindergarten*. At face value these further distance Germany from Britain, where the only state-supported child care is directed at children who are considered to be 'at risk' in some way. In Germany, over 60 per cent of children aged between three and five are in publicly funded child-care facilities compared with only about 40 per cent in Britain (and many of these are catered for in schools). There is no doubt but that of the two countries considered here Germany has gone further in providing a set of supports to assist families with the exigencies of caring for children. But closer examination reveals the limits of the supports, and tempers the cross-national contrast. In line with an ideology that envisions state-sponsored day care as good for the development of the child, this service in Germany is, along with other educational provision, organized around the perceived best interests of the child. Hence the publicly supported child-care services tend to be limited to children over the age of three, to be available only part-time (usually in the mornings) in most cases and to accord no formal priority to the working status of the mother for placement purposes. Only part-time employment is, therefore, possible for women relying on this form of child-care.

One interesting question raised by the comparison of arrangements in Germany and Britain is the extent to which support for families with children goes hand in hand with the maintenance of a traditional role for women. This certainly seems to be the case in Germany, where more services in support of families with children exist but the main orientation of policy is to ease rather than substitute for the traditional role of the mother as the main manager of household and early child education. The relation operates in the opposite way in Britain, where the welfare state is less supportive of caring for children and less concerned about encouraging a traditional mother role in the family. Britain has, for example, long directed its child-related cash payment to the mother or caretaker, whereas fathers form the vast majority of recipients of *Kindergeld* in Germany. This, taken together with the fact that men are the main beneficiaries of tax allowances, suggests that, of the two, the British welfare state is the more interventionist in regard to the division of financial resources between parents, even though it is overall less supportive of families with children.

Support for Caring for the Ill, Elderly and Others who are Incapacitated

In the last two decades, welfare states have begun to recognize the need to extend cash support to caring for the elderly, the ill and those who are in some other way incapacitated. In both welfare systems the effects of such developments have been innovative. The comparative story in this case, however, is one of both differences and similarities, shot through by real questions about the extent to which either welfare state has supported this form of care work. If we conceptualize caring as having two components – financial costs and labour – state subsidies for the contingency of requiring care could go in one of two directions, either to the person requiring care or to the person who provides it. Essentially the two countries have chosen different routes, Germany the former and Britain some of both but mainly the latter.

In Germany, both the health insurance funds and social assistance (*Sozialhilfe*), the main sources of financial assistance with health-related care needs, demarcate illness from care-dependency for income-support purposes. Up to 1995, only illness was accepted as an individual insurable risk. Expenses incurred in meeting the need for care were covered only under limited conditions: being in need of such care carried no entitlement to public funds as long as one's financial means remained above the thresholds for *Sozialhilfe*. In the event, since any public monies paid for needs relating to care were low, they did not enable the person requiring care to purchase it in the marketplace or to fully compensate the carer, usually a relative. The German state therefore has manifested a very clear position: caring for the ill and other incapacitated persons is more or less a private matter; those who require this care merit assistance from public sources only under strict conditions; and those providing the care privately have no right to income replacement from public funds.

Britain resembles Germany to the extent that it also pays cash additions to the person requiring care, subject to fairly strict evidence of impairment. But Britain also offers a nationally organized benefit directly to those who are providing care to ill and disabled people. Introduced in 1975, the non-contributory Invalid Care Allowance (ICA) is intended to replace earnings lost or forgone by a working-age carer who provides full-time care for a severely disabled person. Placing this benefit in its national context highlights its considerable exceptionality. First, hinging on a labour and time input (at least 35 hours' caring a week) on the part of the recipient, ICA resembles an employment contract between the recipient and the state. It therefore represents at the same time a mixture of commodification and de-commodification: individuals are encouraged to exit from the labour market but receive a public payment not for this purpose alone but for the investment of a specific amount and type of labour. Second, access is exclusively linked to the benefit entitlement of the cared-for person – a situation which, as Glendinning and McLaughlin (1993: 24) remind us, is unprecedented outside marriage. The conditions attaching to receipt of this payment tend to be very strict and as a result it is estimated to be received by less than one-tenth of those who are investing the required amount of caring hours (Glendinning 1992: 171). Third, the benefit is located neither in the insurance nor means-tested domains but is poised between them as a non-contributory, categorical benefit. It is among the lowest-level payments in the British system, offering at the time of study income replacement equivalent to only about 18 per cent of average take-home pay. Notwithstanding its uniqueness within the system, one must bear in mind for the purposes of the present comparison that it is possible for carers of ill, elderly and disabled adults in Britain to receive income support from public sources, whereas this was not so in Germany at the time this study is set.

So what is the state's role as a provider of care for the ill, the elderly and disabled, and what place the market? There are quite substantial cross-national differences in both regards. Two are noteworthy. First, the British welfare state has taken a more active role and has since the postwar years been directly involved, through the local authorities, in the provision of both residential and domiciliary services for the ill, the disabled and the elderly. The scale of its involvement in service provision lent the British welfare state a certain social democratic character. The German welfare state, in contrast, as a transfer state has refrained from large-scale direct involvement in service provision but funds non-profit, social service organizations and the voluntary sector to provide services in its stead. This leads to a second cross-national difference, one pertaining to the role of the market. In Britain the 'partnership' between the state and the market is closer, and in recent years the latter has begun to substitute for the former. That is, the state has begun to disengage from this form of provision, cutting down on its direct services and, in the manner of its financial support, encouraging the growth of market provision. Germany differs in that the state has no significant role as a provider of care and strict controls are in place to delimit the market's role in the provision of health-related services. Therefore, the division of care-related labour is between the family and the voluntary, non-profit sector.

Overview of Public Support for Caring

Drawing both sets of provision for caring together, the overall result is in some ways strikingly similar in that the everyday welfare of the young, the ill and the old is a family matter. To the extent that both reinforce private care-giving, there are no huge variations between the two countries. This part of the analysis therefore challenges the representation of the British and German welfare states as significantly different. Furthermore both systems show evidence of a certain amount of 'strain' in making provision for caring. In fact a complex balancing act is involved in assisting with the costs of care and providing a payment that interferes neither with work incentives (especially in Britain) nor the insurance principle (especially in Germany). However, any strains are more readily managed in Britain, where flat-rate benefits, a distributive principle based primarily on need and a higher degree of government control over policies make for less rigidity in the policy process. Germany has been much slower to recognize the need for care deriving from illness, incapacity and old age. Debate there has been dogged by concern about costs, how any new provisions could be integrated with existing *Kausalprinzipien* and provided for in a manner that would interfere neither with the focus on productive labour nor the existing order of family obligations and relations. At the time this study is set, this care was in Germany almost totally 'familized', with little or no state support.

The state's approach to the family goes a considerable distance in separating the two systems and in helping to make sense of differences in provision. Of the two countries, Germany accords protection of the family a much higher and more formal priority. Article 6.1.1 of the 1949 constitutional (West) German Basic Law establishes the primacy of the family in German society and guarantees the institution, along with motherhood and marriage, protection by and from the state.[7] Influenced by social Catholicism, law and practice operate to a subsidiarity model whereby institutions and functions of the state are secondary to those of the family among other primary institutions (Daly 1999). Self-sufficiency of the family is not automatic, however; families have to be assisted towards this end and the state's role is to provide resources in a volume and form that realizes family self-sufficiency. Subsidiarity, in its essence a theory of boundaries, ordains where the line is to be drawn between protection and encroachment on the part of the state. Direct state intervention is a last resort, permissible only to the degree that the natural order of the lower unit is maintained or restored. The balance between supporting the family and not undermining its functioning is a difficult one to strike. It is not the privatization of the family per se that is the desired goal but rather that the family be enabled to carry out its (traditional) functions. One could describe this as self-sufficiency on the part of the family. But what does family self-sufficiency mean? In large part, I believe, it means family solidarity. As translated into institutional rules this ordains: 1) that individuals have a legal responsibility for the care or financial support of other family members; and 2) that access to many of the public resources is delimited by the prior responsibility of first-line relatives (usually members of the immediate family and especially spouses and children) to provide financial resources or care. While the provision of financial support is likely to be a collective enterprise, the provision of care speaks more readily to intra-familial relations and to a particular gender division of labour.

The British state takes a less clear stance on the family. In comparison with Germany, the relationship between the state and the family has been much less clearly, and perhaps rigidly, articulated in British welfare provisions and family law. Policies have shown more change over time, and also less consistency. The effects of an anti-poverty orientation in this regard cannot be under-estimated – sometimes this can and has cut across the liberal concern with market incentives and sometimes also it has made for innovation in policy. In a comparative context, the role of the state in relation to the family in Britain is residual in contrast to the German *Sozialstaat*, which is proactive in regard to the enhancement of the privacy of the family. The British welfare state is generally looser in tying private care to the family and it is also the more willing of the two to intervene in intra-familial processes, for example by paying child benefits to the mother and by treating caring for the ill, elderly or incapacitated as an activity meriting some income replacement from public resources. Furthermore, in its wish to rid itself of a direct involvement in caring, the British welfare state evinces a greater willingness to encourage private provision through the market. Not only this, but public entitlements do not construct it as the natural duty of family members to care for each other, and state provisions do not necessarily 'familize' care to the same degree as in Germany, where private care leads much more readily to family care, as does family care to care by women. British families are left more to themselves to work out the exigencies of care, with public policies offering fewer incentives than in Germany towards a particular gender division of labour.

What is this gender division of labour? The next section moves on to consider how women and men are integrated into the benefit and personal taxation arrangements in the two welfare states.

The Place of Women, Men and their Families in Transfer and Tax Provisions

Following the approach developed in the last chapter, I suggest that women and men's treatment by welfare states can be identified along three axes of analysis: the risk universe, the bases of entitlement, and the treatment of different family types. Each has its own set of empirical indicators, which will be considered in turn. Table 3.2 presents an overview.

The Risk Universe and the Treatment of 'Male' and 'Female' Risks

Their treatment of risks reveals much about welfare states. At their core, cash transfer systems, social insurance especially, act to compensate for income-related risks. But income risks are themselves gendered. Women and men, especially in the light of their differing family-related roles, tend to experience somewhat different risks of income loss. While women share with men the risks of interruption or loss of earned income through illness, accident, unemployment and old age, they experience three additional risks: loss of a male income (through widowhood, divorce and marital separation); loss of personal income through child-bearing; and loss of personal income through the need to care for others (either adults and/or children). These are all risks associated in one way or another with caring. The strategic question for the purposes of comparison is whether and how these and other income risks are covered for income maintenance or replacement purposes.

In terms of the location of risks, income protection in both welfare states has gendered elements (Table 3.2, first two columns). Only two female risks are covered by social insurance: widowhood and maternity. All in all, the two transfer systems are similar to the extent that 1) typically female-specific risks are less likely to be constructed as a right for access to social insurance than those characterizing male lifestyles; 2) female risks are therefore more likely to be made residual, consigned to needs-based social assistance or not covered at all. In other words, both welfare states make a distinction between needs that occur in relation to market activity (which tend to be constructed as insurance rights) and those arising in 'private life'.

To the extent that social insurance is granted as a right and founded on the principles of achievement and independence, whereas social assistance is based on need or dependence, there is evidence, *prima facie*, of a

Table 3.2 Location of risks, replacement rates and inclusion of non-employed home-makers in the main cash transfer programs, c. 1985/86 (%)

	Where risk is located		Average replacement level[a]		Whether home-maker/carer is covered in own right	
	UK	Germany	UK	Germany	UK	Germany
Illness	Social insurance	Social insurance	26	80	No	No but medical costs covered through husband's contributions
Accident	Social insurance	Social insurance	31	50	No	No
Unemployment	Social insurance	Social insurance	27	61	No	No
Old age	Social insurance	Social insurance	27	47	Yes, through special spouse's pension	No
Maternity	Social insurance	Social insurance	44	100	No	No
Survivorship	Social insurance widowhood only	Social insurance	27	43	—	—
Divorce	Social assistance	Social assistance	21	18	—	—
Lone parenthood	Social assistance	Social assistance	21	18	—	—
Caring for children[b]	Not covered	Categorical payment	—	22	—	No
Caring for others	Categorical payment	Not covered	18	—	Yes, payment in own right	No

Notes: [a] Calculated as proportion of the net take-home pay of a single person earning an amount equivalent to average earnings of production workers in the manufacturing sector in 1985/86 (OECD 1988).

      [b] Given the origins of child benefits, they are not treated here as payments for caring for children. The relevant benefit in the German case is paid parental leave.

Sources: Britain: *Social Security Statistics 1986, 1989.*
         Germany: *Statistisches Jahrbuch* 1988, 1990 and 1991.

hierarchy. While this hierarchy undoubtedly draws also on other differentiators (such as career and position in the labour market for instance), Table 3.2 shows that there is both a marked and strikingly similar gender faultline in the risk hierarchies of the two welfare states. Taking wage replacement levels into account (third and fourth columns) strengthens the impression of a gender-related hierarchy showing how female risks consistently yield lower replacement rates than male risks. However, this is a far more entrenched division in Germany, where social insurance replaces around 60 per cent of the average wage compared with only 25 per cent in the means-tested programs. In Britain's 'mongrel' version of social insurance, flat-rate and low-level benefits are the order of the day – the average insurance-based payment is only about 10 percentage points higher than the equivalent means-tested payment, but neither replaces more than 31 per cent of the average wage.

What is not clear from Table 3.2, because of lack of available information, is the extent to which hierarchies based on sex or gender exist within the different programs. While this is something that will be explored empirically in the next chapter, a number of factors lead one to expect such gender hierarchies to be more pronounced in Germany. More precisely, the classical social insurance model contains a number of features likely to generate gender differentials (Scheiwe 1994). First, the emphasis on the contribution principle, which ties the level of benefit to the duration of contributions, disadvantages women relative to men since female involvement in the labour market is either more interrupted or of a shorter duration than that of men. Second, given the close link between transfer height and the former wage, we can expect that transfers to women will reflect their average lower earnings. To the extent that this model is adhered to more closely in Germany, it can be expected to lead to more entrenched gender inequalities.

The Construction of Entitlement and of 'Dependants'

This set of indicators draws out the basis on which people can make claims on public resources. It embraces both the unit of entitlement and the conditions defining entitlement, with particular reference to whether and how women who are wives and mothers are covered.

With regard to the unit of entitlement, there is little variation in that for the purposes of social insurance the unit of entitlement in both systems is the employed individual. What does vary, though, is the degree to and manner in which each system draws in the family situation of the claimant as a factor influencing the level of the payment. In Britain social insurance relates to the collective unit through the inclusion of flat-rate and fixed supplements for adult, and in some cases child, 'dependants'. Social insurance payments in Germany take no direct account of the family obligations of the recipient except in the case of those to the unemployed, which specifically demarcate a different level of wage replacement for recipients with children and also reproduce the family-related allowances contained in the taxation system (since these benefits are calculated on a net rather than gross wage replacement formula). Yet in both national settings these institutional particularities speak more to the level of the benefit for the collective unit than they do to the capacity of the second partner to receive a benefit in her or his own right (to be considered below). When it comes to the unit of entitlement for means-tested benefits, Britain operates a collective unit model, whereas Germany's *Sozialhilfe* is an individualized right. But since the latter rate of payment is subject to conditions about the availability of resources from other members of the household, the individualized nature of the right is very constrained.[8]

A further stage in the distributive process embodied in transfers concerns the construction of entitlement. Here the detailed conditions of eligibility come into play, and for our purpose what is most relevant is how those involved in family-related activities can claim access to public resources. This directs attention in particular to how marriage and motherhood are treated for the purpose of access to benefits in the two systems. Theoretically, the choice of how to integrate those involved in family activities is a threefold one: provide them with benefits in their own right, give them a claim to benefits through their husbands or partners, or accord them no claim at all. The first is akin to extending transfer coverage to those outside the conventional productive labour sector and is a model that has never been fully implemented anywhere. The second and third are variants of a male breadwinner model. As the most widespread policy settlement in developed welfare states, elements of both are to be found in Britain and Germany. To the extent that the woman has derived rights only or receives no benefits at all, the breadwinner model has negative connotations for women's personal income and financial independence. A second element commonly associated with a breadwinner model – a construction of marriage as an institution of private maintenance for spouses – also acts to reduce women's financial autonomy.

Table 3.2 (last two columns) compares the method of including home-makers (that is, non-employed mothers and wives) in the two systems. Strong elements of a male breadwinner model are to be seen in both by virtue of the fact that women outside the labour market for caring-related reasons receive little or no coverage in their own right. But the British system is less traditional in two respects. First, spouses in Britain have derived rights to old-age pensions, which means that those without personal pension rights can claim a part of their spouse's basic pension even when he or she is still alive. Second, as we have seen earlier, only in Britain is it possible for carers of ill, elderly and disabled adults to receive a public payment for the purpose of this activity (albeit at a low level and governed by strict conditions). While neither system could be said to grant strong individual rights to people who are currently involved in or have spent significant portions of their active years caring, the British system is the more 'carer-friendly' in this respect.

The treatment and degree of protection accorded to the institution of marriage is also a telling indicator of the gender tenor of policies. A number of cross-national differences in this respect are noteworthy. In German family law, marriage is accorded a very important place as an institution of private maintenance. This is to be seen especially in the arrangements for marital breakdown. German divorce law, for example, makes provision for an equal division of all economic assets acquired during marriage, including pension credits. Moreover, in a desire to maintain the marital status quo, a former wife can be granted personal maintenance if, for a number of reasons, she was not employed before divorce. In Britain, marriage as an institution is less protected and financial independence within and outside marriage more encouraged. The thrust of the new divorce legislation in 1984 was towards a 'clean break' model with a rather strong emphasis on the possibility of no continuing financial responsibilities between spouses and a once and for all capital settlement. Marriage in this model, says Douglas (1990: 415), is like a business partnership: 'if it doesn't work out, cut your losses and start again with someone else.' Of the two then, the British state is the more reluctant to foster financial dependence on their husbands for no-longer married women and it is also less willing to assume the male maintenance role once the marriage ends, be it through divorce or death. The legal comparison overall suggests that women in Germany should be better protected in the case of divorce. However, since post-divorce maintenance agreements are notoriously unsuccessful, we should keep an open mind about the comparative well-being of divorced women in the two national settings.

The Treatment of Different Household Types

Taxation policy together with income maintenance measures are powerful in shaping family form and economy. In each of the two countries, state policies make a differentiation between households headed by married and unmarried persons. This differentiation is more pronounced in Germany, where the taxation system goes to greater lengths not only to support marriage but to promote a partic-ular form of gender relations within marriage. One-earner couples with or without children are privileged over both single earners and two-earner married couples. Tax-splitting (*Ehegattensplitting*), whereby spousal incomes are added together, halved and then taxed as two separate incomes, is the main vehicle for such privileging. In an examination of the 'tax-benefit package' in fifteen countries, Shaver and Bradshaw (1993) show that, of the two countries under consideration here, Germany provides the greater support for a dependent wife, with an income differential in disposable income of 10 per cent between couples and a single person at average earnings, compared with 4 per cent in Britain. Some idea of the scale of support for a male breadwinner model in Germany's tax system can be gleaned from the fact that in an average year the total volume of *Ehegattensplitting* is almost as much as all other forms of personal tax allowances put together. With such support for a traditional form of marriage in Germany independent of whether there are children in the family, this arrangement speaks primarily to economic relations between spouses. Support of a particular division of labour within the married family clearly rivals support of children as the hegemonic principle of German family policy: in 1991, for example, the cost of *Ehegattensplitting* was DM28.7 billion compared with a total of DM31 billion for the child-related tax allowances, child benefit and paid parental leave (Ostendorf 1997: 380). In Britain at the time the present comparison is set, personal income taxation also favoured married men by awarding them an additional allowance. However the employed woman, married or not, has long had her own tax allowance (equivalent to that of the single earner). Comparing Britain to Germany, then, indicates that while both systems offer some premiums to marriage, the role of a dependent, non-earning wife is more encouraged in Germany.

Within the married/unmarried differentiation lies a distinction between lone-parent and two-parent households. Lone parents, the treatment of whom can be taken as revealing the state's relationship to families without male support, pose something of a dilemma for social insurance-based welfare states, since they lack an active male link to the labour market. The similarities in the response of the two countries are very striking. Both welfare systems have dealt with these families by 1) differentiating among them, especially singling out those headed by widows from others, and 2) generally failing to make specific provision for the latter, therefore consigning them to social assistance. The underlying reference of such differentiations is the marital relationship or that of mothers to the fathers of their children. Family status is arguably given greater priority than women's relationship to the labour market. This is in some contrast to the differentiation made among men wherein the able-bodied/non-able-bodied criterion is to the fore.

Widows receive the best treatment relative to other lone-parent families from both transfer systems. They were the first group of mother-only families to be supported in both countries in the early decades of this century – thereby institutionalizing the risk of 'loss of maintenance' for women (although not for men) into social insurance. Earned on the basis of husbands' insurance contributions, the early widow's pensions laid down no conditions limiting the labour market activity of the recipient. Nor did they enquire into the economic activity of the women involved: being a wife was synonymous with dependence and therefore worthy of state support when reliance on the male income was no longer possible. As the wives of former insurance contributors, these women were automatically de-commodified; they were, indeed, the only category of female-headed families to be so. Their right was founded on the fact of their marriage to men who had paid their dues. Until today, neither the German nor the British system requires widowed claimants to be occupied with domestic duties and, as can be seen in Table 3.2, their benefits are more generous than those for other lone-mother families. To the extent that this is the case, one could say that widows are a privileged group. However, given its more hierarchical nature, the gap between replacement rates for survivorship and other female risks is greater in Germany.

Widows apart, Britain and Germany's treatment of lone-parent families is very similar. Neither has made categorical provision for such families. Divorced, separated and unmarried mothers must, if they require state income support, rely on the 'safety net' of income-tested social assistance. They resort to social assistance, as do all other sections of the population with inadequate incomes and no claim to social insurance, but they receive a slightly higher payment in recognition of their higher living costs. In Britain these lone-parent families are singled out from other social assistance claimants in two important respects. First, at the time this study is set they were not required to register for employment as long as they had children younger than 16 years. This signifies a lack of state expectation that these mothers should, and in reality a lack of motivation for them to, be engaged in paid work. Second, the British welfare state is an increasingly reluctant supporter of these families, especially in recent years. Men's responsibility to maintain their families is emphasized.[9] While case law in Germany is contradictory, it is generally assumed for social assistance purposes that a mother should seek at least part- time employment once her child reaches the age of 10. The German welfare state evinces no great desire to support these families either, but it is concerned that children's standard of living should be maintained after separation or divorce.[10]

Overview

This chapter has pursued a particular line of enquiry, locating the potential for the gendering of welfare state provision in the extent to which differentials and inequalities are constructed or reinforced between women and men in the context of family-related roles and relations. Such processes are seen to reside not only in the income and resources made available through welfare and tax arrangements but also in 1) how a state/family/market distribution of labour is set up and 2) a female/male division of rights to public support established. The availability of public services that support or directly undertake caring is not only a useful guide to the macro-level interactions between state, family and market but it also plays an important role in framing the context within which women and men make choices about how to manage their family responsibilities.

Stepping some paces back from the detail, it is possible to pinpoint the sources of institutional variation that are likely to lead to significant cross-national gender differences. Table 3.3 takes an overview of the comparative framework and in the last column presents some likely outcomes. These propositions, quite general at this stage, will be specified in more detail as the empirical analyses proceed.

In regard to caring, both states operate on a general set of premises that strikes a careful balance in the type of and degree to which caring work is publicly supported. This is one dimension on which the two welfare states are more similar than different; public services and the degree of income support for caring are either very low or are offered in a form and volume that make family caring the norm in both. The two countries therefore are characterized by a relatively similar division of labour between the state and the family. This leads to some similarities in the incentives for particular roles on the part of women and men. The two sets of welfare arrangements are similar to the extent that they urge labour market participation on men. They are also similar in that full-time motherhood, at least for a period, is encouraged. Thus we can expect caring for young children to be full-time in both, with consequent fairly large inequalities in personal income between mothers and fathers. However, cross-national differences in the situation of women other than mothers of young children are to be expected. Those women in Britain who are involved in caring for the ill, elderly and other incapacitated people are more likely to be receiving public income support than in Germany. To frame the likely outcome from the point of view of older German women: they are less likely to have an income of their own in the first place and in the second the gaps between their personal incomes and those of men are likely to be larger.

Table 3.3 Main dimensions of variation between the British and German welfare states from a gender perspective

Dimension	Axis of comparison	UK	Germany	Likely Outcomes
Extent of public service provision for caring for children	The extent to which mothers of young children are 'freed' for labour market participation	Lower	Higher	Mothers of young children are unlikely to be in the labour market; large income inequalities are therefore likely between mothers and fathers in both systems
Extent to which caring for ill, elderly and disabled is publicly supported	The extent to which caring for ill, elderly and disabled earns cash transfers in its own right	Higher	Lower	This form of caring is likely to be more privatized in Germany re-inforcing the tendency of greater income inequality between women and men there
Key features of income support policies re:				
a) General organizational principles	Sex and gender differences in access to transfers, transfer level and tax-related allowances	Flat-rate cash transfers and more individualized taxation	Wage-related social insurance and taxation favours one-earner couples	Sex and gender differences in transfer and taxation levels higher in Germany

Table 3.3 (Cont.)

b) Treatment of male and female income risks	Differences between women and men in their location within the transfer system	The risk hierarchy is less entrenched, therefore 'female' risks less residualized	'Female' risks more residualized relative to those of men	Differences between women and men's location within the transfer system more pronounced in Germany hence higher sex gaps in income inequality and household poverty
c) Construction of entitlement	The intra-household flow of resources	Entitlement individualized but dependence on the part of spouses less emphasized	Entitlement individualized for workers with very strong incentives towards dependence for spouses	Greater female reliance on 'family solidarity' in Germany, hence lower sex differences in individual poverty
d) Treatment of families	How different types of families are treated, especially those headed by a woman	Marriage less privileged	Not only marriage but one-earner couples privileged	Greater incentives for a traditional role for women in Germany plus the risk of lone parenthood is less protected there

Their underlying principles of organization and income redistribution set the two welfare states widely apart. The fact that I compare here one minimum, flat-rate benefit system and one that is earnings-related sets us up for an analysis of the consequences of each type of model for income inequality and poverty in general, as well as sex- and gender-based divisions. To the extent that a social insurance model is closely followed, we can expect it to generate greater sex- and gender-related income inequalities. In particular, the German system, in much more faithfully reproducing wage levels, tying benefits to contributions and emphasizing duration of contributions, seems firmly set in the direction of strong differences between women and men. Female risks of income loss are treated more residually there compared with Britain. The taxation system, encouraging low or no labour market participation for married women, is also important in this regard. The transfer and tax arrangements together mean that German women are less likely to qualify for a (substantial) state transfer in their own right since they are discouraged from the labour market participation through which they could accumulate associated rights. While social insurance also dominates the British welfare system, its flat-rate character, lack of segregation and higher number of individualized elements for women lead one to predict that differentials and inequalities between women and men in Britain will be of a lower order. Moreover, the greater general recourse to means-tested benefits in Britain is likely to limit the scale of male–female differences in transfer height. In terms of income inequality in general then, the features of the two models lead us to expect stronger male–female differentials in the German set of arrangements.

In regard to poverty, the cross-national story is likely to be of greater poverty in the British case, given lower wages and generally lower levels of cash transfers there. When it comes to the distribution of poverty by sex and gender, this will depend to some extent on which income unit, household or individual, is under the spotlight. At the household level, the distribution of poverty by the sex of the head is likely to be negative for women's households in both national settings. The orientation of both transfer arrangements towards market risks leads us to this expectation. Since income need in women's households is less often induced by market-related contingencies, such households will tend to be consigned to the basic level of provision that in turn renders them vulnerable to poverty. However, the gaps in transfer height, the internal differentiation that is an inevitable consequence of wage-linked transfers together with the pervasiveness there of labour market–related risk coverage lead one to expect that the sex differences in household poverty will be more pronounced in Germany. When it comes to poverty among individuals, one can expect a somewhat different cross-national picture. In paying generally high transfers and directing them to the wage-earner, the German welfare state also places greater emphasis on 'family solidarity' as a means of female support. Given this, sex differences in individual poverty rates there should be lower than for Britain. The final parts of the review of the two sets of arrangements considered them in the light of their treatment of different types of household. Here we saw that the traditional couple household, the male breadwinner model if you like, is more favoured in Germany. In a word, marriage is treated as the domain of maintenance for women. This leads me to hypothesize not only that German women will be less likely to participate in the labour market but also that the incentives against marital break-up will be stronger there.

CHAPTER 4

Sex, Gender and the Distributive Principles of Cash Transfer Systems

This chapter, a companion to the last, investigates empirically how the two income-maintenance systems are structured and operate in practice. Its overall objective is to identify the extent to which hierarchies based on sex and gender are to be found in the income programs of the two welfare states and to see how these are expressed in women and men's differential experience of cash transfers. I want in particular to develop a notion of process and social relations when analysing cash benefit arrangements. The analysis to be carried out in this chapter will, in fact, be oriented more to process than to outcome. Cash benefit arrangements are understood as engaging people in a set of practices and social relations that affect their social and gender identity as well as contributing to the more structural phenomenon of social stratification. While I cannot focus directly on the experiential aspects of welfare, I will illuminate the processes whereby women and men are moved through the different cash transfer programs. The chapter has both a descriptive and analytic intent. Descriptively it seeks to identify the manner in which the two transfer arrangements grant access, construct claims and distribute financial resources. Analytically the key thrust is to investigate whether sex and/or gender, in their own right and in the context of other factors, are identifiable principles of stratification in either or both transfer systems. The meaning of stratification will be specified in relation to particular aspects of transfer programs as the analysis proceeds. I begin with individuals, tracing the reach of the income-maintenance mechanisms and identifying the factors that significantly affect both transfer access and size. A similar line of analysis is then undertaken for households.

Focus of Analysis

The twin ideas of hierarchy and differentiated social relations form the heart of my conceptualization of benefit systems as gendered. Hierarchy from a gender perspective is widely taken to refer to the extent to which a sex bias is visible in transfer receipt. Such a bias, often interpreted as sex segregation in cash transfers, has in much feminist work been taken as sufficient evidence that welfare states are gendered (Fraser 1989; Sainsbury 1996). Sex segregation is, however, an imprecise and inadequate specification of the relations between gender and transfers. It is imprecise because it does not make clear whether sex segregation is a general or specific form of the relation between individuals and cash transfer arrangements. It is inadequate because it fails to consider gender, seeing hierarchy more or less exclusively in terms of a typically one-dimensional comparison between women and men as recipients or non-recipients. Working with the concept of sex segregation has, in addition, led to a rather simplistic characterization of benefit systems as dualistic, whereby men are said to predominate in the upper, more generous tier and women in the less generous programs. Such a one-dimensional portrayal may be attributable also to the current state of analysis. Quantitatively, feminist research has remained at rather a rudimentary level. What has been especially missing is work that probes the underlying structure of relationships between gender and other factors. There has been, for example, little or no multivariate analysis to demonstrate how the applicant's sex and family role intertwine with other factors to govern transfer relations. In the context of existing shortcomings two questions become important: how to conceptualize transfer receipt as embedded in a social process, and how to elaborate and establish empirically a more complex view of sex and gender hierarchies in benefit systems.

To understand better the process whereby people get income from public sources, I place the 'transfer relation' at the centre of analysis. This brings to life the idea that transfers are embedded in processes that institutionalize the relationship between individuals' claims on public resources and the apparatus of the state. Working with a concept of transfer relations leads one to differentiate between three dimensions or stages of the process of claiming and receiving income maintenance from public sources. The first is gaining access, the second is the treatment of one's 'claim' in terms of the structure and mode of organization of benefit programs, and the third is the financial return accruing to different kinds of claim. Such a threefold conceptualization uncovers not just the processes that steer people and their claims through the system but also the comparative financial gradations that are to be found there. It thereby makes for a more complex understanding of the hierarchical dimensions that inhere in income-maintenance systems and how they might in turn act as stratifiers.

Moving beyond a simplistic notion of sex segregation also means specifying a broader set of hierarchical elements. Parity, in the sense of equal treatment and equal access to benefits for women and men, has been the most widely used stratification parameter. The reliance on this alone is problematic. It may, for example, be misleading about the gender impact of benefits because it takes too little account of the structure of benefits and their embeddedness within larger income packages and social relations. Hence while some measure of benefit inequality is indispensable to the study of gender hierarchies, it needs to be supplemented by indicators that tap benefit quality. In the latter regard, the degree of income adequacy and income security is essential to any evaluation of benefit quality (Davis Hill and Tigges 1995). On the independent variables side, a number of analytical clarifications – between sex and gender and between individuals and households as units of analysis – are also required. Sex is empirically straightforward as a variable. Gender I define as having two crucial empirical referents: male and female *status in relation to the family*, and male and female *economic activity patterns as they are affected by family-related exigencies*. The first connotes position in relation to the family, the second betokens practice and position in relation to the market and the family. So defined, gender is a characteristic of most meaning for people of working age (defined as under 60 years).[1] Conceptualizing gender in this manner has a sensitivity to both male and female family positions and roles and allows us also to incorporate role combinations more dynamically into the empirical analyses. A key aspect of the individual–welfare state relation is the treatment of individuals relative to their status within the family or household. The potential for gender-based stratification among individuals lies in a systematic privileging of one person over another for the purposes of gaining access to transfers in the first place, and as regards the size of transfers in the second. Below I shall specify the conditions under which transfer systems can be said to be gender-stratified as they relate to individuals, drawing on considerations such as the priority given to the household head and to characteristically male income risks over those of women (as developed in Chapter 2). Logistic regression, a multivariate technique, will be used to determine which factors have a causal imprint on transfer receipt. When the household is the unit of analysis, the sex of the household head[2] is as close as we can come to male/female differentiation. More and more this demographic (in part anyway) characteristic is assuming sociological significance, with women and men heading very different kinds of households. In these two

Table 4.1 Some structural and socio-economic characteristics of male- and female-headed households[a]

	UK		Germany	
	Male	Female	Male	Female
Mean age of head	48	54	48	56
Mean number of children	0.76	0.36	0.61	0.20
Mean household size	2.9	1.6	3.0	1.6
Marital status of head				
% single	10	22	7	23
%married	82	—	85	6
% survivors	} 8	} 78	4	49
% divorced/separated			4	22
Economic status of head				
% in the labour market	67	28	72	35
% retired	19	33	16	40
% other	14	39	12	25
Mean gross adjusted pre-transfer annual household income	£4,860	£2,414	DM22,080	DM12,588

Notes: [a] Based on households for which complete information exists on gross and net income.

national settings as in most others, women tend to be heads of only two types of household: those consisting of just one person (elderly or non-elderly) and those comprising a lone parent with children (Table 4.1). When the household is the unit of analysis, as in the second part of the chapter, the main potential for stratification lies in a systematic differentiation in treatment of one household type over another, specifically, for our purposes, those headed by a man as against those with female heads.

Before we proceed one final analytic clarification is necessary. In order to make incomes comparable across households, collective incomes have to be adjusted to take account of household size and composition and attendant economies of scale. For such an adjustment of incomes in the present case, a standard equivalence scale – the OECD – is used. This distinguishes between the head and other adults (according weights of 1 to the head and 0.7 to all other adults) and between adults and children (each child under 16 years of age being accorded a weight of 0.5). In this manner an adult equivalent income for each household is derived. Unless explicitly stated otherwise, all sources of household income used in the analyses in this and other chapters have been adjusted in this manner for household circumstances. Since these transformations are so central to the household analyses, we should note the most important of the conditions that they impose on the data. In particular, full information is required on the income of all adult household members, both gross and net – a condition with fairly demanding consequences for the valid population base (especially in the German survey).[3] Note that only household income is adjusted in this manner. Where individuals are the focus of analysis, as in the first half of this chapter, the analysis proceeds for the most part on the basis of individual incomes unadjusted for household circumstances.

Male and Female Receipt of Cash Transfers

Male and Female Access to Transfers[4]

Proceeding from all programs to one of the most widely used distinctions, the social insurance/means-tested dichotomy, Table 4.2 shows the proportions of men and women in both countries receiving transfers .[5]

The overall patterns of transfer receipt (the third and sixth data columns) set the general backdrop for sex and gender differences. The direct reach of cash transfers is very similar in the two countries, with about 44 per cent of individuals being in receipt of benefits. A first reading of these figures suggests that variation by sex sunders this general cross-national similarity, with women dominating the population of transfer recipients in the UK and men in Germany. A somewhat different reading of the situation emerges from the data in the second row, however, which arguably provides a truer measure of the reach of the public income maintenance arrangements since they exclude transfers that could be said to be income supplementational in nature – the universal child cash allowances (Child Benefit in Britain, *Kindergeld* in Germany). The resultant fall in the proportion of recipients to 31 per cent in the UK and 28 per cent in Germany illustrates how child-related payments have a roughly similar (but cross-nationally sex-differentiated) effect in inflating recipiency rates. Removing such general transfers to families with children rids the German sample of a significant male–female difference in receipt patterns. A small sex variation lingers on in the UK, with a 34 per cent female recipiency rate compared with a male rate of 28 per cent.

Looking at male and female patterns across program types pinpoints significantly higher female receipt of old-age pensions as the main source of sex differences in the UK (data not shown).[6] Any predominance of women, then, mainly draws on a well-known demographic difference: greater female longevity and hence women outnumbering men in the older age cohorts. Similar demographic patterns in the

Table 4.2   Proportion of men, women and all individual respondents receiving cash transfers[a]

Program type	UK			Germany		
	Men	Women	All		Men	Women	All
All programs	28.5	58.6	44.2	58.0	30.6	43.8
Programs excluding child benefits	27.9	33.7	30.9	27.0	28.4	27.7
Of these:						
Social insurance programs[b]	20.4	28.0	24.4	22.3	25.2	23.8
Means-tested programs[b]	10.0	9.4	9.7	6.1	5.5	5.8
$n =$	7,376	7,979	15,335	3,036	3,248	6,284

Notes: [a]   Based on respondents for whom complete information is available on their personal and household incomes.
   [b]   Because of receipt of different benefits simultaneously, the sum of these two types of benefit may be greater than that in the second row.

German sample are not reflected in old-age pension receipt because, given both the regulations governing pensions and lower levels of female labour market participation, fewer elderly women there qualify for such a pension. This leads to another cross-national difference in the much higher proportion of German women receiving widow's pensions (11 per cent compared with 2 per cent in the UK). This cross-national difference is traceable to both higher numbers of female survivors in the German sample and also to the fact that women there tend to continue to draw survivor pensions throughout their 'transfer career'. In the UK it may be more advantageous to change from survivor to old-age pensions once one reaches the qualifying age for the latter (given prevailing benefit conditions and payment levels). One of the most significant points to remember, however, is that 16 per cent of the women aged 65 years and over in the German sample have neither an old-age nor a widow's pension, compared with 2 per cent of the UK women. Gaining access to a personal pension would appear to be harder for women in Germany. Subsequent analyses will reveal why.

There are further cross-national variations of a programmatic kind. One such variation resides in the use of means-tested benefits. This is considerably more widespread in the UK. A second variation concerns receipt of child benefits. The targeting of this payment on mothers in the UK works well, whereas in Germany *Kindergeld* is effectively a payment for fathers. Regardless of the recipient, however, such benefits are very minor – equivalent to 2 per cent of net personal incomes for both total populations (but 7 per cent for women in the UK). Since child benefits are designed as supplements to income, it seems incorrect to include them on the same basis as transfers that are intended as income replacement. For this reason, and given their strong but largely superfluous (because of very low payment levels) effect on the sex and gender comparison, I shall exclude child benefits from many of the analyses carried out below.

Together these data help to build a picture of both the pattern of transfer access in the two welfare states as well as sex and gender fault-lines. While at first glance both cash transfer systems look to be strongly sex-differentiated, this is an artefact of the wide spread and sex-specific targeting of universal child benefits. Once these are removed, a significant sex difference in transfer receipt is to be found in neither sample, although women form the majority of transfer recipients in both. The analyses undertaken thus far serve to underline the need to look beneath the surface of benefit receipt and transfer statistics.

Identifying Sex and Gender as Factors
Governing Individual Receipt of Transfers

So far only loose patterns of association have been established. I now move on to identify, in the context of the general principles governing access to transfers, how sex and gender predict benefit receipt when other factors are controlled for. Regression analyses, in particular logit analysis (using the SPSS logistic regression program), will be used to examine causally the relationships involved. This technique predicts the log of the odds; in the present case the odds relate to the probability of someone with specific characteristics receiving transfers (p) compared with the probability that they do not $(1 - p)$. The odds for each variable relate to a particular reference category. The difference between the odds for each category and its reference category compares the effect of that category of the variable on the dependent variable with that of the reference category, other factors being controlled for.

Drawing on the analytic considerations set out at the beginning of the chapter, the regression analyses will be used for the specific purpose of testing whether sex and gender independently govern access to transfers. In relation to sex, which is operationalized simply by classifying respondents as either male or female, the ideal test would be to compare how women and men with similar levels of need and/or entitlement fare in terms of securing transfers. It is not possible to do such a comparison directly, however, because women and men's circumstances vary in that they tend to experience quite different risks of income loss, especially in the active years. What I propose to do instead is to control for the effects of factors that give a general indication of neediness in relation to benefit entitlement, in particular income insufficiency (defined in terms of a personal income of below 50 per cent of the population median adjusted income – the cut-off point that will be used to measure poverty in Chapter 6) – and status in relation to the labour market and age, and then test for the significance of the sex variable. This will allow us to ascertain whether sex (as the category of male or female) has an independent effect or not on transfer receipt. Gender, so defined for the purposes of this study as to draw on differentiations between women and men in relation to their family status and economic role, is the more complicated, if not sociological, of the two variables. I suggest that for transfer programs to be identified as gender-differentiated or stratified they must meet certain conditions. In this regard I propose the following three conditions. The first is that the household head be prioritized for transfer receipt. Since most heads of households are men, benefit programs that privilege the head of household indirectly privilege men over women. The second consideration centres upon the coverage of income risks. The specific condition here is that there should be a bias against characteristically female risks. Because of technical problems and some shortages of cases, I can test here directly only for one female-specific risk.[7] This is lone motherhood (defined with reference to women rearing children alone whether they are widowed, never married, or divorced or separated). The third condition for transfer programs to be designated as gender-stratified is that, in circumstances of low income, they should support male family roles over those of women. To test for this, I differentiate a number of male and female family statuses[8] and examine how each status in association with low personal income governs transfer receipt relative to the average.[9] Since gender is most meaningfully defined as a characteristic of prime-age people, separate analyses are run for those aged under 60 years and for the total population including pensioners (only the former are shown because the results for the total population are not significantly different).

As might be expected, given the descriptive results presented in Table 4.2, being either male or female does not significantly predict receipt of transfers on the part of individuals in its own right in either country. This is true for both those under 60 as well as respondents of all ages. Controlling for other factors shows that any sex differences found are a product of other differences between women and men. Table 4.3 helps to identify these other factors by showing how the coefficient and standard error for the sex variable alter when other key variables are added to the model. The results are interesting in a number of respects. First, sex is, neither on its own nor when the effect of other factors is controlled for, a very strong predictor of transfer receipt in either national setting. Of the two countries, though, the sex effect tends to be stronger in the UK. Any sex effects are also very fluid, as can be seen

Table 4.3   Beta coefficients and standard errors for the sex variable on the probability of receiving transfers when different variables are added to the equation

Beta coefficient		Standard error		Variables entered
UK	Germany	UK	Germany	
Those under 60 years				
−0.05	−0.03	0.05	0.04	Being a woman
0.28	0.07	0.06	0.05	Being a woman, low-income father/husband, wife
0.07	0.03	0.06	0.05	Being a woman, low-income father/husband, wife, lone parenthood
0.11	−0.08	0.08	0.05	Being a woman, low-income father/husband, wife, lone parenthood, financial need
0.30	0.09	0.09	0.05	Being a woman, low-income father/husband, wife, lone parenthood, financial need, out of the labour market
All age groups				
0.27	0.03	0.04	0.03	Being a woman
0.35	0.32	0.04	0.03	Being a woman, low-income father/husband, wife
0.29	0.31	0.04	0.03	Being a woman, low-income father/husband, wife, lone parenthood
0.39	0.04	0.05	0.04	Being a woman, low-income father/husband, wife, lone parenthood, financial need
0.25	0.25	0.08	0.04	Being a woman, low-income father/husband, wife, lone parenthood, financial need, out of the labour market

from the way in which the value of the coefficient fluctuates when different factors are added to the model. Again, this is something that is more true of the UK than Germany. What it means in practice is that women and men differ on many of the characteristics associated with transfer receipt, especially so in the UK population. Second, only when people of all age groups are included in the analysis does the sex variable approach significance.

The gender factors prove to be more discriminating predictors of access to transfers, especially in the German case. From Table 4.4, which presents the factors for each national setting as well as those which are significant cross-nationally (in terms of the coefficients, level of significance and computed probabilities[10]), we can see the direction, significance and magnitude of the effect of each factor when the others are controlled for within and across national settings. The German transfer arrangement is the more gender-stratified in that it meets more of the conditions set out above. In particular, in Germany husbands and fathers are in circumstances of low income significantly favoured for transfer receipt. This is not the case in the UK, where the family status of men or women exerts no significant impact on the odds of transfer receipt. Results are a bit more ambivalent on the second condition set out for a benefit system to be gendered – that there be a bias against female risks. Neither system operates an identifiable bias against the essentially female risk of lone parenthood. Indeed in the UK lone mothers are significantly more likely to be receiving benefits, whereas in Germany this status has no significant effect on the probability of receiving transfers. With regard to the third condition, being a household head is a significant precipitator of transfer receipt in both systems. So to the extent that both privilege the household head among individuals, they are gendered. Finally, and on a more general note, while both systems prioritize the risk of loss of labour market income per se, this increases the chances of a person of working age receiving transfers by 40 per cent in the UK and 32 per cent in Germany. As can be seen from the last panel of Table 4.4, which shows the variables that have a significantly different impact across systems, the German transfer system's favouring of low-income husbands or fathers and the lower chances of benefit receipt on the part of wives are the factors most differentiating it from that of the UK.

When pensioners are included in the analysis (data not shown), the gender effects, and the cross-national differences, become stronger, yielding models with generally better predictive utility[11] in both cases (especially in the German case). Although wives with low personal income have in both welfare states a negative chance of receiving transfers, this relationship is significant only in Germany, the status of low-income wife there reducing the chances (by 21 per cent) of receiving a welfare state transfer. The more egalitarian orientation of pensions in the UK welfare state is indicated by the absence of any privileging of husbands or fathers in circumstances of low income. In general the effect of the gender variables makes for a significant difference between the two systems.

To summarize, neither welfare state operates a crude sex division for the purposes of granting individuals access to cash transfers. Any such

Table 4.4 Logistic regression on receipt of transfers (apart from child benefits) by individuals aged under 60 years[a]

Variable[b]	β	se	sig[c]	marginal effect p = 0.15
UK				
Out of the labour market	3.17	0.12	0.000	0.40
Lone mother	1.00	0.13	0.000	0.13
Head of household	3.05	0.10	0.000	0.39
Low-income father/husband	0.41	0.10	0.007	0.05
Low-income wife	−0.65	0.17	0.005	−0.08
Financial need	1.31	0.13	0.000	0.17
Constant	−5.77	0.12	0.000	

McFadden's pseudo r^2 = 0.46

Variable[b]	β	se	sig[c]	marginal effect p = 0.15
Germany				
Out of the labour market	2.48	0.13	0.000	0.32
Lone mother	0.85	0.31	0.025	0.11
Head of household	1.12	0.12	0.000	0.14
Low-income father/husband	2.19	0.38	0.000	0.28
Low-income wife	0.61	0.22	0.036	0.08
Financial need	−0.04	0.15	0.767	−0.01
Constant	−3.30	0.11	0.000	

McFadden's pseudo r^2 = 0.25

Variables with significantly different effects across the two national settings[d]

	β	se	sig[c]	marginal effect p = 0.15
Head of household	−2.1	0.16	0.000	−0.27
Out of the labour market	−0.75	0.18	0.000	−0.10
Low-income father/husband	2.93	0.39	0.000	0.37
Low-income wife	−1.37	0.28	0.000	−0.17
Financial need	−1.36	0.20	0.000	−0.17
Country dummy	2.34	0.17	0.000	0.30

Notes: [a] Based on individuals aged less than 60 years for whom complete information is available on gross and net personal and household income.

[b] The reference category for each of the variables is the opposite of the one listed.

[c] Significance on the basis of the Wald statistical test.

[d] These parameters, computed by creating interactive terms for the variables and the country dummy, measure the differences in slope for each of the variables between the two countries.

differences in transfer receipt are shown by the multivariate analyses to be due to variation between women and men on the factors, such as financial need and labour force non-participation, that normally precipitate transfer receipt. But there are some gendered patterns to be seen. Of the two transfer systems, the German is the more gendered when one understands this with reference to the extent to which it favours men in family statuses for the purposes of transfer receipt and is less likely to grant transfers to lone-parent households. Configured in these terms, the logit analyses tend to show that gender goes some distance in separating these two welfare state cash transfer systems.

Taken on their own, details of access to benefits can say relatively little about benefit hierarchies or gender stratification. It is not immediately self-evident, for example, whether access to welfare state support is positive or negative for women and men. We have to look to other processes and program characteristics to evaluate hierarchy more fully.

Routing into Different Parts of the Transfer System

The second possible hierarchical element in benefit systems is that sex and/or gender may be a basis for channelling people into different parts of the transfer system. This is the classic feminist claim – that women are to be found in the inferior league of benefits. To investigate this let us first consult Table 4.2 again, where we can observe that neither system is particularly segregative. There is, in particular, no evidence of the hierarchical sex effect suggested by previous research (Fraser 1989) in that women are as likely, indeed more so, than men to be situated in the superior tier of insurance-based programs. Against a background of considerably greater general recourse to means-tested benefits in the UK and also a higher prevalence there of receipt of both types of benefit simultaneously, female and male receipt patterns cross the social insurance/means-tested divide. Hence there is no support for a dualistic interpretation of either of these benefit systems. However, I wish to question whether one should accept such a dichotomy as the most meaningful way of identifying a gendered imprint in benefit organization. The insurance/means-tested divide seems to be flawed for this purpose because: 1) it relies on a fairly conventional classification of programs that has no inherent sensitivity to gender considerations, 2) such a twofold labour market/need divide fails to identify specifically claims that arise from family relations and associated activities, and, 3) it conceals differences among programs. I therefore consider it more fruitful to differentiate male and female claimants of transfers on the basis of the source or origin of their claim.

Table 4.5   Nature of claims to cash transfers for male, female and all individual recipients of transfers[a]

All programs	UK			Germany		
	Men	Women	All	Men	Women	All
% with no claim	72	41	56	42	69	56
Those with a claim						
Labour market	63	39	46	30	41	34
Want or need	35	16	22	6	14	9
Family	2	45	32	64	45	57
Programs excluding child benefits						
% with no claim	72	66	69	73	72	72
Those with a claim						
Labour market	64	67	66	77	46	61
Want or need	36	28	31	20	14	16
Family	[b]	5	3	3	40	23

Notes: [a] Based on recipients of transfers for whom complete information is available on gross and net personal and household incomes.
[b] small *n*.

Three types or bases of claim can be discerned in the income-maintenance programs offered in these two welfare states. They are: *claims deriving from the labour market* (e.g. unemployment, retirement, illness), *claims arising from need or want* (e.g. the basic means-tested safety-net programs and in Germany unemployment [*Arbeitslosenhilfe*] and student assistance), and *those arising from either family relationships or family-related work and responsibilities* (e.g. survivorship, lone parenthood, care payments, child benefits). The last type of claim is not usually incorporated as a possible transfer variation despite the fact that welfare states have long provided for 'family failure' – usually the death of the breadwinner – and are increasingly subsidizing care work in the home. As defined here, family claims are mainly, but not exclusively, claims made by women, usually widows and mothers to a lesser extent, who lack financial maintenance from a man. When transfers are classified on this basis, Table 4.5 shows their distribution including and excluding child benefits.[12]

Concentrating first on the general pattern for all programs (the third and sixth data columns of the first panel), family benefits (mainly cash payments for children) dominate, but to a considerably greater extent in Germany where they account for 57 per cent of all transfer transactions compared with a third in the UK. Excluding child benefits changes the picture, with paid work becoming the main source of transfer claim in both (second data panel). However, family-based claims still account for nearly a quarter of all claims in Germany, whereas the British welfare state operates more explicitly to a two-pronged logic of need and/or labour market. Nor is there any great differentiation in the British claims structure in the origins of women and men's claims to transfers in comparison with Germany, where one can really speak of different channels. German men's claims on public resources are typically established through paid employment, whereas those of women derive almost as often from family relations and activities as from paid work. In fact, more than any other group, German women's relationship to public transfers is founded on their status in relation to the family.

At a general level this kind of classification of claims suggests the extent to which individuals' interaction with the cash transfer arm of the welfare state derives from a basis other than paid work. It also has something to say about the general representation of the two welfare states. When considered from the point of the origin of individuals' claims, the labour market is considerably more important than need in the UK. Furthermore, the typical representation of the German welfare state arrangement as resting on labour market entitlement is somewhat questionable given that almost 40 per cent of all individual claims to income maintenance there, child benefits apart, derive from either family relationships or need.

While access to transfers and the channelling of claims are important, the level of transfers received is fundamental to general well-being and welfare state hierarchies. How generous, adequate and income-securing are transfers in the British and German welfare states?

Levels of Transfers Received by Individuals

It is here that one would most expect to find the privileging of particular individuals and therefore the imprint of gender (among other forms of) differentiation. Table 4.6 gives an idea of the average value and general adequacy of transfers for different groups of men and women in terms of mean net wage levels and mean net population income of individuals as a whole.

One important cross-national difference is clear from the outset: it is the low value, compared with Germany, of UK transfers. With recipients' benefits equalling some 55 per cent of average net wages and 71 per cent of average net personal incomes, Germany's transfer system will be seen to much more readily enshrine the principle of income

Table 4.6   Mean net value of cash transfers by sex and family status as a proportion of mean net wages and mean net population individual income (%) [a]

	UK		Germany	
	Average wage	Average income	Average wage	Average income
Men	41	50	69	89
Of those aged under 60:				
Fathers	44	52	63	81
Husbands	41	50	58	75
Others	36	43	31	40
Women	33	42	43	56
Of those aged under 60:				
Mothers	34	42	36	47
Wives	35[b]	43[b]	29[b]	37[b]
Others	34	41	32	41
All	37	45	55	71

Notes: [a]   Based on recipients of transfers other than child benefits for whom complete information is available on gross and net personal and household income.
   [b]   small *n*.

replacement, whereas that of the UK – providing recipients with income equal to only 37 per cent of average net wages and 45 per cent of population average income – is confirmed as close to the notion of a social minimum. The adequacy of benefits in the UK is therefore questionable. Certainly there are very large differences in the generosity of transfers received by individuals in these two welfare states, with the German benefits confirmed as the more generous. In terms of internal stratification, few differentiations are apparent in the British benefit population, whether by sex or by family status. It is only a slight exaggeration to describe this as a transfer arrangement that treats all recipients relatively poorly. While we have long known that the German arrangements are highly differentiated, it has not been so clear up to now just how integral are sex and family status to this differentiation.

   These data are revealing not just about the extent to which a male breadwinner model prevails in the two countries but about the conditions under which such a model is sustained. The differences found in the value of transfers to women and men suggest that the German model is the closer to a strong male breadwinner type. This is confirmed by both Table 4.6 and also by Table 4.7, which shows that the

Table 4.7 Ratio of female recipients' transfers from the main programs to those of male recipients(%)[a]

	UK	Germany
All programs	79	64
Old-age pensions	81	41
Unemployment benefit	79	61
Means-tested income support	65	83

Note: [a] Based on recipients of transfers apart from child benefits for whom complete information is available on gross and net personal and household income.

average benefit received by German women is equivalent to only 64 per cent of that received by men (compared with 79 per cent in the UK case). A general sex difference in the size of benefits is, then, a first characteristic of a male breadwinner model. A second attribute, judging from the results of this research, is the privileging of certain family statuses. Contrary to existing elaborations of the male breadwinner model (Lewis 1992), such a gender order is especially expressed in the privileging of male family statuses. Thus one can see that in the German case married men and fathers receive very high benefits, setting them widely apart, not just from all groups of women but also from single men. In fact, comparing the size of benefits going to different groups of women and men suggests that a strong male breadwinner model is expressed more in differentiations in benefits among men than among women. The British pattern shows little trace of any of these forms of gender privileging – just as it was the case with access to transfers, male and female benefits are quite similar in value and no group of men or women is privileged.

It is important to identify the sources of benefit differentials between women and men where they exist by considering the programs and institutional factors that are responsible. To this end, Table 4.7 presents the average value of transfers to women as a proportion of those to men for the main programs. Judging from these data, the insurance or earnings-related transfers, especially old-age and unemployment benefits, are the culprits in German inequality. Since German social insurance transfers take no direct account of family situation (apart from unemployment payments) or financial need, the lower female transfers stem from either lower wages or a poorer record of contributions. This especially exerts an effect on pensions, with the average pension received by women coming to only 41 per cent of that of men (compared with 81 per cent in the UK). One can identify a number of characteristics in the German benefit arrangements that act against greater benefit equality for women and men. Exclusions and inclusions based on valuations of time lie at the root of much inequality. For example, an hours threshold governs eligibility for membership of the otherwise compulsory social insurance. This operates in such a manner as to have the effect of excluding from both pension and sickness insurance part-time workers who are employed for less than fifteen hours a week and earn less than a specified amount. This kind of regulation is perfectly consonant with a set of benefits that places the highest premium on continuous, lifelong, full-time employment. In such an arrangement people and events not conforming to the characteristically male employment pattern are either ignored or treated as in some way special (read: on inferior terms). In addition to the inbuilt bias in favour of paid time, a further anti-equalization tendency in the German transfer system is the absence of floors and ceilings for benefit purposes. With the height of the benefit dependent on the former net wage, the transfer system continues the privileges and advantages built into both the wage relation and personal taxation.

It must be said that gender inequality is not inherent to social insurance, and certainly not to such a degree as in the German case. The Swedish example shows that one way of countering this form of inequality is to encourage and enable women to improve their labour market presence and progress (by providing services to facilitate, and tax and welfare incentives to encourage, female employment). Such an orientation is foreign to the German welfare state arrangement, which, instead of encouraging employment participation among women, tends to discourage it. Inadequate pension claims can also be compensated for indirectly by payments to survivors. These are clearly very important in German practice, judging from the fact that they sustain more than a tenth of all women in the German sample. Indeed, any equalization effect that occurs between older women and men there is more or less due to survivor pensions (which are equivalent to 60 per cent of the husband's pension entitlement). Another possible way of reducing gender-based benefit inequalities is for welfare states to offer payments for carers and/or to recognize unpaid family labour for pension and other benefit purposes. In both regards the German model has been deficient. Comparison with the British arrangements is instructive. The key to any equalizing tendencies there is the existence of a more or less flat-rate form of social insurance and a wide use of means-tested benefits. These act as automatic ceilings and floors that have the effect of compressing the size of benefits for everybody. In addition, the principle of paying for care (especially for the elderly) has a longer history in the British as compared with the German welfare state. While such benefits are not particularly generous, they still have an overall effect of raising women's incomes in comparison to those of men.

But although it emerges in the more positive light in the present two-country comparison, the British system is far from a model of gender equality. Among its weaknesses is the use of a threshold (in this case based on earnings) to govern entry to social insurance. Just as in Germany, this has the effect of excluding low-paid and part-time workers (most of whom are women) from social insurance in fairly large numbers. A second major problem, from a gender-equality perspective, with the British model of benefits is that because the payments are low, individuals have incentives to seek insurance coverage outside the public system. That they actually do this in fairly large numbers is clear from the present research: almost two-thirds of the retired men and 38 per cent of the women have income from occupational pensions (data not shown). Serious male–female differences are to be seen not just in the numbers but also in the size of the occupational pensions. Among men occupational pensions are equal on average to 38 per cent of their total net income and 80 per cent of their public pension income. For women the respective proportions are 22 per cent and 28 per cent. Hence not only is it clear that recourse to other types of pension is a concomitant of the low-level pension system that exists in the UK but men, with their generally higher employment status and greater resources, have the advantage here. Even if it does lead to alternative forms of provision for old age, however, the UK system still has the edge from a gender perspective in the present comparison: retired women's total personal net income is equivalent to 62 per cent of that of retired men, whereas in Germany it comes to only 49 per cent.

To conclude this section on individuals' transfer relations, it can be said that the comparison of these two systems is in many ways a story of the importance of gender factors. To a large extent, however, such differences as have been uncovered for individuals will be hidden within the 'household exchequer'. This is not to claim that they will necessarily be resolved there, but it does mean that a comprehensive analysis of the transfer process must also consider the collective unit. After all, individuals do not claim and spend transfers only on their own behalf. The next section provides a counterpoint to the picture for individuals by looking at the patterns of transfer receipt and height among households. The gender problematic assumes a different form when households are the unit of analysis. Gender stratification among households, I would argue, takes the form of systematically differentiated treatment of households on

Table 4.8 Proportion of male-, female-headed and all households receiving different types of cash transfer (%)[a]

Program type	UK			Germany		
	Male	Female	All	Male	Female	All
All programs	69.9	85.8	73.7	74.0	78.8	75.2
Transfers excluding child benefits	42.7	80.7	51.8	38.5	69.8	46.0
Of these Social insurance programs[b]	33.4	64.6	40.9	33.4	62.6	40.4
Means-tested programs[b]	14.9	32.0	19.0	6.7	11.7	7.9
n	5,449	1,729	7,178	2,341	736	3,077

Notes: [a] Based on all households for which complete information is available on income.
[b] Because of receipt of different benefits simultaneously, the sum of these two types of benefit may be greater than that in the second row.

the basis of sex of the head. The thrust of the remaining analyses in this chapter, therefore, will compare households with male and female heads, the latter comprising about a quarter of households in both samples.

Male- and Female-headed Households' Relations to Cash Transfers

Receipt of Transfers by Male- and Female-headed Households

Table 4.8 shows the extent and type of transfer receipt across programs by all households, along with a breakdown according to the sex of the household head for both samples.

The two cash transfer arrangements reach much wider for households than they do for individuals, mainly because many of the recipient individuals live in one-person households. In both countries about three-quarters of the population of households (compared with less than half of individuals) are in receipt of transfers. When the child-related transfers are removed (second row), household receipt of what we may think of as 'real transfers' (in the sense of income maintenance) is similar across countries at around a half. As regards transfer receipt for male- and female-headed households, one can see that, in contrast to the pattern for individuals, sex of household head strongly differentiates recipiency rates and to a very similar degree in the two systems. Households headed by a woman are about twice as likely to be receiving transfers. Clearly, then, some process is at work in both societies that results in a greater use of transfers by women's households.

Moving down the table, rows three and four compare receipt of social insurance transfers with those that are means-tested. Limiting the comparison to begin with to all households (columns three and six) confirms that, while social insurance transfers are the more widespread in both, means-tested benefits have a wider reach in the UK. Only 8 per cent of German households receive means-tested transfers compared with a fifth of those in the UK. These 'micro-receipt' data therefore reaffirm the greater reliance in the UK on means-tested transfers overall and indicate that such benefits are more important for the support of households than for individuals. 'Topping-up' of insurance benefits with needs-based benefits accounts for part of the higher prevalence of means-tested transfers: around 20 per cent of the UK households claiming social insurance payments also receive means-tested transfers, whereas the proportion in Germany is only 5 per cent. Two-thirds of these dual recipients in the UK are households headed by a person receiving an old-age pension, whereas in Germany it is households classified as 'other' (mainly three-generation, often immigrant, households) which make most recourse to the two types of benefit simultaneously. There is no significant sex pattern here in either sample.

One must say that from these data access to transfers takes on a different complexion depending on whether one considers it from the vantage point of households or individuals. Not only are public transfers a more important means of support for households than for individuals but receipt is far more sex-specific at the household level. Why is this the case?

Explaining Why Women's Households Make Greater Recourse to Transfers

The first clue lies in the structural differences in households headed by the two sexes (as summarized in Table 4.1). Men and women seemingly head quite different types of household. Women's households tend to consist of just one person, which means that a high proportion of female household heads are elderly; the average age is in the mid-fifties. A second structural difference relevant to transfer receipt is the high proportion of lone-parent households that are headed by a woman: at least 90 per cent. Further variations, many of them critical for the purpose of access to cash transfers, also characterize male- and female-headed households in both populations. Cross-nationally similarities are to the fore: women-headed households are smaller in size, have fewer child dependants, and have heads who are most likely to be widowed, divorced or separated and with a low probability of being in the labour market (Table 4.1). Given this, one finds a large difference in household income levels. In the UK female-headed households' gross pre-transfer mean adjusted income is equal to 50 per cent of that of male households; in Germany it is 57 per cent. So when we compare male- and female-headed households cross-nationally, we are in fact comparing very similar entities but, within each national setting, households headed by a woman are quite different to those headed by a man.

This raises two questions of analytical import. When they are constituted similarly, do male- and female-headed households have similar access to the transfer system? And how far do differences in the structure of their households go to explaining sex differences in patterns of transfer receipt?

In answering the first question, of whether similarly constituted male- and female-headed households have similar recipiency rates, we run into a problem of comparability. Because men and women tend to head quite different types of household, there are insufficient cases to compare recipiency rates across the full spectrum of households. There is then only one analytic option: to limit the comparison to those households with sufficient numbers of male and female heads for comparison. This means in effect comparing one-person households, whether elderly or non-elderly. Such analyses indicate that there are no differences by sex of household head for either elderly or non-elderly households in the UK, but in Germany non-elderly, one-person households are more likely to be receiving transfers when they are headed by a woman (data not shown). But structural differences between such male and female households are also implicated in this result: the men who head one-person households tend to be younger and economically active, whereas women in this situation are older and less likely to be in the labour market. It appears, then, that differences between female and male household receipt of transfers is largely due to structural differences in the types of household which each sex heads.

To test for these effects and to identify those independent variables that are most influential in predicting the probability of a household receiving transfers,[13] I used logit analysis, just as I did with transfers to individuals. One of the main purposes here is to ascertain if male- and female-headed households have a similar probability of transfer receipt when they experience the contingency of low income. Age is again controlled for by carrying out separate analyses for those under 60 years of age. The detailed results can be consulted in Table 4.9 (note that the model in both cases has quite good predictive utility for the total sample but considerably less for those under 60).

In the event, the sex of the household head exerts no independent effect on a household's probability of transfer receipt in either sample. It is the level of household income need that counts most, and when the

Table 4.9 Logistic regression on household receipt of transfers (apart from child benefits)[a]

UK Variable	β	se	sig[b]	marginal effect p = 0.26
Households with head aged less than 60 years				
Low-income female households	1.22	0.17	0.000	0.23
Low-income male households	1.79	0.28	0.000	0.34
Head out of the labour market	2.85	0.11	0.000	0.55
Constant	−1.57	0.04	0.000	
McFadden's pseudo r^2 = 0.62				
Germany				
Low-income female households	0.80	0.16	0.000	0.15
Low-income male households	0.70	0.19	0.000	0.13
Head out of the labour market	2.22	0.16	0.000	0.43
Constant	−1.57	0.06	0.000	
McFadden's pseudo r^2 = 0.24				
All households UK				
Low-income female households	0.95	0.16	0.000	0.24
Low-income male households	1.73	0.27	0.000	0.43
Head out of the labour market	3.00	0.09	0.000	0.75
Head aged 60 years or over	1.90	0.09	0.000	0.47
Constant	−1.58	0.04	0.000	
McFadden's pseudo r^2 = 0.54				
Germany				
Low-income female households	0.98	0.15	0.000	0.24
Low-income male households	0.73	0.16	0.000	0.18
Head out of the labour market	1.60	0.17	0.000	0.40
Head aged 60 years or over	2.45	0.15	0.000	0.61
Constant	−1.65	0.06	0.000	
McFadden's pseudo r^2 = 0.45				

Notes: [a] Based on households for which complete information on gross and net income is available.
   [b] Significance on the basis of the Wald statistical test.

contingency of low income occurs women's households, compared with all other households, are as likely as those of men to be receiving transfers, and more likely in the UK. So there is no evidence of embedded sex discrimination of this type in either system. Neither is there any great mystery as to why women's households have a higher prevalence of transfer receipt: it is because they have fewer other means of financial support than those of men, especially since they are less likely to have a head who is active in the labour market. There are really only minor cross-national differences, and these conform to what we already know about the two systems: the stronger need orientation of Britain's welfare state and the greater demarcation between pensions and other benefit programs in Germany. In both countries we find a fairly standard set of factors predicting household access to transfers and, since none of the variables have a significantly different cross-national effect; these two cash transfer systems are not very different in how they grant access to households.

Streaming of Claims and Size of Transfers to Households

Other differences prevail, however. As was the case for individuals, one finds that household claims are also structured differently in the two welfare states. While the labour market is the predominant mode of claims-making in both, family claims take second place in Germany, whereas in the UK means- or needs-tested benefits closely rival those deriving from the labour market. Just as was the case for individuals, family relations and activities are quite insignificant as a source of households' claims on public transfers in the UK. Against a background of its more differentiated benefit arrangement, Germany's is also the more strongly sex-patterned. Family-based claims account for around 60 per cent of transfer receipt among female-headed households there, in comparison to just 6 per cent for those headed by a man. The vast majority of claims of male households derive from the labour market, but there are no significant sex of head differences in the use of needs-based claims. The UK sample manifests fewer sex of head differences in the nature of households' claims to welfare state transfers.

Table 4.10 compares the levels of income yielded by each transfer system in the context of average income in the household samples as a whole.

Two important cross-national variations set the context for any sex differences that exist. First, as we have come to expect, income-maintenance transfers to households are far more generous in Germany. When child benefits are excluded, for example, benefits approximate 58 per cent of mean adjusted household income compared with only about a

Table 4.10 Mean value of transfers for different types of program to recipient households as a proportion of mean net household income (%)[a]

	UK			Germany		
	Male	Female	All	Male	Female	All
All programs	20	24	21	27	53	34
Programs excluding child benefits	27	23	26	55	63	58
Of these:						
Labour market	26	23	25	60	70	62
Need	29	24	27	24	35	27
Family	[b]	22	22	32[b]	66	60

Notes: [a] Based on adjusted incomes of all households in receipt of each type of transfer for which complete information on household income is fully available.
  [b] small *n*.

quarter in the UK. Second, the general pattern of national variation in the height of transfers by type of claim found for individuals is also reproduced for households. As with individuals, it is the work- and family-related transfers that yield the most generous claims in Germany. Needs-related transfers are fairly similar in relative value cross-nationally. One pattern which reverses that found for individuals is that transfers account for a higher proportion of total adjusted income in women's households as against those of men. This is true both for claims deriving from the labour market and the family.

Higher transfers to women's households could arise from a number of sources. They may be a function of the fact that more female-headed households are receiving old-age or widowed pensions, which we now know to be among the most generous benefits in Germany. Or they could be associated with the type and size of household. Therefore the final set of analyses seeks to identify, through ANOVA (a bivariate statistical technique) whether the sex of household head has an independent effect on the size of transfers received by households. The analysis focuses only on the total population of recipient households because the numbers of recipient households with heads aged less than 60 years tend to be low. The dependent variable is the size of transfer (apart from child benefits) received by recipient households adjusted for household size and composition. Gross income before transfers was entered as a covariate for the purpose of removing extraneous variation from the dependent variable.

Along with the covariate, four factors emerged as having a significant effect on the amount of equivalent adult transfers received by households

Table 4.11 ANOVAS – Unadjusted and adjusted effect of significant factors on levels of transfers (excluding child benefits) received by households, expressed as % deviation from the grand mean[a]

All Households		UK			Germany	
	n	Unadjusted	Adj. for other factors and income	n	Unadjusted	Adj. for other factors and income
Sex of household head						
Male		—	—	865	−5	8
Female		—	—	508	8	−14
β					0.10	0.15
Age of head						
17-59	184	−34	−21	507	−44	−19
60+	260	24	15	866	26	11
β		0.53	0.33		0.48	0.21
Type of claim						
Employment based		—	—	821	7	3
Need-based		—	—	178	−45	−18
Family-based		—	—	374	7	2
β					0.25	0.10
Household size/type						
1 person	222	21	11	438	35	34
Couples	110	6	6	430	17	1
Two parents with children	43	−63	−41	282	−39	−15
Lone parents	38	−35	−21	10-3	−48	−35
Other	31	−43	−17	120	−45	−32
β		0.54	0.32		0.51	0.38
multiple r²		0.41			0.35	

Notes: [a] Based on households receiving the relevant transfers for which complete information exists on all income.

in Germany, two in the UK (see Table 4.11). The significant factors and covariate together explain around 40 per cent of the variance in each case. The two factors common to both samples are the *age of the household head* and the *type of household* (differentiated on the basis of one-person, couples, two-parent, lone-parent, and other households). For the German sample the two other significant factors are: the *sex of the household head* and the *basis of the claim to transfers.*

It is the significance of the latter two factors that sets the two systems apart. These data are especially important in indicating that in Germany the effect of the sex of head varies before and after the effects of other factors are controlled for. When taken on their own, female-headed households receive higher transfers (as we have seen in Table 4.10 above), but when the effects of the other factors and the covariate are controlled for, households headed by a woman in Germany receive adult equivalent transfers that are 14 per cent lower than the grand mean. The independent significance of both the sex of household head and type of claim variables is notable and suggests that differences in the size of transfers going to male- and female-headed households in Germany are not totally attributable to the practice of streaming claims on the basis of their source of origin. In other words, sex of household head is a source of variation, albeit relatively weak, in transfer height in Germany independent of how the household's claim originates. Now from these data the British welfare state shows no evidence of operating a division on the basis of sex of household head per se. Rather, its primary concern is with household type and the support of households headed by the elderly, these being the only factors significantly determining the height of transfer received by households.

Overview

It is fairly easy to identify both of these transfer systems, and perhaps also others, as being sex-differentiated. Relying on descriptive analyses, as most of the research to date has tended to do, women dominate the population of individual and household recipients of transfers. But this superficial kind of analysis is insufficient grounds for assuming that sex is the basis for the differentiations. In point of fact, much of the female dominance of transfer receipt statistics, especially among households, is traceable to women's predominance in the population sectors that have the greatest need of and recourse to transfers, the elderly for example. So the larger numbers of women among transfer recipients are grounded in a set of demographic and social phenomena which, while sociologically interesting, do not of themsleves give much manoeuvre in interpreting them as part of a gender design in welfare states. Deciphering welfare state hierarchies as they relate to gender requires a more penetrating analysis, and it is for this purpose that I developed in this chapter an approach that treats the transfer relation as involving three stages –

access, the structuring or ordering of claims, and the financial treatment of claims – and specified the conditions under which cash transfer programs could be empirically identified as gender-stratified. The analysis was revealing, along the way elucidating some hitherto hidden elements as well as confirming some of the general features of the British and German welfare states.

The main thrust of the evidence confirms the British and German to be two quite different transfer systems, especially as they relate to individuals. In the context of two key structural differences between them – a less differentiated claims hierarchy in the UK as well as generally lower rates of payment – gender as a characteristic of individuals performs relatively well in pinpointing differences within and across systems. When defined to embrace both family status and differentiations in the kind of economic risk to which men and women in family situations are prone, there is considerable evidence that of the two the German *Sozialstaat* operates in a manner that is more gender-stratified. When relating to individuals, such a process of differentiation is manifest by a privileging of male income risks and male family statuses over those of women. While the British system also showed a tendency to favour household heads, especially with regard to access to transfers, there is less evidence there of systematic differentiation on the basis of women and men's family positions.

When we moved from the individual to the household level of analysis, the results were generally consistent, with stronger male–female differences again visible in the German transfer model. It is in this system that the sex of household head matters more, especially in relation to how claims are constructed and treated financially. The nature of the relationship is such that female-headed households are more likely to be receiving transfers, but when other factors are controlled for, the amounts they receive are significantly lower than those going to male-headed households. The British welfare state showed no evidence of systematic differentiations between male- and female headed households. Rather, apparent sex differentiations in levels of transfers to households were shown by the multivariate analyses to be a function of household income levels.

Overall, these data tend to confirm that the German model of transfers is the more hierarchical of the two in a number of ways. For one, claims in Germany tend to be more differentiated in terms of their source of origin and how they are associated with different payment levels. Furthermore, such distinctions intertwine more closely with sex and gender in Germany to lead to higher inequalities between transfers to male and female recipients in different family statuses as compared with the UK.

One must say that from these results access to transfers takes on a different complexion depending on whether one considers it from the vantage point of households or individuals. Not only are cash transfers a more important means of support for households than for individuals, but receipt patterns are far more sex-specific at the household level. Such is the scale of the differences that it seems inadequate to study transfer systems by considering only households or individuals alone. This is certainly the case for analyses that go in search of the gender dimension in cash transfer arrangements.

Taking a broader view of stratification, what the information on the UK case suggests is that the main line of gender (and other forms of) cleavage in that society may well lie outside the population of benefit recipients. That is, a main axis of stratification may lie on the line that divides benefit recipients from the rest of the population. In Germany it is more likely that the deeply drawn set of divisions and differentiations that characterizes the benefit population is a mirror image of the stratification pattern in society as a whole. The following chapters, in searching for the outcomes associated with these two welfare state models, will seek to consider questions such as these by placing the transfer arrangements and their beneficiaries in their wider context. The next chapter begins the more detailed exploration of stratification-related outcomes by looking at income inequalities and how they are altered by cash transfers and taxation.

PART III

Gender and the Impact of the British and German Welfare States

CHAPTER 5

Income Inequality and Resource-based Relations

Having seen how the two transfer systems operate, in this and the following two chapters I turn to outcomes. Viewing income inequalities as the result of a set of interactive processes and structures, here I take up the question of the welfare state and family's[1] effects on the relative financial well-being of women and men. Along with the effects of cash transfers, I also consider how the taxation arrangements in each case redistribute income and alter the comparative financial situation of individuals and households. Against a backdrop of transfer-related and other differences in the organization of the two welfare states, the accent will be on economic inequalities between women and men and among the households they head. The chapter's centrepiece is a comparison of the degree to which the welfare state and the family or household system are each involved in the redistribution of income. The first step is to understand how the well-being of women and men as individuals and as household members is secured and the role of the tax and transfer arrangements in that process within a comparative perspective. If income inequalities are the result of a series of interactions, then it follows that the family/household system is a potentially vital player. Intra-household processes, especially the degree to which access to the collective income changes the relative income position of women and men, form, therefore, the chapter's second theme. The third and final part of the chapter seeks to establish the degree and nature of redistribution achieved among different types of households, with a particular eye to how transfer and taxation arrangements affect the relative income levels of households headed by women and men. So I begin with individuals, investigating first the distribution of personal income and related inequalities and then how individuals are placed relative to other members of their household, before moving on in the final section to consider income disparities among households themselves.

Focus of Analysis

Three main considerations set the analytical backdrop to the study of gender and redistribution. The first relates to how the income distribution process can be modelled to allow for the conceptualization of effects on the part of both transfer and taxation policies and the family. The second issue is the type of analysis that should be undertaken to identify such effects. Third, there is the question of what influence the welfare state and family/household could be expected to exert on relative economic well-being in the two states under consideration. Serving as an introduction to the line of analysis that I wish to develop in this chapter, each will be considered in turn.

Modelling the Welfare State and the Family in Relation to the Income Process

The welfare state can be understood as a set of policies aimed, in part anyway, at equalizing the distribution of economic welfare in a population. Opinions differ on its success in this respect. For some the welfare state is a relatively effective instrument of equalization, other writers consider it as advantageous mainly for the middle classes, while still others regard it as a surface phenomenon unable to modify basic class structures (Ringen and Uusitalo 1992: 69). While there is considerable variation in perceived outcomes, it is generally accepted that welfare states' effects are a product of their service provision, cash transfer and taxation policies. Through their particular configurations of such policies, welfare states influence not only the level of living available to individuals and households but also the domains from whence income is obtained.

Intra-familial distributive practices are crucial to inequality theory in general, for as Curtis (1986: 169) rightly points out, no matter how rewards are distributed in society people can and do organize themselves (e.g. in families) to redistribute them. The family or household plays a crucial role in determining at once levels of well-being of members and their labour market participation patterns. Limiting consideration to the economic dimensions of the family or household, two key aspects must be differentiated: the family as a site of production or reproduction, and the family as a locus of consumption. Both dimensions are extremely important for gender differences and inequalities. First, family-based productive and reproductive activities bear on men and women in diverging ways: the male role is mainly conceptualized as that of financial provider, whereas the role of women is closely associated with the caring, and hence labour, functions of the family. Second, the family is not only one of the most important sites of redistribution between women and men but the norms governing redistribution within it rest centrally on gender (along with age).

By conceptualizing the income redistribution process as involving a number of different components, it is possible to model the likely effects of both institutions, as well as the market, on income and well-being. Adapting an earlier model of Ringen and Uusitalo (1992), the income redistribution process can be understood as involving a number of stages in which the state and the family exert either direct and/or indirect influence at certain points. This is modelled as follows:

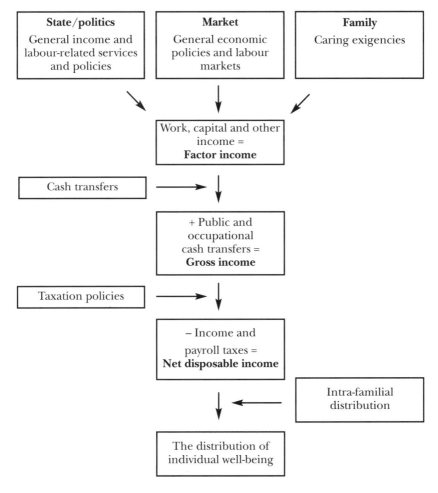

Figure 5.1   Model of the income redistribution process

This relatively simplified model (it contains no feedback loops or interactions for instance) differentiates three main points in the income redistribution process. The first is factor income, which includes income from paid work along with that from self-employment, capital investment and other sources. Adding cash transfers, from both public and other (e.g. occupationally derived pensions[2]) sources, brings us to gross income, which is essentially all money income. Net disposable income, the third level of income, is derived by deducting income and payroll taxes.

In the income redistribution process as modelled, I attribute an indirect role to the market as well as both direct and indirect roles to the state and the family. Differentiating between income distribution and redistribution helps to clarify what are conceived as direct and indirect effects for the present purpose. Although the boundaries between them are somewhat arbitrary, income distribution refers to the *allocation of scarce values or goods*, whereas redistribution invokes *intervention(s) aimed at reallocating market inputs or outputs* (Shanahan and Tuma 1994: 733–7). Hence general economic and market conditions, social and economic policies and caring exigencies stemming from the family, while primary for the distribution of income, are secondary for the purposes of income redistribution. In other words, while the particular elements of the three institutions as specified in the first row of the figure affect access to income and its general distribution, they exercise only an indirect effect on income redistribution.

Moving on to the redistribution process proper, the welfare state is conceptualized as having two direct effects.[3] First, through cash transfers it influences the transformation of factor income into gross income. The second direct effect of the welfare state is to be found in the configuration of personal income and payroll taxation, through which gross income becomes net income. With regard to the family or household, I am most interested in the extent to which, through pooling and sharing of resources, it can alter individuals' standard of living in comparison to what they could achieve on their personal incomes. Comparing people's personal incomes with those assumed to be available to them as members of households gives a measure of the extent to which the household can act as a redistributive unit. The second empirical part of this chapter will, therefore, focus on individuals' comparative positions as income-holders in their own right and as members of households. The kinds of financial independence or dependence that exist between women and men in the context of different welfare state models will be explored in detail in Chapter 7.

Types of Redistribution and Mode of Analysis

The income security system is defined by a double process of redistribution, its allocative terms setting up financial circuits on the basis of both relative income situation and family structure and life cycle (Shaver 1991: 158). Two types of redistribution, therefore, prevail in the literature. Vertical redistribution, by far the more widely studied, concerns the degree of change effected by the fiscal process among income groups or classes. Horizontal redistribution focuses on the degree of change or stability effected in the incomes of individuals and families at different stages of life. When sex and gender are the focus, horizontal redistribution is, arguably, of greater relevance than redistribution across income classes. This is so for two reasons. First, focusing on vertical redistribution de-emphasizes, and to some extent conceals, the scale of income inequalities between women and men and their households. Second, what is most relevant to evaluate from a gender perspective is how the income security system sets up circuits of redistribution between women and men on the basis of family form, life-cycle stage and income. So by comparing individual women and men as well as their households at different points of the life course, we can see how gender processes are expressed in the complex of exchanges within and across life-cycle stages.

The standard method for the analysis of the redistributive impact of cash transfers and taxes is the so-called 'fiscal incidence method' in which income levels at the various income stages are compared. The difference between the distributions before and after a particular policy intervention is taken as a measure of its redistributive impact. While this is customary in the field, it is not entirely uncontroversial. Its main limitation is that it captures only direct effects and therefore allows for no behavioural adaptations. The underlying difficulty is the absence of a proper counterfactual. The pre-transfer situation is hypothetical and so we cannot be sure that 'pre-transfer' income would be as it is in the absence of state transfers. In other words, 'pre-transfer' income is itself dependent in many ways on state provision, because other areas of social policies (such as education, housing, taxation for example) affect income patterns and also because people adapt their behaviour and income situation to the existence and nature of social provisions.

In addition, restricting the study to direct effects tends to exaggerate the degree of redistribution and to simplify the process whereby such effects occur. In favour of the method, however, the estimated redistribution is real in that it reflects existing flows of income and services and clearly portrays important stages in the process of income redistribution. In order to minimize the counterfactual problem, I shall take care to distinguish between those under and over 60 years of age and exclude the latter from some of the analyses of redistribution. This is advisable because the assumption of no behavioural adaptations in the light of existing provision is least tenable for the elderly. After all, people are highly likely not only to plan for income shortages in their old age but to develop their strategies for long-term income security around the existence and nature of public provisions.

To establish the redistributive impact of the family or household is considerably more problematic, mainly because so little is known about how family members share and redistribute their income. While neither data set (nor indeed any known) gives explicit information on this, it is possible to approach the question through a consideration of assumed intra-household transfers. To identify their possible scale, I shall focus on the differences between the individual's personal income and the standard of income available to him or her as a member of a household. To compute such a household standard for individuals, the combined household income is, as before, adjusted in accordance with the OECD equivalence scale, yielding an equivalent household income that is the same for all household members. Even though such adjustments are standard practice in income research, their hypothetical nature should be noted, not least for the assumption they make that all income is both pooled and shared equally among household members.

Welfare State Models and Income Redistribution: the Comparative Context

The analyses undertaken so far depict the comparative framework as involving both similarities and differences. Drawing the two welfare states closer together are their low levels of services in support of the family and a prioritizing of heads of households for the purposes of transfers. The gender implications of these are quite obvious. Low public service provision hinders women's participation in the labour market and thereby encourages not only a traditional, home-based role for mothers and others with caring responsibilities but also an inferior income situation for women within the household. Transfer programs which prioritize male support have the effect of reinforcing what is also a traditional pattern of intra-familial or intra-household income flows – from man to woman. Redistributively, however, Germany's use of a high wage replacement model of *Sozialversicherung* sets it apart from the British welfare state in which benefits are flat-rate and means-tested payments rival social insurance as the main mechanism of public income support. We have seen from the last chapter that, of the two welfare states, the German is the more gendered in the manner in which it makes income from public sources available to women and men in different family situations. Bringing the personal tax system into the analyses, as I shall do in this chapter, should serve to amplify such gender effects. More precisely, Germany's tax model of *Ehegattensplitting*, in favouring couples with only one income or those where the second partner has a low income, encourages no or only minor labour market participation on the part of married women. Furthermore, this set of arrangements in association with the configuration of civil and marital law makes the German welfare state more supportive of the institution of the family, as compared with the UK, but also less likely to intervene in the redistribution process within families.

In terms of predicting the likely effects, one has to differentiate between the individual and household levels of analysis. For individuals my view is that the British welfare state will be the more effective in regard to redistribution between women and men. This is likely to be the case because its orientation towards alleviating poverty and providing a minimum income means that 1) there are fewer differences in the size of transfers in the UK between women and men, and 2) to the extent that they experience low incomes, women in the UK are more likely to receive transfers than their German counterparts. To frame the argument from the perspective of individuals in Germany, one expects the welfare state there to effect less redistribution between women and men because 1) transfers there are founded on a model that reproduces market-generated income inequalities so that women are in the first place less likely to receive transfers than men and in the second likely to receive lower transfers, and 2) the taxation system with its high subsidies for certain (married) men is more likely to redistribute income among different categories of men than between women and men. What, then, of the likely redistributive effects of the family or household? In this regard, we expect that the family in Germany will be more important than the welfare state as an agent of income redistribution between women and men. This would be more consonant with the 'familized' cast of German society. For opposite reasons, in the UK the state will be to the fore in both general income redistribution and that between the sexes. In terms of redistribution among households, the evidence from the last chapter of significantly higher transfers to women's households in Germany leads us to expect that German transfers will be more equalizing between women and men's households than are those of the UK.

Individual Incomes and the Role of Transfers and Taxation

The Composition of Individual Income Packages

Using the model of income formation outlined above, Table 5.1 shows how women and men's personal income packages were composed in each country in the mid-1980s.[4]

Table 5.1   Composition of individual income packages (%)[a]

	UK			Germany		
	Men	Women	All	Men	Women	All
Wages and salaries	71.6	60.4	68.0	76.2	66.5	73.4
Self-employment income	10.6	2.9	8.1	6.4	1.9	5.1
Property/asset income	3.8	5.8	4.4	1.8	5.3	2.8
Private transfers	—	—	—	0.2	1.1	0.5
Other income	0.5	2.7	1.2	—	—	—
Factor income	86.5	71.8	81.7	84.6	74.8	81.8
Cash transfers	8.4	24.5	13.7	15.2	25.1	18.0
Occupational pensions	5.0	3.7	4.6	0.2	0.1	0.2
Gross income	100.0	100.0	100.0	100.0	100.0	100.0
Income tax	15.7	11.2	14.2	13.4	14.6	13.8
Employees' payroll tax	4.7	3.5	4.3	9.2	8.0	8.8
Net income	79.6	85.3	81.5	77.4	77.4	77.4

Notes: [a]   Based on personal incomes of those for whom complete information
is available on their gross and net personal incomes as well as those
of their households.

Concentrating first on the general patterns (third and sixth data columns), we see that people in Germany and the UK derive their income from more or less similar sources. Some minor differences do exist, as can be seen by looking at the components of factor income. Wages and salaries (including financial bonuses linked to paid employment) account for a higher proportion of income in Germany, as does self-employment in the UK. Financial yields from property and assets (which include investment and dividend income[5]) also matter more as a source of income in the UK, although they comprise a relatively minor share of income in both. Private transfers are to all intents and purposes inconsequential in both national settings (in the UK data these are classified as 'other' income). All of these sources together bring factor income to a similar 82 per cent of gross income in both countries. Transfers make up the difference. It is notable, but consistent in the light of the analyses of the last chapter, that public transfers make a higher contribution to the typical German income package – almost a fifth compared with 14 per cent in the UK. Coming to the final income stage, net disposable income, while income taxes are roughly equivalent as a proportion of gross income, German payroll taxes at 9 per cent of gross income are about double the average for the UK. These together with income tax slice a hefty 23 per cent off the average gross income in Germany whereas the British system is somewhat more generous, taking only 19 per cent. The German model is clearly the more expensive.

When it comes to women and men's income packages, it can be seen that in both national settings women derive significantly less of their income from market sources and more from cash transfers. Table 5.2 compares male and female incomes directly. It first presents women's income from each source as a proportion of that of men. Since male–female income inequalities may arise also from divergences in the numbers with no income from a specific source, the proportions of women and men with income from each source (in the case of taxes the proportion that pays them) is also shown and, for these, the female–male ratios.

For the two total populations (first two data columns), we can see that sex-based inequalities in personal incomes are really very large and that they reach right across the income formation and redistribution process. While there is considerable fluctuation in the sex ratios by income sources, women's incomes generally come closest to those of men for the minor income types, for example property and asset in-come, private transfers. Public transfers offer an exception to this pat-tern, however. In Germany they are one of the most 'equal' sources of income – although it is rather ironic to observe that a female–male ratio of 0.6 defines equality here. For the UK population a rather different version of equality emerges, with women's transfers being 24 per cent greater in value than those received by men. Taking a cross-national view, sex-based income inequalities are considerably more pronounced in the German popula-tion. Factor income serves as a good example; the female–male ratio is 0.40 in the UK whereas in Germany it is only 0.33. Such a cross-national divide is carried through to the final stage of the income process.

These results are illuminating also because they give us an idea of where male–female income inequalities originate. Here the labour market is hugely important. Women's earnings in the UK equal only 40 per cent of those of men on average, and less again in Germany at 32 per cent. Part of the cross-national disparity is due to a lower proportion of women with any earnings at all in Germany – 41 per cent compared with 49 per cent in the UK. Apart from women aged over 60 years, mothers form the bulk of the non-employed women in both popula-tions. However, the fact that wives[6] in the German sample are consider-ably less likely to be employed than their UK counterparts is further evidence that the breadwinner/home-maker model is more widespread in Germany (to be considered further in Chapter 7). The lack of labour

Table 5.2 Female–male income ratios (based on the mean) across income sources for all individuals, % of men and women with income from each source and female–male ratios for those with income from each source[a]

	All: ratio women's/men's		% with income from source				Of those with source: ratio women's/ men's	
	UK	Germany	UK		Germany		UK	Germany
			men	women	men	women		
Wages and salaries	40	32	56	49	68	41	55	54
Self-employment income	11	11	10	3	5	2	37	34
Property/asset income	68	109	57	52	35	33	74	113
Private transfers	—	178	—	—	1	2	—	97
Other income	60	—	23	13	—	—	62	—
Factor income	40	33	88	79	83	63	40	43
Cash transfers	124	60	28	59	59	31	59	116
(less child benefits)	(93)	(68)	(27)	(34)	(26)	(28)	(76)	(64)
Occupational pensions	32	42	14	9	3	2	53	55
Gross income	44	37	99	97	100	79	45	44
Income tax	38	40	71	59	95	81	53	46
Employees' payroll tax	40	32	48	28	67	40	56	53
Net income	47	37	100	97	100	79	47	45

Notes: [a] Based on personal incomes of those for whom complete information is available on their gross and net personal incomes as well as those of their households.

market income together with the fact that German women are generally less likely than their counterparts in the UK to have other sources of income leads to the situation that only 63 per cent of them have any factor income at all, compared with 79 per cent of the UK women. When the picture is broadened to include public transfers, all but 3 per cent of women in the UK sample now have some personal income, whereas 21 per cent of the German female sample still have no personal income at all. In this context, the significance of the policy of paying child benefit to the mother in the UK should not be underestimated. Notwithstanding its low level, 4 per cent of UK women would have no personal income without it.

The final data columns in Table 5.2 show that even when the proportion without each income source is controlled for, sex-based inequalities remain more entrenched in Germany. Wages and salaries provide an exception to this in that employed women in both countries earn around 55 per cent of the wages of employed men. But it is also the case that more of the sex-based income inequality in the German as compared with the UK case is traceable to women having no income at all from a number of sources. Of these, the non-receipt of public transfers and wages is especially significant.

Table 5.2 also sheds some light on how the transfer and taxation systems affect male–female income inequalities. There are two issues here worth separating in terms of the 'inequality problematic' faced by welfare states. One is the degree to which income from the welfare state itself is unequal. The second is the scale of the income inequalities characterizing other sources of income. With regard to the latter, both welfare states share a problem of enormous magnitude, with female factor incomes no more than 43 per cent of those of men. Given this, it could be reasonably expected that the tax and transfer systems should then bias their transfers towards women. The next section takes up this question in more detail within the context of the general degree of horizontal redistribution achieved in both national settings.

The Redistributive Effects of Transfers and Taxation

Horizontal redistribution is arguably one of the most important functions of modern welfare states, for it is part and parcel of societies' generational contract and their support of the family. It can be configured as the degree of improvement in average incomes (measured in terms of the mean net income) effected by the process of transforming factor incomes into net disposable incomes. This transformation, what we can call the fiscal process, embraces both transfers and taxation. Redistribution takes place to the extent that the fiscal process effects the largest increase in average income of those groups and individuals who are low in pre-fiscal income. Two types of redistribution are of central interest here: that between individuals at different stages of life and, within life-cycle stages, that between women and men. To capture life stage and family status here, I divide the population into four groupings, in essence treating the cross-section as if it were a panel. The first grouping comprises all individuals aged 60 years and over; the second consists of parents of children aged 16 years or less; the third is spouses aged less than 60 years with no dependent children; and the fourth is a catch-all 'other' category that includes those under 60 years who are neither married nor parents. Table 5.3 presents a comparison of factor and net incomes on the basis of the post-transfer mean, thereby capturing the transformation effected in average well-being by the fiscal process overall.

Table 5.3   Mean factor and net income, as a proportion of mean population values, and the % change effected on individual incomes[a]

	UK			Germany		
	Factor	Net	% change	Factor	Net	% change
All individuals aged						
60 years or over	29.5	79.2	+168	25.5	85.1	+234
Men	48.9	108.2	+121	49.8	131.1	+163
Women	14.5	56.6	+290	8.6	53.1	+517
All parents of depen-						
dent children	110.3	101.4	−8	146.4	125.3	−14
Fathers	167.9	138.0	−18	256.7	218.0	−15
Mothers	51.0	63.6	+25	51.0	45.2	−11
Spouses less than 60						
years with no de-						
pendent children	151.7	124.2	−18	144.8	113.3	−22
Husbands	222.3	183.1	−18	225.8	179.1	−21
Wives	110.1	81.2	−26	73.8	55.5	−25
Others less than						
60 years	118.4	101.6	−14	93.9	73.3	−22
Men	167.0	138.4	−17	101.3	77.4	−24
Women	66.1	62.0	−6	83.8	67.6	−19

Note: [a]   Based on personal incomes of those for whom complete information is available on their gross and net personal incomes as well as those of their households.

Beginning with the pre-fiscal situation (the first and fourth data columns), there are three main stories here, some more surprising than others. The first – and least surprising – is the very disadvantaged situation of those aged 60 and over in the absence of fiscal redistribution, cash transfers especially. The second theme is the significance of family status and in particular the existence of quite large pre- and post-fiscal income disparities according to family status. The overall degree of variation, or the range of pre-transfer inequality, indicates that German taxes and cash transfers are called on to address the greater degree of income inequality. Third, although the clues from these data are only indirect, very large sex gaps in personal incomes before transfers are indicated, with differences among the elderly and between male and female parents being especially pronounced in both national settings. In general, family roles are associated with quite different income levels for women and men before the fiscal process, although such inequalities are more pronounced in Germany.

Unsurprisingly, the elderly are the main beneficiaries of redistribution in both welfare states. Notwithstanding this, however, the degree to which this age group benefits from redistribution is much higher in

Germany. We may take this as evidence of the greater status maintenance and indeed horizontal redistributive orientation of the German
transfer system. Here we see the generational contract, in the sense of a
commitment to the security of living standards across the life cycle,
brought to life. As might be expected also, people of working age pay
for this redistribution towards the elderly. The extent to which they are
called on to do so varies according to their family status, however. Most
noticeably, we see evidence here of how the German fiscal and social
protection system operates in favour of people with family responsibilities, whereas the British system makes no consistent distinctions on the
basis of family situation. Looking within family status categorizations
helps to identify some of the consequences of arrangements in both
systems for women and men. Apart from those aged 60 and over, male
incomes are privileged in both national settings, judged in terms of how
the redistribution process affects their relative income levels. But this is
much more extreme in Germany, where the fiscal system has a more or
less equivalent effect on male and female incomes even though
women's personal incomes are much smaller than those of men to
begin with. One of the starkest outcomes of this cross-national contrast
can be read from the situation of mothers: they benefit somewhat from
horizontal redistribution in the UK, while their German counterparts
suffer an overall disimprovement in their situation relative to what it was
before transfers. A similar result occurs for German wives, again a very
negative outcome in the context of their low pre-transfer incomes and
given the favourable treatment, relatively speaking, accorded their
husbands' income. All in all, these results suggest that there is a process
at work in both transfer and taxation systems for people of working age
which 1) benefits men in certain family situations over similarly placed
women, 2) has the result that male–female income inequalities are not
radically altered by tax and transfer transformations, and 3) takes a
more extreme form in Germany.

Sex and Gender Variations in the Redistributive Impact of Transfers and Taxes

One of the most interesting questions raised by these analyses is how
the transformations exert their impact on the incomes of women and
men. It is important to pinpoint where exactly the different effects
occur. In order to explore this in greater detail, I now disaggregate the
fiscal process into its transfer and taxation components. For the
purposes of this analysis I concentrate on those aged under 60 years. To
explore the effect of transfers and taxation I compare the position of
each grouping relative to the before and after mean. Thus in Table 5.4
we can observe how each group of individuals is placed relative to the

average for pre-transfer and tax income (equivalent to factor income in the conventions used earlier), transfers, gross income and the tax paid respectively. To give an example, the data in the first row of the first panel show that men aged under 60 in the UK have a mean pre-transfer income that is equivalent to 124 per cent of that for the UK sample as a whole and that they receive transfers equal to 42 per cent of the average transfer paid there to all individuals.

Beginning with the transfer process (first data panel), one cross-national difference is very clear: the British transfer system treats male and female incomes more equivalently than its German counterpart in terms of the size of the transfer people receive relative to how well off they are before transfers. One can identify in this system a disfavouring of men for transfer purposes and a corresponding favouring of women. If we interpret equal treatment as referring to how individuals are treated in relation to the average, then this model clearly targets those with lower incomes. In Germany the size of transfers relative to how one is placed before transfers is, to say the least, unbalanced. Male incomes are clearly privileged. German men aged under 60 have a pre-transfer income that is 47 per cent above the average, but they also receive transfers 32 per cent in excess of the norm. Female incomes are relative losers in this process, women's pre-transfer incomes and the transfers they receive both being considerably below the average (53 per cent and 67 per cent respectively).

Following the first two data columns down, we can see that these transactions are played out differently across family statuses. Among the most noteworthy of the effects is a distinct 'privileging', for transfer purposes, of mothers in the UK. This is in large part an effect of child benefits and transfer receipt on the part of lone parents. Since neither pattern of receipt typifies men in the same age group, the result is that UK fathers receive much lower transfers relative to the average. Despite this, however, while the British welfare state tends to treat mothers favourably in regard to the large gaps between their incomes and average incomes, it still falls far short of equalizing incomes between mothers and fathers (as we have seen from Table 5.3 above). In comparison to mothers, wives receive no privileging at all. But if we want to see a transfer system which takes little or no account of 'need' in terms of pre-transfer income then we should look at the German model. If confirmation was needed that the overwhelming emphasis here is on privileging men with family responsibilities for benefit purposes, it can be drawn from any number of statistics in Table 5.4. The 'pro-male' family status focus of the German model is to be seen not only in male–female disparities but also in the treatment of 'other' men. These receive transfers that are considerably lower than those of

Table 5.4 Pre-transfer income, transfers, gross income and tax paid in relation to the average (as a proportion of the mean for each type of income) for individuals aged under 60 years[a]

	Transfer Process		Taxation Process	
	Pre-transfer income	Transfers	Pre-tax gross income	Taxes paid[b]
All under 60				
UK				
Men	1.24	0.42	1.52	1.73
Women	0.68	1.12	0.66	0.56
Germany				
Men	1.47	1.32	1.46	1.43
Women	0.53	0.67	0.54	0.57
Parents				
UK				
Fathers	1.68	0.39	1.44	1.66
Mothers	0.51	1.21	0.58	0.33
Germany				
Fathers	2.00	2.08	2.00	1.73
Mothers	0.40	0.87	0.43	0.41
Spouses				
UK				
Husbands	2.21	0.38	2.32	2.13
Wives	1.00	0.12	0.84	0.92
Germany				
Husbands	1.76	1.17	1.72	1.74
Wives	0.58	0.28	0.56	0.63
Other				
UK				
Men	1.66	0.66	1.44	1.63
Women	0.66	0.50	0.62	0.60
Germany				
Men	0.79	0.78	0.79	0.94
Women	0.65	0.85	0.66	0.70

Notes: [a] Based on personal incomes of those for whom complete information is available on their gross and net personal incomes as well as those of their households.

[b] Including both income and payroll taxes.

fathers and husbands, even though their pre-transfer incomes are also lower.

Moving on to the taxation process (second data panel), neither system presents a particularly egalitarian scenario when considered through the lens of sex and family status, but again, of the two, the situation of UK respondents is the better. Thus the tax paid by women as a

proportion of the average is lower than their gross income as a proportion of the average, whereas men carry a heavier taxation burden relative to their general income advantage. In Germany the taxes paid by
women tend to be greater than the proportion that their incomes form
of the average. To understand how these effects occur, we should pause
for a moment to consider how personal income taxation is organized
in each country. Germany's is such that it offers strong incentives not
only for couples to pay taxes jointly but for no or low income on the
part of the second partner. Under its particular arrangement couples
electing for this option aggregate their income, which is then halved;
the tax due is calculated on this half and then multiplied by two. Given
that this is the most popular procedure for couples (the vast majority of
couples in the German sample paid tax jointly) and the manner in
which I divided the tax burden between members of joint tax-paying
units (see Appendix I), one would expect both a close correspondence
between women and men's tax contributions and also that male
incomes would be favoured. Both of these effects are visible: women
and men's taxes are almost exactly proportional to the size of their
income relative to the average, and taxation has the effect of enabling
husbands and fathers to retain their considerable income advantage
over other men and over all women as a group. These results, and in
particular the cross-national pattern, are consistent with other analyses.
For example, Vermeulen et al. (1995: 19) calculate that the effective
tax rate for women in two-earner couples working average hours was 41
per cent in Germany in 1991 compared with an effective tax rate of 29
per cent for a one-earner couple. Divisions among men are part and
parcel of the differentiation generated by this kind of joint taxation
regime. We can observe from the earlier Table 5.3 (fifth data panel)
that the incomes of German fathers and husbands remain very high in
relation to the average after the fiscal process has taken its effect,
whereas those of women, already low, are actually reduced still further.
The British taxation system was based on a joint taxation arrangement
for married couples around the time of study, although it has since
moved towards separate taxation. In the mid-1980s it also tended to
privilege male incomes but did so to a lower degree than the German
taxation regime. In more recent times the British system has become
more neutral towards labour market participation of married women:
the effective tax rate for the second earner in a couple in 1991 was 16
per cent compared with a tax rate of 21 per cent for one-earner
couples (ibid.).

Some of the cross-national male–female difference is also due to the
fact that more married women in the UK sample have personal incomes
and, relatedly, that the income inequalities between married women

and men there are of a lower order to begin with. One final observation underlines the cross-national contrasts. The tax system treats men and women with no primary family status more or less equivalently in terms of their tax burden in relation to their level of income. In Germany, these men in particular, despite considerably lower incomes, pay for the privileging of men with family responsibilities. Women are not alone, then, in helping to underwrite the tax privileging of German husbands and fathers.

While couples are likely to work out their financial arrangements between them, the effects of the German taxation and transfer arrangements are clearly to the detriment of women's personal incomes and to the benefit of those of men. Table 5.5 shows this plainly, presenting the degree of change effected in female–male income ratios by the transfer and taxation processes. It offers some telling details.

First, in both national settings it is the transfer rather than the taxation provisions that are the main vehicle of income redistribution. Second, any equalization occurring between female and male incomes is due to transfers. When all age groups are included in the analysis, there is quite a considerable difference cross-nationally in the degree of equalization effected by the transfer and taxation procedures individually and the fiscal process as a whole. Pre-transfer inequality in women's incomes as a proportion of those of men is reduced by more than a quarter in the UK, compared with only 13 per cent in Germany. The treatment of the elderly plays a pivotal progressive role in any of the effects that occur. However, when we exclude those over 60, we see that all of the equalization occurring in the German case is limited to the pensioner population, whereas the redistribution is greater and has a wider spread over different life stages in the UK. In fact for those aged under 60 female–male income inequality is reduced by 19 per cent in the UK, whereas in Germany inequalities within this age group are more or less unaltered by the fiscal process. The bulk of this improvement in the UK is accounted for by an increase in mothers' incomes as a proportion of those of fathers, and it is transfers that are largely responsible for this and indeed most other reductions in gender-based income gaps in the UK sample. The German transfer provisions also effect some improvement in income inequalities between women and men outside primary family statuses, but, this group apart, the general effect of both transfers and taxation there is for either no or only a minuscule improvement in the income position of working-aged women vis-à-vis men. The consequences are ominous: after transfers and taxation German mothers' personal income comes to only a fifth of that of fathers and that of wives to no more than a third of the income of their husbands. Compare this to the situation in

Table 5.5 Ratio of female to male incomes pre-cash transfers, post-cash transfers, and post-tax and the % change effected[a]

	UK			% change		Germany			% change	
	1	2	3	1–2	2–3	1	2	3	1–2	2–3
	Pre-transfers	Post-transfers	Post-tax			Pre-transfers	Post-transfers	Post-tax		
All individuals	36.1	43.5	46.7	+20	+7	32.5	36.6	36.6	+13	–
Individuals aged 60 years and over	28.0	48.3	52.3	+72	+8	17.9	38.8	40.7	+117	+5
All individuals less than 60 years	38.1	43.2	46.0	+13	+6	35.9	36.7	35.8	+2	–2
Of which:										
Parents of dependent children	29.5	40.5	46.0	+37	+14	19.9	21.3	20.7	+7	–3
Spouses no dependent children	44.4	45.1	46.4	+1	+3	32.7	32.3	31.0	–1	–4
Others	40.1	43.2	44.8	+8	+4	81.6	83.1	86.6	+2	+4

Notes: 1   Pre-transfers; 2 Post-transfers, pre-tax; 3 Post transfers and taxes;
   [a]   Based on personal incomes of those for whom complete information is available on their gross and net personal incomes as well as those of their households.

the UK – granted a far from equal scenario as well – where mothers and wives' personal incomes reach 46 per cent of those of fathers and husbands.

To summarize, when it comes to reducing income inequalities between women and men, the British fiscal system emerges in the more positive light. Although female–male income gaps are somewhat lower there to begin with, the British manner of organizing transfers and taxes leads to the greater sex and gender equalization. Only for those aged over 60 is the degree of equalization greater in Germany. Despite this, however, the net personal incomes of older women come to only 41 per cent of those of men compared with 52 per cent in the UK. Among people of working age, the German welfare state is even more deficient as an agent of redistribution between women and men. There are two keys to the greater redistribution effected in the UK case. One is the targeting of mothers for the purpose of receiving family benefits; the second is the more favourable treatment of (inferior) female incomes by taxation.

This, then, is the situation facing people as individuals. To get a view of how these personal incomes relate to collective incomes and a measure of the situation facing households and families as agents of redistribution, I shall now consider how individual income-holders are placed relative to each other within the household. Since the relationship between personal and collective income will form a large part of Chapter 7, it is considered here mainly for what it reveals about the scale of the redistributive task facing households and families. Chapter 7 will examine the dynamics of male and female incomes from the perspective of support obligations among family members and how people's personal income situation compares with that of other members of their family or household.

The Role of the Family/Household in Redistribution

Supporters of both of these welfare state models might well argue that inequalities in personal income between women and men are not all that important since most people live within some kind of household or family arrangement and therefore have the opportunity to have personal income gaps or shortages made up. This might well be the case, but for our analytic purposes it remains a hypothetical situation. Given this, it is important and helpful to pose the question of whether it is even possible for people to have income inequalities made up by transfers from others inside the household or family. This question leads me to investigate 1) the proportions of women and men that live in households where it is technically possible to get a transfer, and 2) assuming that such a transfer is made, the extent to which male–female income inequalities could be altered by it. While the patterns here depend very much on the structure of households, and the relevant cross-sample variation in this regard, intra-familial transfers are still important as an outcome measure in two respects. First, to the extent that people share living arrangements they engage in economic exchanges. In this regard focusing solely on personal income cannot be the full story of male and female well-being. While our income adjustments follow customary practice and redistribute the collective income equally between members, this at least gives us some measure of the potential of the household as a redistributive agent between men and women. Second, while the degree of redistribution or equalization of male and female incomes is dependent on the type of household in which people live, and therefore cross-country variation here is closely tied to the distribution of household types in the two samples, it is still relevant to enquire into the potential extent to which people have available other household members who may be able to make up shortages in their own income.

Table 5.6 shows female–male income ratios on the basis of the household income distributed equally among members for all those who share a household. It also presents the female–male income ratios for those who live alone, since these ratios also contribute to the picture for the total population as presented in the fourth row. The second part of the table compares the relative roles of the fiscal process and the household (this hypothetically) in reducing female–male income inequalities overall.

Basically we see from the first four rows of data that the living situation of individuals in the two samples is such that female–male income inequalities are vastly reduced when the household income equally distributed is the unit of analysis. Assuming equal sharing of collective income, there is a disparity of only 7 percentage points between female and male incomes in both samples. The comparisons with those who live alone suggest that women are considerably better off when sharing a household with somebody else. Yet as will be apparent from a comparison of the ratios for those who live alone with those who share a household, for women in the UK having someone to share income with does not make as great a difference as it does for German women. In other words, large disparities between male and female incomes in Germany offer a strong encouragement for women there to share a household.

When we compare the redistributive effect of the state with that technically possible for the family or household, it can be seen (from the last two rows of Table 5.6) that the expectations of the greater importance

Table 5.6 Ratio of female to male incomes for different population sectors on the basis of household income distributed equally among members and the % reduction in female–male income inequalities effected by the fiscal system and the household[a]

	UK	Germany
All those who share a household	0.93	0.96
Individuals under 60 who live alone	0.76	0.77
Individuals 60 and over who live alone	0.82	0.73
Total population	0.93	0.93
% reduction effected by fiscal system in female–male income gaps (total population)	27	13
% reduction effected by household in female–male income gaps (total population)	46	56

Notes: [a] Based on adjusted household incomes of those for whom complete information exists on their gross and net personal incomes as well as those of their households.

of the private sphere in Germany are confirmed. Female–male income inequalities are reduced by 56 per cent by (assumed) intra-household transfers there compared with 46 per cent in the UK. In the latter case, state transfers, in the form of both cash payments and taxation, play a smaller role in reducing female–male income inequalities than does the family or household, but the public transfer and tax mechanism is still much more significant than in Germany.

Redistribution among Different Types of Household

Welfare states' treatment of households may not necessarily follow from their treatment of individuals or vice versa. It is plausible not only that transfer and taxation systems would pursue different objectives at the two levels but indeed that the treatment of individuals may itself flow from considerations about collective units. In any case, assumptions about intra-household responsibilities and internal flows of support may generate a degree of tolerance or *sang froid* about individual income inequalities that cannot be tolerated for collective units. To the extent that policy goals pertain to the collective unit rather than to the individual, there are limits to the degree of welfare states' tolerance of high levels of income inequality, and poverty, among households. Since the German welfare state holds income security over the life course in much higher esteem, one would expect fewer income inequalities among households there after the fiscal process has taken its effect. There is also a second interesting dimension to the individual/collective unit emphasis of policy. It pertains to the degree of variation between how women and men are treated as individuals and how the households that they head fare. In this regard, the treatment of men as individuals and as household members has a smaller range of variation than that of women because transfer payments and tax arrangements more often reflect an assumption that men are heads of their households. Table 5.7 allows us to judge the national and cross-national policy nuances by showing the pre- and post-fiscal incomes of different types of household in relation to the net (post-tax and transfer) mean for all households and the degree of change achieved.

The situation facing the transfer and taxation provisions, in terms of the degree of income inequality among households that they must try and counter, is similar to that for individuals in that the scale of inequality is again slightly greater in Germany. In both cases, however, the degree of pre-transfer income inequality among households is less than it is for individuals. It is the treatment of different types of household though, and the comparison of before and after relative well-being, that makes these data most interesting. And here also we find cross-national similarities as well as differences.

Judged in terms of their pre-fiscal incomes, the types of household most in need of transfers and favourable treatment for taxation purposes do not vary a lot between the two countries. We can see that households headed by married and single men under the age of 60 tend to be both relatively well off and similarly placed in relation to average incomes. Nor is there a lot of variation in the type of household that is worse off. These tend to be women's households for a start, with those headed by single women at or above pension age and lone mothers especially in need of a public income subsidy. The relative income position of lone-mother households differs markedly across national settings. So great is their need of a public subsidy that such households in the UK resemble elderly households more than they do other households headed by a person of working age. In Germany lone mothers' households' pre-fiscal situation, although also comparing poorly with that of other households with a head in prime age, is such that they are much less dependent on transfers as compared with their UK counterparts. Widows and divorcees also tend to be very poorly off in the UK.

The general direction of the fiscal effects and the resulting reordering of household types are in many cases rather similar cross-nationally. So, as one would expect, households headed by an elderly person are the main beneficiaries of redistribution in both settings. Among female households, those headed by a single woman aged 60 and over or a widow are the most favoured. Among male households

Table 5.7 Mean factor and net income, as a proportion of mean population values, and the % change effected for different types of household[a]

Marital status/ age of head	UK			Germany		
	Factor	Net	% change	Factor	Net	% change
Married men						
Under 60	128.7	111.7	−13	140.8	102.7	−27
Over 60	66.1	86.3	+31	52.1	92.1	+77
Single men	163.1	138.7	−15	163.3	124.0	−24
Divorced men/widowers						
Under 60	119.0[b]	109.3[b]	−8	165.1	130.0	−21
Over 60	58.6	85.8	+46	31.2	108.4	+247
All men's households	114.1	107.3	−6	121.8	103.5	−15
Single women						
Under 60	112.4	105.0	−7	147.7	113.4	−23
Over 60	44.7	99.1	+122	20.0	95.8	+379
Divorced women/ widows	42.0	73.5	+75	35.8	82.7	+131
Lone mothers[c]	31.1	54.2	+74	58.7	63.8	+9
All women's households	55.6	77.0	+38	64.7	88.7	+37

Notes: [a] Based on adjusted household incomes of those households for which complete information exists on their factor and net incomes.
[b] small *n*.
[c] Includes all households consisting of a woman rearing dependent children alone. The head may be never married, widowed or divorced or separated women.

those of divorced men aged at least 60 years and widowers do relatively well in both national settings, but in the UK the redistributive bias towards households headed by a married man aged 60 or over is much weaker than it is in Germany. The effects of the more generous pension arrangements in Germany are noteworthy in this respect. There are similarities in the treatment of households headed by a lone mother, but in the sense of uniqueness within the national context rather than cross-nationally. The British welfare state is, in cross-national terms, the more generous to these households, although within the national context the degree of redistribution is low in the light of both their very high need and how other needy households are treated. In Germany these households are very unusual in that transfers and taxes effect hardly any improvement in their relative income level or their position in the income hierarchy. Comparing outcomes in terms of net incomes (second and fifth data columns) suggests that both welfare states fail lone-mother households. The British welfare state fails to transfer sufficient income to these households; the German response is inadequate because its fiscal process effects hardly any improvement in their relative income position. The result is that lone mothers in both national settings end up in the most disadvantaged position of all, with the equivalent of 54 per cent of average household income in the UK and 64 per cent in Germany. Households headed by divorced or separated women and widows have the second-next lowest incomes in both national settings. But there is a cross-national difference in their standard of living, with the income of these women-headed households in the UK coming to only 70 per cent of the average, whereas it reaches over 80 per cent of the German national mean.

This latter point touches on a set of important cross-national differences. One dimension of such variation is that the German fiscal process achieves a greater degree of inequality reduction overall and, as a result, the dispersion in final incomes is smaller there than that characterizing British households. This is not without its gender dimension. But now we have a reversal of the cross-national pattern seen hitherto in that the German welfare state emerges, for the first time, as the less gendered of the two. For evidence of this, one can see that the net income gaps between women and men's households are lower in Germany (varying only 15 per cent around the mean compared with 30 per cent in the UK). Furthermore, while the two welfare states raise women's households' income levels in relation to the average by a similar degree, that of Germany effects a greater reduction in the incomes of male households. One of the outcomes is that at the end of the process women's households are short of the average standard of living by 11 per cent in Germany, whereas they fall 23 per cent below the average in the UK.

The contrasts between the two states' means of dealing with individuals and households are very striking. Germany performs better at the household level, both in terms of the overall degree of reduction achieved in income inequality and also in terms of the improvement in the situation of women's households vis-à-vis that of men's. The British welfare state is, in contrast, the better at equalizing individual incomes. Germany, therefore, can be characterized as concerned more with collective than individual well-being. This interpretation helps to make sense of the very different gender-related outcomes of the German welfare state for individuals as against households and of its greater willingness to tolerate income inequalities among individuals. But it has to be emphasized that Germany's concern with income security over the life course acts to benefit women's households also because it leaves widows considerably better off than in the UK, for example. While it cannot be fully attributed to welfare state effects, Germany is the better place of the two for women to head households on their own, in terms of income inequalities anyway.

Overview

While neither welfare state promises income equality between women and men, both evince a concern to affect financial relations between the sexes. The British fiscal system takes care to direct some benefits to women, either as mothers or as wives of pensioners. In Germany there is no such flow of transfers to women as family members while their husbands are still alive, but once widowed they are relatively well provided for. Married men and fathers are privileged there for receipt of cash transfers and for favourable income tax treatment. Sometimes this occurs at the expense of female incomes and almost always it eliminates the possibility of a significant reduction in income inequalities between working-aged women and men in family roles. It is as if the state refuses to step across the threshold, preferring to entrust the benefits to the main income-earner and setting up a series of incentives to ensure that it interacts with just this member on behalf of the household. The underlying assumption is clear: covering male risks of income loss and offering a promise of income security over the life course to the main earner is automatically to take care of his or her family members as well. As a result, German women in family roles not only have very inferior personal incomes in comparison with men but the fiscal process does little or nothing to change this, except where women are of or near pension age and heading their own household. What it means in real terms is that the German welfare state is only as good for married women as their men are in sharing their incomes with them. It is somewhat ironic to report that, in the context of what could be said to be generally more modest aspirations on the part of the British welfare state, it is the British rather than the German that goes further in equalizing incomes between women and men as individuals. However, all of this has to be set in context. The most important aspect of the background is that both welfare states and societies are willing to tolerate quite large income gaps between women and men within the family.

A rather interesting sociological trend to emerge from this chapter is that these two welfare states differ in their treatment of individuals as against households. Such differences are much more marked in the case of Germany, which displays a lower tolerance for income disparities among households than among individuals. This is consistent with my depiction of the German state as refusing to cross the threshold and speaks to a particular redistributive division of labour between the state and the family. So for women of working age, especially those who are married, the family is the main redistributive channel, with the man/husband as the family's 'public representative'. But this does not tell the whole story of how the German welfare state is gendered. For a greater concern with household or collective well-being than with that of individuals is completely plausible as a key dimension of this model, and the results do point in this direction. Another side of the gender dimension of the German welfare state is therefore that women fare better as household heads than as individual members of marital units (in terms of how their incomes are treated by taxation and transfer policies). And this is also an important part of the cross-national comparison, for there is less income inequality between households headed by women and men in Germany than there is in the UK.

It is actually rather difficult to identify a clear logic in the British set of taxes and transfers. While it is better than the German in ameliorating sex- and gender-based income inequalities among individuals, this is neither an unambivalent nor a completely consistent tendency. For example, some apparent desire to reduce income inequalities between mothers and fathers is not matched by a push to render wives' incomes more equal to those of husbands. In this regard the policy of paying child benefits to mothers, while significant in outcome terms, is inconsistent in the context of the overall logic of policy. In aiming to effect greater equality between male and female parents, it is isolated in policy terms. All in all, there is some evidence to suggest that British income policies appear to treat individuals on the basis of their income level rather than their sex or family position. But this may be to over-interpret the extent to which the British welfare state operates to a consistent policy logic.

Certain policy issues arise from these findings. One can raise the question, for example, whether male–female income inequalities have to be directly targeted by income-maintenance and redistribution policies for a significant reduction in income inequality to be effected. There is not a great deal of direct targeting of women in either of these two systems, and perhaps this plays a part in the unequal outcomes. Another issue raised is the extent to which women's households may benefit from policies that do not have any explicit sex equality aspect. One can give the example of Germany, where the policy orientations towards income security over the life course and the protection of marriage turn out to be of considerable advantage to households headed by widows. These and other policy issues will be further discussed in the final chapter. Now I turn to another outcome associated with the welfare state, poverty, and examine the effect of policies on the (re)distribution of poverty between women and men and the households in which they live.

CHAPTER 6

Sex, Gender and Poverty

The feminization of poverty has become a favoured theme in recent years, and as Dey (1996: 1) remarks, it has placed gender issues at the heart of the poverty debate. This chapter, concentrating on the lower end of the income continuum, sets itself the task of comparing the variation in poverty around sex and gender in the two national settings. Descriptively the chapter seeks to uncover how the interaction between individual, family and social policy works out in the context of poverty incidence and depth. Analytically it searches after the role played by the cash transfer provisions in redistributing the risk of poverty among women and men. In this regard we should remind ourselves that certain poverty-relevant features of their organizing logics set the two welfare states widely apart. Germany's close adherence to a high wage replacement, social insurance model confers on it a strong bias towards compensation and income security, rendering poverty reduction somewhat of a by-product. The British welfare state, in some contrast, is centred around a dynamic of poverty alleviation wherein benefits are low-paying and based on proven need. However, examining their broader mechanisms and distributive processes as they relate to gender and the family casts the comparative framework in a somewhat different light. In particular, comparison along the axes of risk coverage and the construction of entitlement, as undertaken in Chapter 4, suggests a commonality in approach that is likely to lead to some cross-national similarity in the distribution of poverty between women and men and on the basis of gender status and role.

The aim is to explore how the structure of poverty varies on gender grounds cross-nationally and to link differences found to social policy programs and the organizational features of the welfare state as a whole. Since cash transfers are much more important for poverty reduction than is taxation, the spotlight is placed here on cash transfers. Welfare state outcomes will be evaluated, therefore, by a comparison of the poverty-alleviating effects of cash transfers, that is, the impact of transfers on redistributing the risk of poverty. For this purpose, I shall rely on the relatively simple procedure of comparing poverty rates 'pre' and 'post' transfers. While this is completely static by nature and assumes that the different components of income are determined independently of each other, it still illustrates something meaningful about the effects of transfers on poverty. Again I shall carry out analyses for both households and individuals, this time beginning with households because the collective unit is more often the target of poverty-related policies.

Some Propositions in the Context of the Comparative Framework

The systematic comparison of welfare state provision in both national settings allows one to develop some propositions in relation to a number of relevant analytic dimensions: the internal and cross-national incidence of poverty; sex- and gender-based variation in poverty at both the household and individual levels; and the relative roles of state transfers and 'private' transfers in reducing poverty.

The first, and broadest, point of comparison is between a model of transfers organized according to a framework of rights-based, high wage replacement benefits and one resting on a combination of low-paying social insurance and needs-based payments. Comparison on this axis speaks especially to the general incidence of poverty in both societies. Differences in the generosity of transfers and in income levels more generally lead us to expect that people in the UK will experience significantly greater poverty.

Moving beyond this broad level, the expected degree of variation is tempered by a more precise comparison of the two models. With regard to the distribution of poverty between women and men's households, the orientation of both transfer systems towards market-related risks, in its own right and in the light of the tendency for low income in female-headed households to be less induced by employment-related contingencies, leads us to expect a strong sex-based differentiation in the incidence of household poverty in both national settings. This sex differentiation will be to the disadvantage of female households (Pfaff 1992). However, the cross-national gaps in the size of transfers, the internal differentiation that is an inevitable consequence of wage-linked transfers, together with the pervasiveness there of labour market–related risk coverage, suggest that sex differences in poverty will be more pronounced in Germany. In other words, with poverty as a specific target, the British system of flat-rate and low-level transfers is likely to exert a more equalizing effect on male and female household incomes at the lower end of the income continuum.

When it comes to individual poverty rates, the features of the two transfer models lead us also to certain predictions about their effects in redistributing the poverty risk between women and men within and across national settings. Both transfer systems tend to interact with the family through the person of the productive worker, who is treated as a (potential) head of household. Thus, instead of individualizing entitlements to those with no direct link to the labour market, both states utilize the worker as the conduit of benefits for the collectivity, channelling resources to other members through him or her. To the extent that this is the case, women receive lower transfers than men. Into this breach should step the family. But to a varying extent cross-nationally. Germany's strong attachment to a principle of subsidiarity not only affords a guarantee of protection to the institution of the family as such but makes the state unwilling to intervene directly into familial distribution processes, for poverty alleviation or other purposes. Britain's welfare state has no formal commitment to the protection of the family and, with poverty reduction as one of the main motors of transfer access and generosity, women with low incomes in the UK should have easier access to transfers than is the case in Germany. Overall, then, one would expect a less important role for the state in Germany and a correspondingly greater role for the family in poverty reduction among individuals, with the pattern the other way around in the UK.

Poverty Distribution and Variation among Households

Incidence and Extent of Household Poverty by Sex of Head

Following Wright (1992, 1993), poverty in the main analyses will be measured in three ways. The first is the customary head-count measure that enumerates the proportion of people falling below the poverty line. The second is the standardized poverty gap that taps the average income level of the poor and therefore reveals what percentage more income people would need not to be classified as poor. The third is a composite measure, encompassing both of these indicators as well as the variation in incomes among the poor (Appendix II details how each of these measures of poverty is derived).[1] Their beauty in the present context is that they can be decomposed into relative poverty shares. Since each incorporates a different dimension of poverty, all three sets of results need to be considered simultaneously, keeping an eye especially to the consistency of findings across them. To take account of economies of scale and variations in need arising from household size,

Table 6.1 The incidence and intensity of poverty among male-, female-headed and all households[a]

	% poor all	% poor male	% poor female	Ratio fp/mp	Ratio fp/fn
Head counts[b]					
UK	12.6	9.6	21.9	2.28	1.74
Germany	7.2	5.8	11.7	2.02	1.63
German as % of UK rate	57.1	60.4	53.4	88.6	
Standardized poverty gap					
UK	23.8	20.7	33.3	1.61	1.40
Germany	16.0	11.6	30.0	2.59	1.87
German as % of UK rate	67.2	56.0	90.0	160.9	
Relative deprivation[c]					
UK	8.3	7.7	10.5	1.36	1.26
Germany	6.1	4.1	12.8	3.12	2.10
German as % of UK rate	73.5	53.2	121.9	229.4	

Notes: [a] Based on adjusted household income for those households for which income information is complete.
[b] Estimates have been multiplied by a factor of 100.
[c] Estimates have been multiplied by a factor of 1,000.
fp = standardized proportion of female poverty; mp = standardized proportion of male poverty; fn = females as a proportion of total population.

the aggregate income is as before adjusted according to the OECD equivalence scale. The income base is net disposable household income. The poverty line is set at 50 per cent of median, equivalenced, net household income.[2] Table 6.1 presents the poverty results for households classified by sex of head yielded by this configuration of measures. From it, the two ratios especially interest us: the sex/poverty ratio (the female poverty rate as a proportion of that of men) in the fourth column and the standardized ratio of female poverty (column five), which is an indicator of the risk of poverty among female-headed households relative to the share they form of the total population.

Across measures there are significant and consistent differences between the two samples in the incidence of household poverty in general and on the basis of sex of head. The expectation of higher poverty rates in the UK context is confirmed. Depending on which indicator one chooses, the poverty rates for households in the UK are between 57 per cent and 74 per cent higher than those for German households. Consulting the range of poverty indicators shows that not only are more households in the UK poor, but those falling below the poverty line have a greater shortfall of income and are more deprived than their German counterparts.

These findings confirm existing information, so that comparing them with other research finds fairly ready consistency. Mitchell's (1991: 49) estimate for Germany in 1979 is 0.4 of a percentage point lower than that of the present study. Since considerable controversy surrounds poverty estimates in the UK, especially those provided by government, it is probably best to locate poverty estimates within a range. This range is bounded at one end by O'Higgins and Jenkins' (1989) figure for the year in question of 9.8 per cent for household poverty in the UK and on the other by the 13 per cent estimate provided by van den Bosch (1998). My figure of 12.9 per cent for the UK is at the top end of that range. In terms of how these poverty figures fold into trends over time, we now know that poverty in the UK in the mid-1980s was on a steady upward trend. A modest decline in the 1970s was superseded by a growth in the first part of the 1980s. This accelerated to such an extent that by the early 1990s poverty would touch a fifth of the population, the poverty rate having more than trebled since 1978 (ibid.). The German figures have a somewhat different context. There the poverty trend was quite stable during the 1980s, but since reunification at the end of the decade the poverty rate has started to climb upwards (Döring et al. 1990; Krause 1992; Hauser 1995). The gap between poverty levels in the UK and Germany remains very large, however.

Returning to the mid-1980s, our analysis reveals considerable economic privation among female-headed households. In both countries the female poverty rate is more than double that of men. In the UK women's households have a head-count poverty rate of 22 per cent compared with a 10 per cent rate for men's households; for Germany the respective rates are 12 per cent and 6 per cent. In terms of sex differences then, we also find some of our expectations confirmed. That is, despite very significant cross-national variation in the overall incidence of poverty, the two countries are roughly equivalent in terms of the sex distribution of household poverty on the head-count measure, with female-headed households outnumbering those of men among the poor by about two to one. But consulting the other two poverty indicators in Table 6.1 – the poverty gap and relative deprivation measures – indicates that on these two measures the sex differences are stronger in Germany. That is, although in the UK women outnumber men among the poor to a greater extent than in Germany, sex differences in what one might call the quality of poverty – how much below the poverty line the poor fall and how deprived they are in relative terms – are greater in Germany. In

other words, while women's households are significantly more likely to
be poor in both national settings as compared with those of men, the sex
differentials are more pronounced in Germany. These findings are
particularly noteworthy in the light of the results of the last chapter,
which showed the income gaps between women and men's households
to be lower in Germany. It seems then that while the majority of female-
headed households are not all that unfavourably placed in relation to
those of men, there is a small group of women's households in Germany
that is very badly off.

In order to flesh out the socio-demographic background to the
poverty picture, Table 6.2 sketches poverty profiles for women and men's
households. These demonstrate how a number of demographic characteristics are associated with poverty, and they also indicate whether those
households below the poverty line receive transfers. For comparative
purposes, this information on poverty profiles shows two immediately
striking kinds of patterns. The first concerns a cross-national difference,
the second a similarity. Cross-national differences in the poverty incidence of elderly households are very striking: these households have one
of the highest poverty rates in the UK case (up to 20 per cent poor),
whereas the German figures confirm the relative success of its transfer
system in releasing the elderly from the spectre of poverty (poverty rate
no higher than 4 per cent). This variation in the situation of the elderly
is in fact one of the major sources of variation in poverty between the UK
and Germany (couple-with-children households, which tend to have a
considerably higher poverty rate in the UK, showing the next greatest
variation). The cross-national similarity concerns how economically
marginalized lone parents are in both national settings. These households have the highest poverty rate of all, 44 per cent in the UK, 34 per
cent in Germany. That this is an effect especially associated with lone
motherhood is confirmed by the data on the relationship between the
number of children in a household and poverty rates (Table 6.2, second
panel). For while increasing numbers of children are a 'poverty pressure
point' for all households, this is much more pronounced when the
household is headed by a woman.

The last panel of data in Table 6.2 shows that poor households in the
UK are more likely to be receiving transfers than is the case in Germany.
With only 12 per cent of poor households not receiving transfers,
poverty in the UK can be said to be less a failure of access to the transfer
system than a product of transfers that are too low in value. In Germany,
on the other hand, the high proportion of poor households with
employed heads (41 per cent) implicates the labour market centrally in
poverty in that country. Both transfer systems are, however, more likely
to fail women than men's households. In Germany this is by and large a

Table 6.2 Poverty rate (head counts) for male-, female-headed and all households by household characteristics and the income sources of those households below the poverty line[a]

	UK			Germany		
	Male	Female	All	Male	Female	All
Type of household						
All one-person	15.3	20.0	18.2	3.7	6.2	5.4
Of which:						
One person > 60	14.8	21.1	19.5	2.9	4.5	4.2
One person < 60	15.6	17.0	16.2	4.1	10.0	7.0
Elderly couple	11.1	3.1[b]	10.6	3.0	b	3.0
Couple no children	3.6	b	3.7	2.9	11.6[b]	3.8
Couple with children	13.0	b	13.0	6.9	27.8[b]	7.5
Lone parent	b	47.0	43.8	8.3[b]	35.6	34.0
Other	3.9	7.5[b]	4.5	14.5	17.8	16.3
Number of children						
No children	8.0	16.6	10.5	4.2	8.1	5.4
One	7.0	40.2	13.0	6.5	24.1	9.1
Two	10.2	42.6	13.9	8.0	66.7	11.6
Three or more	25.5	47.5[b]	28.1	19.6	28.6[b]	20.2
Age of head						
Less than 35 years	12.7	41.6	18.1	10.2	20.0	12.6
35–59 years	7.1	16.0	8.5	4.7	14.8	6.1
60+	10.9	18.1	13.7	4.8	6.6	5.5
Economic status of head						
Full-time employed	3.1	1.0	2.9	3.8	5.6	4.0
Part-time employed	6.3	10.8	8.6	11.3	24.1	18.0
Retired	11.6	18.2	13.9	4.9	6.1	5.4
Unemployed	43.3	58.6	45.4	28.6	32.1	29.5
Sick/disabled[c]	48.0	42.9[b]	46.9	—	—	—
Housewife/man	34.8	35.3	35.1	12.1	21.9	16.3
Those below the poverty line						
% receiving transfers[d]	81.9	95.0	87.4	63.2	77.9	68.9
Of these:						
% receiving social insurance	39.4	42.1	42.1	38.2	44.2	40.5
% receiving means-tested benefits	60.6	57.9	57.9	33.8	52.3	41.0
% with head in labour market	22.7	6.1	15.7	50.0	29.1	41.0

Notes: [a] Based on households for which complete information exists on gross and net income.
 [b] small *n* or *n* too small for a proportion to be calculated
 [c] No data on sickness/disablement are available for Germany.
 [d] Excluding child benefits.

failure of the safety-net, means-tested programs, although for some women's households very low widow's pensions are also a cause of poverty. In the UK in contrast, receipt of social insurance as against means-tested benefits does not significantly reduce the risk of poverty among households headed by a woman.

Sex of Household Head Among Other Factors
Explaining the Incidence of Poverty

To what extent are the poverty differentials between women and men's households attributable to the sex of the head, or do they result from structural differences, especially the fact that women and men tend to head quite different types of household? In order to answer this question and to test for the robustness of the sex of household head among other effects, I again use logistic regression. In this case I want to test the capacity of each factor to predict poverty among households[3] when the effects of other factors are controlled for. For the purpose of this analysis I included those factors that most differentiate women and men's households, drawing especially on characteristics of both household heads (age, sex and labour market status) and households themselves (size, type, dependency burden). In the end, quite a parsimonious model emerged with just two common factors significantly predicting household poverty – the *labour market status* and *sex of the head* – and the addition in Germany of *type of household*. Table 6.3 shows the size and direction of the effects in each case.

One of the most important findings for our purposes is that in both countries the sex of the household head is an independent predictor of poverty among households. Although it is not by any means a strong predictor – having a female head raises the 'odds' of poverty in both cases by 3 per cent – nevertheless its emergence in both cases is noteworthy. By virtue of the sex of their head then, women's households are prone to poverty independently of other household characteristics. Notwithstanding this effect, the factor that best predicts poverty is whether the head is in the labour market. When she or he is without a job, a household's likelihood of poverty jumps by 20 per cent in the UK and 17 per cent in Germany. In Germany one other factor has a significant effect on the odds of household poverty: the type of household. This is really an age effect. All households with a head aged less than 60 years are significantly more likely to be poor than are households with heads over that age threshold. The poverty risk of lone-parent households is especially high.

What role do transfers play in the poverty situations of women and men's households?

Table 6.3 Logistic regression on head-count poverty for all households[a]

Variable	β	se	sig	Marginal effect p = 0.10
UK				
Female head	0.30	0.08	0.000	0.03
Non-labour market				
participation	2.17	0.10	0.000	0.20
Constant	−3.30	0.24	0.000	
McFadden's pseudo r² = 0.18				
Germany				
Female head	0.30	0.09	0.000	0.03
Non labour market				
participation	1.87	0.18	0.000	0.17
Type of household[b]				
Singles and couples				
without children	0.74	0.36	0.038	0.07
Lone parents	2.31	0.47	0.000	0.21
Two parent with				
children and 'other'	1.66	0.30	0.000	0.15
Constant	−3.32	0.17	0.000	

McFadden's pseudo r² = 0.19

Variables with significantly different effects across the two national settings[c]

Non labour market				
participation	−0.94	0.20	0.000	0.08
Country dummy	−3.52	−0.09	0.000	−0.32

Notes: [a] Based on households for which complete information exists on gross and net income.
[b] The reference category here is households with a head aged over 60.
[c] These parameters, computed by creating interactive terms for the variables and the country dummy, measure the differences in slope for each of the variables between the two countries.

The Effects of Cash Transfers on Household Poverty

To approach this question I examine what poverty levels would be in the absence of cash transfers, using a reduction coefficient to measure the extent of the decrease effected by public transfers in market-generated poverty. On its own the head-count measure is an insufficient gauge of the change effected by transfers since it ignores the effect of transfers to those still below the poverty line. That is, as a measure that tells us only what proportion of the population falls below the line, the head-count statistic fails to register the relative poverty-alleviating impact of transfers. In investigating the effects of income transfers I shall, therefore, use both head counts and poverty gaps. The first could be said to reveal the impact of transfers on poverty *elimination*, the second the effects on poverty *alleviation* (Ritakallio 1994: 10–12). Table 6.4 shows the before and after poverty rates for households.[4]

The pre-transfer picture is, as one would expect, one of much more widespread poverty. But what comes as something of a surprise is the high degree of similarity cross-nationally in households' need of transfers to keep poverty at bay. All other things being equal, about a third of households would fall below the poverty line without public transfers, and the average poverty gap would be between 69 per cent and 85 per cent. The cross-national patterns are also strikingly similar in the divergence between the need for transfers in women and men's households. Obviously, prime-aged women's households are much more reliant on transfers for reducing poverty than those of men in the same age group. Without cash assistance from public sources, the poverty rate of households headed by a woman aged less than 60 years would be 41 per cent in the UK (54 per cent higher) and 32 per cent in Germany (about double). Before transfers, though the male–female divergences tend to be greater on the head-count measure than they are on the poverty gap. That is, although women's households also tend to be further below the poverty line than those of men, the income shortfall of poor men and women's households is more similar than the actual numbers of each that are poor. Among elderly households, pre-transfer poverty levels and hence dependence on transfers is more extreme in Germany, the existence of fairly significant occupational pensions in the UK reducing the extent to which elderly households need public transfers to keep them out of poverty. In general, though, before transfers sex differences, on both head counts and poverty gaps, are less significant among elderly households compared with what they are for those headed by a person of working age. How do the two transfer systems interact with this pattern?

The general background is that cash transfers to households have a consistently higher anti-poverty effect in Germany, reducing the head-count poverty rate by 80 per cent compared with 60 per cent in the UK. German transfers also achieve a higher degree of reduction in the poverty gap, but the variation between the two countries is minimal. But different systems have particular strengths and weaknesses. The British transfer system is better at reducing the poverty gap and therefore at alleviating poverty than it is at eliminating it. In considerable part, however, any cross-national differences found are attributable to the superiority of the German pension system, which renders transfers there especially good at reducing head-count poverty among households with an elderly

Table 6.4 Pre- and post-cash transfer poverty rates and degree of change effected by transfers on head counts and poverty gaps among households[a]

Head counts	UK			Germany		
	Pre-transfer poverty	Post transfer poverty	change effected %	Pre-transfer poverty	Post transfer poverty	change effected %
Households with head aged less than 60 years						
Male	12.6	9.1	−28	15.2	6.1	−60
Female	40.7	26.4	−35	32.2	16.0	−50
Total	17.3	12.0	−31	18.1	7.9	−56
Sex–poverty ratio	3.23	2.90	−10	2.12	2.62	+24
Households with head aged 60 and over						
Male	50.0	10.9	−78	74.3	4.8	−94
Female	71.2	18.1	−75	88.3	5.5	−94
Total	58.1	13.7	−76	79.9	5.2	−93
Sex–poverty ratio	1.42	1.66	+17	1.19	1.15	−3
All households						
Male	23.0	9.6	−58	29.4	5.8	−80
Female	57.2	21.9	−62	60.9	11.7	−81
Total	31.2	12.6	−60	36.9	7.2	−80
Sex–poverty ratio	2.49	2.28	−8	2.07	2.02	−2
Poverty gaps[b]						
Households with head aged less than 60 years						
Male	0.65	0.27	−58	0.57	0.20	−65
Female	0.79	0.22	−72	0.79	0.27	−66
Total	0.73	0.25	−66	0.64	0.22	−66
Sex–poverty ratio	1.22	0.81	−33	1.39	1.34	−4
Households with head aged 60 and over						
Male	0.63	0.09	−86	0.94	0.20	−78
Female	0.70	0.06	−91	0.97	0.23	−76
Total	0.66	0.08	−88	0.96	0.22	−77
Sex–poverty ratio	1.11	0.67	−40	1.03	1.14	+11
All households						
Male	0.65	0.22	−66	0.80	0.20	−75
Female	0.73	0.15	−79	0.92	0.26	−72
Total	0.69	0.19	−72	0.85	0.22	−74
Sex–poverty ratio	1.12	0.68	−39	1.16	1.29	+11

Notes: [a] Based on adjusted household income for those households for which complete information exists on gross and net incomes.
[b] (poverty line − mean of those below the line)/poverty line.

head. The provisions in the UK also achieve their largest poverty reduction for elderly households but, with a 76 per cent drop in head-count poverty – compared with one of 93 per cent in Germany – considerable numbers of elderly households in the UK remain poor after transfers.

When it comes to the redistribution of the risk of poverty among households on the basis of sex of head, neither system performs particularly well and there are no significant differences between them on the head-count measure. The overall effect is for a slight reduction (8 per cent in the UK, 2 per cent in Germany) in the propensity of women's households relative to those of men to be poor. However, transfers in the UK reduce sex differences in the poverty gap by 39 per cent, whereas the overall impact of transfers in the German case is to widen the female–male income shortfall, by 11 per cent. One can see in Germany the effect of the absence of a floor below which the value of benefits cannot fall. Transfers to male and female non-pensioner households have an especially unequal effect there, increasing the extent to which women's households outnumber those of men among the poor by a quarter. The UK case is a contrasting one. To the extent that its transfer arrangement has any gender-equality strengths, they lie for the most part in its treatment of households with heads aged less than 60 years. One good outcome for this age group is that transfers have the effect of reducing by 10 per cent pre-existing sex differences in head-count poverty. Thus while the overall degree of poverty reduction is lower there, transfers in the UK operate in a manner that favours poverty reduction among non-elderly, female-headed households as compared with those of men. But note that at the end of the day sex differences in the numbers of prime-aged households falling below the poverty line are greater there than in Germany. The arrangement in the UK is also more equalizing than the German with regard to the poverty gap among working-aged households, actually overturning the pre-existing sex differences. But it is not very effective in changing the distribution of poverty among elderly male and female households, significantly reducing the poverty-gap differences but increasing head-count differentials. When one looks at the scale of the inequalities remaining after the British transfer system has had its effect, it is clear that a major weak point from the perspective of gender equality is that it does not do enough to reduce either poverty in general or its unequal distribution between women and men. In the latter regard, it is nevertheless somewhat better than its German counterpart.

How are such outcomes brought about? In seeking an answer to this question, I shall concentrate on households with a head aged less than 60 years since it is among these that the behavioural adaptations are least predictable and the variety of policies in operation greatest.

The Detailed Effects of Transfers Explored

In order to investigate for structural effects, I disaggregate transfers on the basis of the broad orientation of particular programs and investigate how each individually affects the sex ratio on the head-count and poverty-gap measures. Modifying slightly the threefold claim structure used in Chapter 4 to incorporate a duration dimension, I find that transfers in the two systems are differentiated into four broad types: those that are intended as *family benefits* (cash benefits for families with children and cash support for survivors); those designed to facilitate *short-term exit* from the labour market (e.g. sickness, maternity and unemployment benefits); those oriented to *more long-term exit* (retirement pensions and long-term illness); and those oriented to *minimum income/poverty* (means-tested benefits to cover general and specific income shortages). Table 6.5 disaggregates (in the above sequence[5]) total transfers into these four types in order to evaluate the effects of each on poverty elimination and alleviation and on the sex–poverty ratio.

The results confirm some key structural differences between the two welfare states. For one we can see that poverty elimination and alleviation is in Germany a function of social insurance, while in the UK means-tested transfers bear the main burden of the fight against poverty. Overall the UK model emerges in the more positive light in terms of decreasing sex differentials in poverty. Of the two transfer models, it is also clear that Germany's programs are much more differentiated, in general and in terms of how they affect the poverty distribution between women and men's households. A first way in which German programs can be said to be more differentiated is that the poverty-reduction burden is spread more widely across different programs there than it is in the UK, where means-tested transfers are the main line of defence against poverty. A second source of internal differentiation in Germany is that poverty reduction in women and men's households is achieved by quite different types of program. For German men's households labour market exit programs effect a large part of the poverty reduction, whereas 'family' and 'minimum income' programs are the transfer programs of most significance for reducing poverty among women's households. In the UK the ubiquity of means-tested benefits makes for fewer sex differences in terms of which programs effect poverty reduction, although there is also a slight tendency for social insurance transfers to be more important for reducing poverty among male-headed households as compared with those of women.

The impact of labour market exit programs is to increase sex differences in both countries. In the UK, where such programs have been less significant as a component of social protection policy, their effect is

Table 6.5 Effects of transfers on poverty head counts, poverty gaps and the sex–poverty ratio for households with heads aged under 60 years[a]

	UK			Germany		
% poor head counts	Male	Female	Sex–pov. ratio	Male	Female	Sex–pov. ratio
I Before transfers	12.6	40.7	3.23	15.2	32.2	2.12
II After family transfers	11.8	34.8	2.95	12.5	25.8	2.06
III After short-term exit transfers	11.3	34.4	3.04	9.8	24.7	2.52
IV After long-term exit transfers	11.0	34.2	3.11	7.9	22.5	2.85
V After 'minimum income' transfers	9.1	26.4	2.90	6.1	16.0	2.62
Total change achieved I–V (%)	−27.8	−35.1	−10.2	−59.9	−50.3	+23.6

Distribution of change by type of policy:	Of total change:		Change from stage to stage	Of total change:		Change from stage to stage
% achieved by family transfers	24	41	−9	30	42	−3
% achieved by short-term exit transfers	14	3	+3	30	7	+22
% achieved by long-term exit transfers	8	1	+2	19	14	+13
% achieved by minimum income transfers	54	55	−7	21	37	−8

Average poverty gap of those who are poor

	Male	Female		Male	Female	
I Before transfers	0.65	0.79	1.21	0.57	0.78	1.39
II After family transfers	0.64	0.68	1.06	0.57	0.67	1.18
III After short-term exit transfers	0.61	0.64	1.05	0.53	0.63	1.19
IV After long-term exit payments	0.55	0.60	1.09	0.41	0.60	1.46
V After 'minimum income' transfers	0.27	0.22	0.81	0.20	0.27	1.34
Total change achieved I–V (%)	−58.5	−72.2	−33.1	−64.9	−65.4	−3.6

Table 6.5   (cont.)

Poverty gap	UK			Germany		
	Male	Female	Sex–pov. ratio	Male	Female	Sex–pov. ratio
Distribution of change by type of policy:	Of total change:		Change from stage to stage	Of total change:		Change from stage to stage
% achieved by family transfers	3	19	−12	—	22	−15
% achieved by short-term exit transfers	8	7	−1	11	8	+1
% achieved by long-term exit transfers	16	7	+4	32	6	+23
% achieved by minimum income transfers	73	67	−26	57	64	−8

Note: [a]   Based on adjusted household income for those households for which complete information exists on gross and net incomes.

weaker than in Germany. In both national settings means-tested trans-fers have an equalizing effect on the sex distribution of poverty. This is important because means-tested benefits are often criticized and tend to be generally unpopular with social policy researchers. But the results of this analysis highlight their equalizing strengths from a gender perspec-tive. Note, however, that the positive effects of these programs are more pronounced in the UK. As we might expect, family transfers also tend to benefit women's households more than those of men, thereby reducing sex poverty differentials in both national settings. In comparing the positive effect of family benefits cross-nationally, it is important to be clear that the effects are brought about by different programs. In Germany it is survivors' benefits that are more or less single-handedly responsible for the equalizing effect. These benefits tend to be more generous there (being linked to the spouse's former wage) and, at the time of study, had fewer conditions limiting access than in the UK. When one speaks of the equalizing impact of family programs in the UK, one is referring mainly to the effects of child benefits. The results in this respect highlight the advantages of directing such benefits to women. Unlike their German counterparts, where men actually benefit more from family transfers than do women, family-oriented transfers in the UK have a consistently positive effect on both female poverty rates and the sex–poverty ratio.

The poverty comparison among households and the role of cash transfers, then, can be summarized as follows. Before and after transfers, women's households in both national settings outnumber those of men among the poor by a ratio of two to one. Sex differences in the poverty gaps and relative deprivation indicators are more pronounced in Germany, however. In the UK the pattern of effects is more complex: the head-count differences remain strong but the differentials in the poverty gap are overturned in favour of women's households. So what the UK system does is increase the income of women relative to that of men at the lower end of the income scale but not to such a degree that it makes a significant dent in the sex differentials in poverty among households. Regression analyses indicated that the sex of head effect, although not all that strong, is independent of other factors in both countries. In other words, these are both societies with an inherent tendency towards a sex differential in household poverty. In both national settings, transfers are very important for poverty reduction among households. Women's households in the UK are marginally greater 'winners' from the transfer system than those headed by a man, especially when the head is aged less than 60 years. Women and men's households in Germany either benefit to a more or less similar degree (true of those headed by an elderly person) or those of men benefit more (true of households with a head under 60) from the poverty-reducing effects of transfers. The outcome – and a key difference cross-nationally – is that German transfers overall leave sex–poverty differentials among households more or less unchanged or else increased, whereas in the UK sample transfers act to reduce such differentials. Variations in both the structure and the pervasiveness of social insurance transfers lie at the root of the cross-national differences here. That is, Germany's high wage replacement model together with the widespread use of social insurance as the main form of transfer act to increase sex differentials. The equalizing thrust of family and minimum income programs is not enough to offset the tug of labour market exit programs pulling the other way. In contrast, the UK strategy of flat-rate social insurance and a more widespread recourse to means-tested transfers is more equalizing in regard to differences in the risk of poverty between male- and female-headed households.

Poverty Distribution and Variation among Individuals

Measuring Poverty among Individuals

When it comes to measuring poverty rates among individuals, one has the choice (or dilemma) of relying on household incomes or basing the calculation on respondents' personal incomes. The literature offers little comfort on which yields the more reliable poverty figures, although individual poverty statistics tend to be most widely computed on the basis of collective income. But this type of analysis requires important decisions about how to distribute the aggregate income among individual household members. To a very real extent, this remains somewhat of an arbitrary decision because so little is known about the actual allocation of income within households – Jenkins (1990: 10) labels it the 'unobserved redistribution process'. On the other hand, relying on personal incomes assumes that each individual operates as an independent financial unit, neither providing nor receiving financial support – an assumption that is highly likely to be counterfactual and almost certainly subject to variation by household type, and perhaps also social class (Vogler 1989). Given the lack of information in either sample on how collective income is actually shared between members, I decided to follow standard procedure and distribute it equally. Note, however, that adopting this method means that the poverty rates as presented for individuals are likely to underestimate the extent of poverty among women (for children also, but they are not considered here).

Sex, Gender and Individual Poverty

As can be seen from Table 6.6, with 12 per cent of individuals poor on the head-count measure in the UK and 6.6 per cent in Germany, the poverty rates for individuals are more or less similar to what they are for households.

The most significant variation from the household pattern lies in differences between the female poverty rates cross-nationally (compare Tables 6.1 and 6.6). In both national settings the effect of moving from the household to the individual level of analysis is to decrease the incidence of female poverty. The sex differential practically disappears, especially in Germany where there is no significant sex difference in individual poverty rates. Presuming that the collective income is shared equally then, German women are much better off in the poverty stakes as members of households than they are as household heads. To put this into numbers, 6.8 per cent of all women are poor as individuals compared with a poverty rate of 11.7 per cent for women's households. The real significance of this contrast is that female poverty rates in Germany are very sensitive to whether the household or the individual is the unit of analysis for poverty calculations. This is true to a much lesser extent in the UK, where women have a significantly higher risk of poverty than men, both as individuals and as household heads. This cross-national disparity is a function of three things. Incomes in general

Table 6.6 Incidence of poverty among men, women and all individuals[ab]

	% poor All	% poor Men	% poor Women	Ratio fp/mp	Ratio fp/fn
Head counts					
UK	11.7	10.2	13.2	1.29	1.13
Germany	6.6	6.4	6.8	1.06	1.03
German as % of UK rate	56.4	62.7	51.5	82.2	
Standardized poverty gap					
UK	24.2	22.1	26.5	1.20	1.10
Germany	14.2	13.7	14.5	1.06	1.03
German as % of UK rate	58.7	62.0	54.7	88.3	
Relative deprivation					
UK	8.4	7.9	9.3	1.18	1.11
Germany	5.2	5.0	5.6	1.12	1.07
German as % of UK rate	61.9	63.3	60.2	94.9	

Notes: [a] Based on adjusted household income equally distributed for those individuals for whom complete information exists on their own as well as their household incomes.

  [b] Methodological notes as for Table 6.1.

are lower and spread more widely in the UK population, making for higher poverty rates there as compared with Germany. Second, as we saw in the last chapter, the income gaps between women and men's households are larger in the UK. Third, fewer British women as compared with their German counterparts have access to the income of a male household head.

Examining the Relationship between Sex and Gender Factors and Individual Poverty

In order to test for the more detailed aspects of sex and gender in relation to poverty, I ran logistic regressions, which once again treated poverty as an outcome variable. The main purpose here is to see the effects of different components of gender status and role (such as marital status, family status and the family economy) on the 'odds' of poverty for individuals,[6] and especially to identify cross-national differences. The results from the best-fitting models are reported in Table 6.7. From them we can see that the gender factors create a complex pattern. Parenthood, employment status, the nature of the household economy (in terms of whether it has at least one worker or not) and in some cases marital status and age have significant effects on whether a person is

Table 6.7 Logistic regression on head-count poverty among women and men by family status and labour market status[a]

Factor	UK				Germany			
	β	se	sig[b]	marginal effect (p = 0.10)	β	se	sig[b]	marginal effect (p = 0.10)
Women								
Mother	0.98	0.14	0.000	0.09	1.18	0.16	0.000	0.11
Employed	−1.67	0.08	0.000	−0.15	—	—	—	—
Married	—	—	—	—	−0.58	0.15	0.000	−0.05
At least one worker in h'hold	−2.57	0.11	0.000	−0.23	−1.59	0.17	0.000	−0.14
More than 60 years of age	—	—	—	—	1.01	0.20	0.000	−0.09
Constant	−0.09	0.10	0.978		−2.33	0.15	0.000	

McFadden's pseudo r[^2] = 0.21   McFadden's pseudo r[^2] = 0.13

Factor	β	se	sig[b]	marginal effect	β	se	sig[b]	marginal effect
Men								
Father	0.88	0.14	0.000	0.08	0.91	0.16	0.000	0.08
Married	0.64	0.11	0.000	0.06	−0.57	0.15	0.000	−0.05
At least one worker in h'hold	−2.87	0.15	0.000	−0.26	−1.76	0.18	0.000	−0.16
More than 60 years of age	—	—	—	—	−1.16	0.25	0.000	−11
Constant	−0.10	0.12	0.417		−1.07	0.17	0.000	

McFadden's pseudo r[^2] = 0.19   McFadden's pseudo r[^2] = 0.13

Variables significant cross-nationally

Men

Factor	β	se	sig[b]	marginal effect
More than 60 years of age	−1.66	0.51	0.000	−0.15

Notes: [a] Based on those for whom complete information exists on their gross and net personal incomes as well as those of their households.

[b] significance on the basis of the Wald statistical test.

poor or not. In most cases each has a direct and independent effect on the odds of poverty. Age is, however, the only variable having a significantly different effect across countries (although this is true only for men). One can read the results to say that poverty among British and German women is predicted by more or less similar factors and that for men cross-nationally the only factor significantly altering the odds of poverty is whether they are under or over pension age. The following discussion should therefore be taken as reflecting tendencies within the national context rather than robust differences across them.

First, of the three family-related statuses, we see confirmed here that only parenthood is a significant risk factor for poverty. That is, being a mother or a father significantly increases the odds of poverty both for German and British women and for men once other factors are controlled for. Parenthood is in general a poverty risk factor for both women and men and to a largely similar extent cross-nationally (raising the odds of poverty by about 10 per cent). The family economy, defined in terms of whether at least one member of the family has a job, is, however, closely intertwined in the relationship between poverty risk and family status. As was the case with households, this is truer of the UK, where employment reduces married women's chances of poverty by 15 per cent. Underlying these findings is a point about the importance of two incomes in helping married women and men in the UK to avoid poverty. The poverty odds in Germany are less tightly governed by the number of workers in the family, and the woman's own employment status exerts no significant effect. There is some evidence here also to confirm the more adequate nature of German transfers. Consider the effect of the age variable, for example. In the UK age has no significant effect on the likelihood of poverty for either sex. Both women and men are as likely to be poor below as above pension age. In Germany however, the poverty-reducing effects of pensions are reflected in the finding that being 60 years or over lessens the chances of poverty for both women and men by around 10 per cent.

Moving on to consider marital status, we can see that it has one main significant effect. This occurs in Germany for both women and men, for whom being married significantly reduces the odds of poverty (although only by a very modest 5 per cent). A link between non-marriage and low personal income is, therefore, highlighted in Germany, suggesting that subsidies through the family, together with high earnings for married men, are important in reducing the chances of poverty there for both women and men. For men age is the underlying factor here in that it is mostly younger men who are unmarried. Age is also the key factor for women, but in a different sense in that women who are currently unmarried are older and therefore less likely to have an income from employment.

The Effects of Cash Transfers on Individual Poverty

The above analysis highlights a key characteristic of how the British welfare state functions in real life: labour market participation is the

Table 6.8 Poverty head counts and female–male poverty ratios before and after transfers for all individual respondents as well as for those under 60 years by gender role and the % change achieved by transfers in each case[a]

	UK				Germany			
	Men	Women	All	Sex–poverty ratio	Men	Women	All	Sex–poverty ratio
Before transfers								
All	21.7	28.9	25.4	1.33	23.3	19.3	21.2	0.83
Of those under 60:								
Parents	17.3	24.7	20.9	1.43	14.7	13.3	13.9	0.90
Spouses	8.3	7.6	7.9	.92	9.1	4.4	6.6	0.48
Other	11.7	15.4	13.5	1.32	12.9	12.1	12.6	0.94
After transfers								
All	10.2	13.2	11.7	1.29	6.4	6.8	6.6	1.06
Of those under 60:								
Parents	13.2	18.1	15.6	1.37	6.7	10.2	8.6	1.52
Spouses	4.3	3.9	4.0	0.91	3.6	3.4	3.5	0.94
Other	6.8	8.4	7.6	1.24	8.6	7.6	8.2	0.88
% Change achieved 1–2								
All	−53	−54	−54	−3	−73	−65	−69	+28
Of those under 60:								
Parents	−24	−27	−25	−4	−46	−23	−38	+69
Spouses	−48	−49	−49	−1	−60	−23	−47	+96
Other	−42	−45	−44	−6	−33	−37	−34	−6

Notes: [a] Based on adjusted household incomes equally distributed for those individuals for whom complete information exists on their gross and net personal incomes as well as those of their households.

surest route to non-poverty for individuals, men especially. To get a picture of how the two transfer systems are implicated in the poverty risks of individuals, we can carry out a similar exercise as we did for households by comparing pre- and post-transfer poverty rates. Table 6.8 gives the before and after poverty scenarios among all individuals as well as those below 60 years of age by gender role.

To begin with the pre-transfer poverty scenario (first data panel), while individual poverty rates are always higher for the UK, averaging 25 per cent compared with 21 per cent in Germany, the sex distribution of poverty varies cross-nationally. For the UK the pattern is the now familiar one of significantly higher female poverty. But the German results are especially interesting. Now the pattern is reversed compared with the UK and with that for German households in that it is men in Germany who have a higher pre-transfer poverty rate. In other words, German men are more reliant on public transfers for poverty reduction than are German women. Disaggregating the patterns for those aged less than 60 years by family status indicates further variation in the need for transfers. In the UK mothers would have a much higher poverty rate relative to fathers without transfers, whereas in Germany the most significant family status difference is husbands' heightened poverty risk without transfers. Differences between 'other' women and men's need of transfers play a large part in increasing the pre-transfer sex–poverty differential in the UK also, with women having a considerably greater need of transfers.

Comparing pre- and post-transfer poverty rates reveals that the cross-national differences in the overall effects of transfers are greater for individuals than they are for households. But there is at least one constant: just as it did for households, the UK welfare state effects a small improvement in female–male differentials, whereas the overall effect of the German transfer arrangements is to significantly increase sex–poverty differentials from their pre-transfer level (by 28 per cent). These findings cast in a different light the lower sex–poverty differentials for individuals in Germany as reported in Table 6.6, showing that the overall effect of transfers is to overturn the pre-transfer sex–poverty balance, raising women's poverty risk higher than that of men. Now some of the results of targeting transfers primarily on men are being revealed. For against a background of greater poverty reduction overall in Germany, it is male poverty rates that are most affected. Tracing the patterns for those under 60 on the basis of family status shows that parents in both cases tend to be under-targeted for poverty-reduction purposes, but in the UK there is no differentiation made between male and female parents. The German system is, in contrast, at its most unequal for women and men within the family and, obversely, at its most equal for those outside primary family roles. The only 'pro-woman' bias that is visible is for those with no primary family status, and the general tendency is for males in family roles to be privileged over females in corresponding roles. We see here confirmed the propensity of the German welfare state to support prime-aged women only when they could be expected not to receive support from a man. The British welfare state, while not wholly consistent in its treatment of men and women in different family statuses, directs its transfers in such a manner as to have the effect of avoiding direct differentiation between women and men inside and outside the family. The sex–poverty differential therefore remains largely unchanged by transfers.

In order to see how particular kinds of transfers are associated with these outcomes, we can in Table 6.9 break down the transfer impact in the same manner as earlier, differentiating between family-oriented, short- and long-term labour market exit programs and those transfers that are oriented towards a minimum income. These effects are calculated only for the head-count measure but are presented for people aged under 60 as well as for the total population.

Table 6.9   The effects of transfers on poverty head counts and the sex–poverty ratio for all individuals as well as for those aged under 60 years[a]

	UK			Germany		
	Male	Female	Sex–pov. ratio	Male	Female	Sex–pov. ratio
All						
I Before transfers	21.7	28.9	1.33	23.3	19.3	0.83
II After family transfers	21.4	28.0	1.31	22.1	17.4	0.79
III After short-term exit transfers	20.8	27.6	1.33	20.6	17.0	0.83
IV After long-term exit transfers	11.9	15.7	1.32	7.7	7.9	1.03
V After 'minimum income' transfers	10.2	13.2	1.29	6.4	6.8	1.06
Total change achieved 1–V (%)	−53.0	−54.3	−3.0	−72.5	−64.8	+27.7

Distribution of change by type of policy:	Of total change:		Change from stage to stage	Of total change:		Change from stage to stage
% achieved by family transfers	3	6	−2	7	15	−5
% achieved by short-term exit transfers	5	3	+2	7	3	+5
% achieved by long-term exit transfers	77	75	−1	77	73	+24.1
% achieved by minimum income transfers	15	16	−2	−9	9	+2.9

Under 60s						
I Before transfers	13.6	17.5	1.29	12.4	10.1	0.81
II After family transfers	13.0	16.1	1.24	11.0	9.0	0.82
III After short-term exit transfers	12.3	15.6	1.27	9.2	8.6	0.93
IV After long-term exit payments	11.0	14.1	1.28	6.5	7.2	1.11
V After 'minimum income' transfers	9.2	11.4	1.24	6.5	7.2	1.11
Total change achieved 1–V (%)	−32.4	−34.9	−3.9	−47.6	−28.7	+37.0

Table 6.9   (cont.)

	UK			Germany		
	Male	Female	Sex–pov. ratio	Male	Female	Sex–pov. ratio
Under 60s Distribution of change by type of policy:	Of total change:		Change from stage to stage	Of total change:		Change from stage to stage
% achieved by family transfers	14%	23%	−4%	48%	38%	+1%
% achieved by short-term exit transfers	16%	8%	+2%	16%	14%	+13%
% achieved by long-term exit transfers	30%	25%	+1%	16%	14%	+9%
% achieved by minimum income transfers	40%	44%	−3%	20%	34%	+11%

Note: [a]   Based on those individuals for whom complete information exists on their gross and net personal incomes as well as those of their households.

What they show are some differences and similarities in how both transfer models, as well as particular programs within them, operate to bring about a reduction in poverty among individuals as against households. One of the most notable differences from the situation for households is that family-oriented programs are much less important for reducing women's poverty as individuals as compared with when they head households. The results for the UK are notable for highlighting the continuing importance of social insurance transfers there, although means-tested benefits retain some importance for reducing poverty, especially among those aged less than 60.

Taking the population as a whole, the bulk of the poverty reduction among women and men in Germany is effected by long-term labour market exit programs. But these programs are also the main culprit in increasing the sex–poverty differentials there. To be more precise, the higher incidence and absolute value of pensions and early retirement payments to men actually overturn the sex–poverty ratio in men's favour. Of all the four types of transfer, only those here labelled as 'family benefits', principally widow's payments, act to reduce women's risk of poverty vis-à-vis that of men in Germany. The potentially unequal effects of long-term labour market exit programs are tempered in the

Table 6.10 % change in head-count poverty rates effected by transfers from the state and the family/household[a]

	UK		Germany	
	State	Family[b]	State	Family[b]
All				
Men	−40.0	−12.0	−70.0	−49.8
Women	−42.4	−60.0	−34.6	−87.8
All	−41.2	−51.0	−58.5	−67.5
Under 60s				
Men	−32.0	−20.5	−44.6	−45.5
Women	−39.3	−61.5	−22.7	−87.3
All	−36.4	−49.7	−34.9	−67.6

Notes: [a] Based on those individuals who do not live alone for whom complete information exists on their gross and net personal incomes as well as those of their households.
  [b] Note that the effects for the family are computed net of the state's effects.

UK case by the more basic nature of (old-age and retirement) pensions plus the practice of paying to women a part of their hsuband's pension even when he is still alive. But finally the British programs tend to be relatively neutral between women and men.

The State and the Family's Effects on Poverty Reduction

The final question of interest is the degree to which the family or household is relied on to reduce individual poverty. The effects of the family or household are calculated here as the difference between poverty rates computed on personal incomes and those that are calculated for individuals on the basis of the equal distribution of household incomes. In order to control for the cross-sample variation in the number of one-person households, the calculations in Table 6.10 of the poverty-reducing effects of transfers from the state and those from the household or family are limited to people who do not live alone.

Family sharing of income is a more important means of reducing poverty in Germany. For example, operating with the collective income equally divided has the effect of decreasing head-count poverty by 68 per cent in Germany compared with 51 per cent in the UK. In both national settings then, private (familial) transfers are more important than state transfers in reducing poverty, but this is a more pronounced tendency in Germany. There is some variation of note. When it comes to countering women's poverty, private transactions are in Germany much more important than public transfers, whereas for women in the UK the poverty-reduction burden is shared more equally between the state and family. It is, however, the relationship between the two institutions and poverty reduction among men that leads to the most significant cross-national variation. Male poverty rates in the UK are only slightly reduced by having the benefit of access to the collective family or household income, whereas poverty among men in Germany drops sharply when they are assumed to share equally in the household income. These are not necessarily husbands or fathers but rather younger unmarried men who, like their female counterparts, tend in Germany to be dependent on their family of origin for a longer period and to a greater degree than is customary in the UK.

So in a sense, while women in both national settings need both the state and the family to stem their poverty, women in Germany need the family more. Men in Germany also benefit from the family as a 'poverty preventive' institution, whereas men in the UK tend overall to be only marginally affected by the poverty-reducing effects of what I have called here private transfers. Yet it should be borne in mind that these conclusions, along with all those relating to individual poverty in this chapter, assume that household income is not only shared but shared equally among members.

Overview

It is never easy to identify clear objectives in cash transfer programs, nor are the goals or aims of social policies self-evident. Yet it does seem reasonable to associate contemporary welfare states with the aim of reducing poverty. There is, however, no sure route between such a broad policy objective and particular outcomes for women and men. In this chapter I have approached the British and German cash transfer systems in terms of how their allocation procedures act to shape and redistribute poverty risks between women and men. I have demonstrated that issues of poverty can, partly at least, be explained by reference to gender.

I began by focusing on the household. The results suggest that, for seemingly very different welfare states, they have remarkably similar outcomes in terms of the distribution of poverty between women and men's households. Thus Germany is a low-poverty country, and the UK a high-poverty one, but in both cases women's households have double the poverty incidence of households headed by a man. I also expected, however, that, while both national settings would exhibit strong sex differences in poverty, these would be more pronounced in Germany. The results showed this to be the case: German women's households are more disadvantaged relative to those of men in poverty terms. While the sex of the head is not a very strong influence on a household's likelihood of being poor, it does exert a significant effect in both national settings. Hence in neither case is the sex of head effect reducible to labour market participation or other differences between women and men's households.

The two transfer systems are implicated in the poverty outcomes as identified. In both cases transfers have a large anti-poverty effect. However, against a background of greater poverty alleviation in Germany, the sex–poverty differentials there are either unchanged or increased in comparison to what they are assumed to be in the absence of transfers. Inequalities in transfers to male and female households of working age are especially important here. While the prevailing provision in the UK could not be said to be especially egalitarian either, it at least effects a reduction in the differential propensity of male- and female-headed households to be poor and the degree to which they fall below the poverty line. In terms of accounting for these particular cross-national variations, the German transfer system was shown to be the more internally hierarchical with regard to poverty reduction in men and women's households. This is true in two respects: while social insurance is by far the most pervasive type of provision, different types of social insurance program are oriented to male- and female-headed households, and the sex-differentiated effects of each type of program are more pronounced than in the UK. While one would not wish to exaggerate the policy implications, the role of minimum income transfers has to be emphasized. These are important in reducing both poverty in households headed by a woman and differentials between women and men's households.

Focusing on individuals reveals a more complicated sex and gender faultline. The sex–poverty differentials are lower than they are for households in both national settings, but especially so in Germany. That is, if we assume that the household income is shared equally, women in Germany are significantly less likely to be poor as individuals than they are as heads of households. Pursuing the analysis of poverty among individuals further showed that parenthood is the family status most closely associated with poverty, with lone motherhood a significant risk factor in both cases. This analysis also revealed the close connection between labour market participation and avoidance of poverty for both men and women in the UK, thereby confirming the relative 'meanness' of the British welfare state. Probing the detailed effects of transfer programs on individual poverty rates suggests that the more consistent and extreme bias of German transfers towards men makes male poverty rates the main beneficiaries of transfers there. One important outcome is that, while before transfers women have lower poverty rates than men, their comparative poverty risk is actually higher once transfers have had their effect.

There is evidence to suggest that in Germany the family or household is relied on as a 'poverty absorber' to a greater degree than in the UK. While this is more true for women, German men too require a redistribution of the family or household income for poverty-reduction purposes. What most emerges from this chapter is the importance of the family, specifically having access to the income of other members, in combating poverty. Redistribution through the family is actually more important than that effected by the state in reducing poverty in both national settings. The family is, however, comparatively more important in Germany. The German set of welfare arrangements clearly relies heavily on two assumptions: first that transferring income to some men as the presumed heads of their households is a sufficient guarantee of household well-being; second that women's welfare is secured within the household. To the extent that the second condition is met – and I, just like the German welfare state, assume this rather than test it – German women are not significantly disadvantaged in poverty terms relative to men. In the UK, where less reliance is placed on the family, women are as individuals significantly more likely to be poor than men.

The gender-sensitive aspects of the approach to poverty measurement that I developed and applied here should be noted. Poverty was not unquestioningly accepted as a household phenomenon, for example. Care was taken throughout the chapter to juxtapose individual and household poverty. The analysis was also carried out in a manner sensitive to life-course patterns, for the results of other research suggest that female poverty tends to be precipitated by life-course transitions, whereas that of men is related more to labour market developments (Ruspini 1997). But the analysis has limits. I have found no solution to the vexed question of how to share household resources but rather followed the conventional practice of assuming equal sharing. The limitations of the approach to measuring poverty as a general phenomenon also need to be made explicit. What I have done here is equivalent to taking snapshots of poverty at one point of time. As such my analysis is wide of the latest fashion in poverty research, which searches after duration and movement (Buhr 1995; Leibfried et al. 1995; Leisering and Walker 1998). However, none of the recent work on the dynamics of poverty gives cause to assume that the structures of poverty uncovered here would be any different to those found by dynamic analyses. For what is often under-emphasized by the duration-oriented analyses is that those moving out of poverty are replaced almost immediately by somebody else. As a result, the overall structural pattern tends to be reproduced although poverty as an individual experience would be different. Gender is a key facet of that structural pattern and there is no reason to suspect that the gender inequalities in poverty alter quickly.

CHAPTER 7

Marriage, Financial Relations and Women's Economic Risks

It is one of the guiding themes of this book that individuals' well-being is defined by the interaction between family, state and market. Up to now most attention has been focused on investigating the cash transfer and taxation arrangements along with some of their connections with the family and, less often, the market. In this, the final empirical chapter, I want to look both inside marriage and also at what might be termed the 'margins of marriage'. An important aspect of different models of social provision from a gender perspective is how national policy configurations coexist with and affect patterns of intra-familial sharing and financial support. While conventional welfare state analysis prioritizes the treatment of earners for comparative purposes, my approach suggests that welfare states exert an influence in fashioning aspects of life choices more broadly. Such welfare state effects are indirect and more qualitative. Drawing on Dahrendorf's (1979) idea of life chances, I consider the incentives contained in existing policy configurations for certain economic behaviours and in turn patterns of financial support on the part of women and men. In particular, income, taxation and service provision policies influence individuals', women's especially, capacity both to maintain a household on their own and to be financially independent within households. In part, the chapter focuses on the present reality of support relations and obligations between married or cohabiting women and men, seeking to identify not only if different models of marriage exist in the two national settings but the conditions that underpin them and some of their most significant consequences. In its second part the chapter is more speculative. It looks forward in the life course of those individuals who comprise the study population, returning to the theme of differential female and male income risks and investigating some of the most serious of such risks for women: divorce, separation and lone parenthood.

A key thrust of the analysis thus far suggests a differential construction of marriage and family in the two societies. Germany is protective of what would today be described as a traditional form of marriage in which the man's status as breadwinner and male incomes are both deemed worthy of public support. Britain could be described as an 'ambivalent family model' in two senses. First, its set of policy arrangements is less consistent in reinforcing a particular pattern of gender relations. Second, the male breadwinner norm does not appear to be as predominant there and certainly not at the expense of other family members' income to the same degree as in Germany. Before we can characterize these as two distinct models from a gender perspective, however, we need to know more about the male–female financial patterns with which they are associated and their consequences for women's broader life choices. Two aspects are central. The first is intra-familial economic relations and the relative benefits and disbenefits involved in marriage for women and men. The second is the contingency of marital breakdown and the spectre it casts on adults' (and children's) financial well-being. The perpetuation of marriage as the most important institution of private maintenance and the growing instability of marriage at once justify an interest in the complexion of marital financial relations. The broader referent in both cases is the degree to which a male breadwinner norm prevails and the consequences this has for families and for the women and men who comprise them.

The Role of Marriage and Male Support

Some Theoretical Foundations

The core of income-based relations between women and men is to be found in the connection between income secured oneself and that obtained by other members of the collectivity. Here lies the potential to be independent of or dependent on others, with consequences for life opportunities, power relations and the standard of living of both the collective unit and its individual members. Economic relations between women and men within the household or family are crucial to an understanding of gender relations and individual well-being for a number of reasons. On the one hand, financial relations between spouses provide the context within which many decisions and choices are made by partners; on the other, they impose constraints on the options available to one or both partners. It is now a well-established sociological fact that the household or family is not necessarily a unit of shared interests. While the traditional division of labour may be rational from the family's point of view, it is, to say the least, problematic in terms of women's access to a personal income (Sørensen and McLanahan 1987). For it is equally true that one of the consequences of a traditional family model is low income on the part of women and consequential financial dependence on men.

What significance should be attributed to women's financial dependence? It is possible to identify a number of associated processes. First, at the most general level the assumption of female dependence provides a rationale for paying higher wages and social security benefits to men. The ideology of male support, therefore, potentially governs the lives of all women, including those not personally dependent on male incomes. Second, for the women directly involved – married and cohabiting women – financial dependence may endanger both their income security at any one time and their income stability over the life course. Having to depend on others for their income renders women's financial well-being problematic should their partner not share his income or do so only minimally. Over the longer term, the growing incidence of marital breakdown and divorce imperils women's income stability since the greater a woman's dependence in marriage the greater is her potential loss of income should the marriage end. This is true for both widowhood and divorce. Apart from the economic risks, financial dependence is likely to affect the power balance of relationships, and it is this which has called forth feminist fire.

Research, Anglo-Saxon for the most part, has begun to identify some meanings of women's financial dependence. Lister (1990: 451) draws attention to three aspects identified by research: lack of control; lack of enforceable rights; and a sense of obligation towards the provider. Theoretically feminist analyses have raised female economic dependence to great heights. Some feminist theorists, in fact, consider married women's economic dependence to be one of the crucial mechanisms maintaining women's subordinate position in society (Hartmann 1979; Delphy 1984). Dependency relations are viewed as relations of power in which women's personal dependence on income secured by men acts to bolster male power and traditional authority patterns within and outside the family. Hence women as dependants are rendered exploitable. While there is a counter-argument emphasizing interdependence (Land 1989; Arber and Ginn 1991), by and large dependence is imbued with a strongly negative imagery, similar in some ways to neo-right representations of a climate or culture of benefit dependency on the welfare state.

I don't want to argue against the existence of a power structure within families nor that women's inferior income position may place them at a disadvantage when it comes to negotiations over resource distribution or the pursuit of goals or activities that may be seen (or represented) to be in their individual self-interest. Nor would I deny that traditional forms of marriage embodied a very strange trade indeed, she 'trading' her right to disobey for an 'equality' that gave him all the rights of resource disposal.[1] I do, however, draw attention to the danger of 'economic determinist' type of thinking here and also to cultural differences between the two countries. Economic resources do not define the full range of exchanges taking place within the family, just as economic rules of exchange are unlikely to govern alone (see Curtis 1986). There is also a danger of assuming that financial dependence has the same connotation across national settings. Here it is relevant to point out that, of the two countries studied, the ideal of independence, especially as it relates to financial autonomy, is more entrenched in Britain. Financial independence was never as prominent in political activity around the 'woman question' in Germany (and other continental European countries) as it was in Britain and the USA. Furthermore, the philosophical underpinnings of the German welfare state and German society tend towards a collectivist rather than an individualist outlook. The influence of social Catholicism, which holds to a relational perspective on the social – individuals and groups are seen as embedded in a nexus of interdependent relations and are able to achieve self-realization only through such relations – is strong on the Continent. In a philosophy that emphasizes duties rather than rights and social embeddedness rather than individualism, both women and men are defined in the first instance by their family membership. Independence is a relatively foreign concept in this way of thinking.

At the minimum the potential range of financial benefits and disbenefits in marriage for both women and men requires empirical validation. While I do not have the necessary information on intrafamilial dynamics to explore fully the extent or nature of the exchanges involved, it is possible to identify the scale of support needs and demands and some of the likely financial consequences of being married for women and men. To begin I look at income relations between partners in marriage, interpreting these in terms of the degree to which one partner requires support from the other and the extent to which the other spouse is required to share his or her personal income with adults and children. To identify the financial benefits in marriage, the second set of analyses in this part of the chapter compares the living standards of individuals in different marital and family situations.

Table 7.1   Respective contributions of men and women to household income (%) [a]

Household type	UK		Germany	
	Men	Women	Men	Women
Elderly couples	69	31	80	20
Couples < 60	60	40	70	30
Parents with children	76	24	84	16
All of these	70	30	80	20

Note: [a]   Based on individuals who are either married or cohabiting for whom complete information is available on personal and household income.

Resource-based Relations within Married Couples[2]

Financial Relations and Status within Marriage

The majority of married women and practically all such men make some financial contribution to their household or family.[3] However, there is an important cross-national contrast here in that 28 per cent of married German women have no personal income. This means that over a quarter of German married women are completely financially dependent on income secured by their husbands. For the men involved it signifies a breadwinner role. The vast majority of such women are either mothers of young children or in their late forties and older. All but 5 per cent of married women in the UK sample have some personal income, even if only monies deriving from child benefits.

Such personal income patterns carry through into intra-couple income inequality. When we measure each spouse's contribution to the joint income as in Table 7.1, we can observe that married women in Germany contribute no more than a fifth, compared with an average contribution of 30 per cent on the part of equivalent British women.

Unsurprisingly, the size of a woman's financial contribution varies with her family and demographic circumstances. Women make the lowest contribution when they have dependent children – 16 per cent in Germany, 24 per cent in the UK – and the highest when they live in couple households where the head is below pension age and there are no dependent children. In the latter type of household, men and women's contributions approach parity in the UK, but 30 per cent is as high as married women's contribution gets in Germany. The fact that elderly German women personally contribute no more than a fifth of the collective income – compared with 31 per cent on the part of similar British women – can be taken as a further indication of cross-national differences in both women's access to retirement and old-age pensions and male–female gaps in public transfers.

What do such income inequalities mean for support patterns between spouses and with regard to children? We can, following Sørensen and McLanahan (1987, 1989), distinguish between the prevalence and degree of income support needed by or from each spouse. The first step is to assign to each a *support status*, classifying them on the basis of the size of their contribution to the collective income. Spouses are either supporters (when they contribute at least 60 per cent of the household's financial resources), interdependent (if they provide between 40 and 60 per cent of the household income) and supported (if they provide less than 40 per cent of the household income). We can also treat of the *degree of support* by distinguishing the average extent to which each spouse is required to support or is supported by the other. This analysis turns on the comparison between a spouse's personal income (from all sources) and her or his share of all collective income equally divided. Degree of support is calculated as the proportion of one spouse's personal income that needs to be transferred to the other for the second partner to have an equal share of the collective income. In other words, it is the excess of one's personal income over one's equal share of the collective income for those individuals whose personal income is greater than their household share. Dependence characterizes those whose personal income is less than their household share, and its degree is calculated as the proportion of that person's share of household income that is a transfer from the other spouse.[4] For all of these calculations we also take account of parents' support of children (Table 7.2), allocating such obligations between partners in proportion to their contribution to the total income.[5]

In both national settings marriage plays a key role as a conduit of financial support, but reliance on marriage is greater in Germany. There scarcely more than one out of ten married respondents (compared with 17 per cent in the UK) are interdependent in the sense of making a roughly equivalent financial contribution to the joint income. Such a low level of male–female income equivalence leads to both heavy financial demands on male incomes and high support needs on the part of women. In fact 80 per cent of German married men are required to provide some financial support to their wives to enable them to share equally in the collective standard of living. In the UK the proportion of married men who should transfer part of their personal income to support their wives in this manner is somewhat lower at 75 per cent. The other side of this coin is that 25 per cent of wives in the UK are in a financially independent position in their household, being either equal contributors or having a sufficiently high income to be in a position to provide a transfer to their husbands. Less than 20 per cent of

Table 7.2 Support status of men and women within the household and degree of financial support provided and received (%)[a]

	UK		Germany	
	Men	Women	Men	Women
Supporter of spouse	74.8	7.8	80.3	5.9
Interdependent	17.4	17.4	13.8	13.8
Supported by spouse	7.8	74.8	5.9	80.3
(% totally supported)	(6.6)	(6.7)	(1.4)	(27.9)
% of personal income to support spouse[b]	23.0	8.0	35.0	3.0
% of support needed from spouse[c]	5.0	43.0	3.0	64.0
% of personal income to support children	14.0	14.0	12.0	7.0
Total support obligations from personal income	38.0	17.0	47.0	10.0

Notes: [a] Based on individuals who are either married or cohabiting for whom complete information is available on personal and household income.
[b] computed as (personal income – household share)/personal income.
[c] computed as (household share – personal income)/household share.

the married women in the German sample are so situated. While requiring support from one's spouse is paradigmatically a female experience, we should also note that 8 per cent of the men in the UK sample and 6 per cent in the German contribute less than their wives and are therefore in need of some financial subsidy from them. Still, in both cases women tend to be the supported and men the supporters. Interpreting these results as speaking to the degree of 'familization' of women, this process is more entrenched in Germany.

Support status tells us too little about intra-household financial relations. The degree of support should also be considered. It is not only the incidence of female reliance on male incomes that is greater in Germany but also the degree (fourth row of Table 7.2). Under circumstances of equal sharing, the average married German man is required to devote 35 per cent of his personal income just for the support of his wife; this is a third more than the proportion required of husbands in the UK. The degree to which wives are called on to subsidize their husbands is modest by any standard – no more than 8 per cent of a woman's personal income in either national setting on average needs to be allocated to that of her husband so as to equalize his share of the joint income. The more normal situation for married women in both national settings is to rely on their husbands. But this is a pattern which is again more pronounced in Germany. We can observe from the fifth row of Table 7.2 that German married women on average rely on their husbands to provide 64 per cent of their economic support, whereas British women's personal income is short of their household share by 43 per cent.

To round off the picture of family support patterns we have to add child support obligations. These are generally heavier in the UK sample – because households there tend to have more children and also less income – absorbing an average of 14 per cent of all married couples' joint incomes compared with around 10 per cent in Germany. But note that men in Germany bear a disproportionate share of the cost of children (sixth row of Table 7.2), since so many married German women have no or very low personal incomes. All in all, when their child and spousal support obligations are aggregated, the average German married or cohabiting man is required to devote 47 per cent of his personal income for the support of his wife or partner and dependent children compared with 38 per cent for equivalent British men (final row of Table 7.2). It is interesting to observe that the transfer required for the wife is on average three times that needed for children in Germany, whereas in the UK the difference between what men pay for the support of their wives and that for their children is much smaller (23 per cent and 14 per cent respectively). Overall, married women in the UK pay 17 per cent of their income for the support of others and German women pay about half that amount. In both cases women's support obligations are dominated by their support of children rather than of their husbands or partners.

Considering the variation in support obligations and needs by age and income level helps to identify the sources of married women's economic dependence (Table 7.3). The pattern of female dependence over the life course, both in terms of the proportions requiring a subsidy from their husbands and the size of the subsidy needed, follows a somewhat different path in the two national settings. Such a pattern is simplest in Germany: both aspects of women's dependence increase more or less progressively over the life course. Women are least likely to require a subsidy from their husbands in the early years of marriage, but by the time they reach the age of 65, 88 per cent of German women require some subsidy from their husbands and their personal income is on average two-thirds short of their household share. Thus the extent of German women's dependence intensifies over the life course. It is as if once begun, German married women find it impossible to escape financial dependence on their husbands. Once out of the labour market, women's income falls behind to such an extent that the income gap is too large ever to be made up. Female dependence on male incomes in the UK not only varies over the

Table 7.3   % of married women requiring financial support, degree of support required by them, and % of men's income needed for the support of their wives across different age groups and income quintiles[a]

Age Groups	All	17–24	25–34	35–44	45–54	55–64	65+
UK							
Women requiring support	74.8	75.9	77.0	79.0	70.9	77.9	77.5
Average shortfall of women's personal income[b]	43.0	43.5	48.6	38.3	38.9	51.3	35.6
Average proportion of men's personal income needed for the support of their wives[c]	23.0	26.8	21.8	18.8	20.4	32.1	26.8
Germany							
Women requiring support	80.3	53.9	67.0	81.3	83.7	85.5	87.6
Average shortfall of women's personal income[b]	64.0	40.1	56.2	64.8	67.2	73.4	66.3
Average proportion of men's personal income needed for the support of their wives[c]	35.0	13.6	22.3	28.2	37.9	39.2	38.1

Income Quintiles	All	Quin 1	Quin 2	Quin 3	Quin 4	Quin 5
UK						
Women requiring support	74.8	79.8	81.6	81.8	76.5	65.1
Average shortfall of women's personal income[b]	43.0	28.6	47.9	53.7	47.5	39.3
Average proportion of men's personal income needed for the support of their wives[c]	23.0	17.0	25.6	26.8	24.9	22.4
Germany						
Women requiring support	80.3	83.1	90.2	86.4	78.1	64.2
Average shortfall of women's personal income[b]	64.0	57.3	73.7	63.9	57.3	41.2
Average proportion of men's personal income needed for the support of their wives[c]	35.0	40.8	34.9	32.3	28.7	24.2

Notes: [a]   Based on individuals who are either married or cohabiting for whom complete personal and household income information is available.
[b]   computed as (women's household share – their personal income)/ household share.
[c]   computed as (men's personal income – their household share)/ personal income.

life course but is much more closely associated with child-related exigencies – being lower in the early and late phases of the life cycle and high in the middle. The contrasts in the situation of elderly women across national settings is once again evidence of the greater equalizing tendency of welfare state transfers in the UK. These are not so equal, however, as to eliminate British women's need of an income subsidy from their husbands. Still, when couples reach pension age and above in both national settings, he is required to devote only a fifth of his income to her in the UK compared with 38 per cent in Germany.

Moving on to income quintiles (Table 7.3 second data panel), the cross-national patterns are more similar than for age groups. The general tendency is for both support obligations and requirements to decrease as the collective income rises. In short, a class pattern can be identified here in that women make a greater financial contribution when the collective income is higher. The fact that the tendency is for spouses to become interdependent as collective income rises rather than for her to support him suggests that many of these families are in the higher income brackets because they are two-income families. But it is really only from the fourth income quintile on that a dramatic change takes place in both the proportion of women requiring support and the size of the transfer needed. A common pattern in both cases is for women in the poorest quintile to be less financially dependent than those in the two adjacent quintiles. However, again we have to note that German men never devote less than 24 per cent of their personal income for the support of their wives and in the lowest income quintile the transfer required for their spouse alone comes to a hefty 41 per cent of their personal income.

One would not be distorting reality too much if, by way of summary, one simplified and said that marriage in Germany follows a traditional pattern and adheres closely to a sole male breadwinner model. The family is much more the locus of female support, and within the family women and children's welfare hinges very closely on male incomes. As contrast, couples in the UK are more likely to be interdependent and are in general called on to devote less of their personal incomes to the support of the other. Furthermore, the German model is such that the support of wives is the main demand on male incomes, whereas the support burden of UK husbands and fathers is more equally divided between the needs of wife and children.

The Financial Benefits and Costs of Marriage to Individuals

A good gauge of the financial benefits and disbenefits involved in marriage is to compare the relative income levels of those who are married and unmarried. Table 7.4 presents, for those aged less than 60, married women and men's personal and household incomes, the latter adjusted for household size and composition, as a proportion of those of women and men in a range of family situations.

Beginning with women, the first impressions for both national settings are of financial advantage for married women compared with other groups of women. That is, although married women's personal incomes tend to be lower, their equivalent household standard is always either similar to or higher than that available to all non-married women (whether single women, widows or mothers rearing children on their own). Marriage, therefore, has considerable potential financial gains for women in both national settings. Comparing the information on personal incomes gives an idea of the extent to which married women provide for themselves. Cross-nationally there are very big differences here. The thrust of the contrast is as indicated earlier: the low degree to which German married women secure their own financial well-being. Income divergences between lone and married mothers are especially large: the latter have a personal income that is only a third of that of lone mothers in Germany (60 per cent in the UK). But when it comes to the household standard of living, married mothers' households have a considerable income advantage over those of lone mothers (fourth row of Table 7.4). While this is true also in the UK, the scale of the potential financial gain to German women in marriage is higher across household types. The financial gains to women from marriage in the UK are of a considerably lower order. Admittedly, the household income of married women is always in excess of that of non-married women there, but the gaps in personal incomes are not as large. Judging from these results overall, the comparative financial advantages of marriage to women in the UK are less than they are in Germany.

Interpreted another way, this information suggests that there are costs as well as benefits involved in marriage for women and that such costs are greater in Germany. If we regard the lower personal incomes of married women in comparison to other women as a cost of marriage – in the sense of personal income forgone – then marriage costs German women very dearly. Their personal incomes come to only 61 per cent of those of all non-married women compared with 105 per cent in the UK. One result of this we have seen above in the high dependence of German married women on financial transfers within the family. There is another sense in which the costs of marriage could be said to be higher for women in Germany. This comes to light when we compare their household standard of living with that of other women (see rows one and two of Table 7.4). Here we observe that married women forgo the opportunity to earn a personal income in return for a household standard of living that is similar to that of non-married

Table 7.4 Ratio of married women's and men's net personal and adjusted household incomes to those of women and men in other marital situations(%)[a]

| | UK | | Germany | |
	Personal Inc.	Household Inc.	Personal Inc.	Household Inc.
Women				
Married women/all non-married women	104.7	112.4	61.4	104.6
Married women/single women, no children	137.6	107.2	73.0	100.6
Married women/widows[b]	64.5	128.6	46.8	110.4
Married mothers/ non-married mothers[c]	59.9	169.4	32.1	144.4
Men				
Married men/all non-married men	120.6	114.0	257.5	99.4
Married men/single men, no children	115.2	102.1	297.8	102.6

Notes: [a] Based on individuals aged less than 60 years for whom complete information is available on personal and household income.
[b] Since it was impossible in the UK database to distinguish between widows, separated and divorced women, this comparison for the UK is for women who are in any of these categories.
[c] The comparison in this case is with lone mothers whether single, widowed or divorced or separated.

women. Only in comparison with lone mothers, and to a lesser extent widows, are married women's households significantly better off in Germany. In the UK some idea of the financial contribution made by married women to their households is also clear from these data. Not only is married women's personal income significantly higher there than in Germany but married men's income is lower than it is in Germany. In fact it is among men that the contrasts are at their starkest. German married men have personal incomes at least two and a half times greater than those of all unmarried men, whereas in the UK married men's personal incomes are no more than 20 per cent higher than those of other men (as a result of tax treatment and different labour market participation patterns).

To be sure, such costs and benefits are a matter of interpretation, for it could also be argued to be an advantage of marriage for women in Germany that they are enabled to attain, without significant labour market participation on their own part, a household standard of living similar to that which other women attain mainly through their own earnings. Whatever the nuances of interpretation here, the comparison with the UK is illuminating. For there married women could be said to have something of both in that their personal incomes are greater than those of all other women by 5 per cent, while their collective income is on average 12 per cent higher. But we cannot really treat this 'advantage' independently of the extent to which the women themselves contribute to it by their own earnings.

The relation of women to the labour market, understood not only in terms of participation rates but also with reference to whether they work full- or part-time and the average contribution of their earnings to the collective income, is fundamental to the calibre of intra-familial financial relations. As Table 7.5 reveals, married mothers and wives in the UK are not only employed in larger numbers than their German counterparts but they are more likely to be in the labour market full-time and through their earnings to make a larger contribution to the household income. In both cases though, mothers have the lowest rate of labour market participation, confirming each as countries where women withdraw from the labour market for child-rearing purposes.[6] A comparison of the employment participation rates and patterns of wives suggests, however, that such an exit is of a more permanent nature in Germany, with only 54 per cent of wives with no child-care responsibilities employed there compared with 72 per cent in the UK sample. Comparing the employment situation of other women indicates that married women come closer to the 'female norm' in the UK, where female employment is higher across family statuses (with the exception of lone mothers, of whom more later) than it is in Germany. The low level of employment participation (about 40 per cent) among non-married women in both samples is remarkable. This is mainly a function of the divided nature of the category, which tends to consist of women who are either fairly young, and hence still in education or unemployed, or fairly old and therefore out of the labour market.

There is a relationship between wives' earnings and the income standard of the household as a whole (data not shown). In both countries there is a tendency for the proportion of women with earnings to rise as household income rises. But, consistently across quintiles, the proportion of households with female earnings is greater in the UK than in Germany. Women's earnings also make a greater contribution to household income in the UK, except for the lowest quintile. The cross-national differences in the contributions of female earnings are especially marked for the middle quintile and reach a peak in the UK for the fourth quintile. In general, therefore, in the UK higher living standards of households depend more closely on female earnings. Hence married women there achieve a higher standard not just by their access to the pooled and equally shared income of a male

Table 7.5 Labour market situation of women and men aged under 60 years[a]

	UK				Germany			
	Parents	Spouses	Lone mothers	Single no ch.	Parents	Spouses	Lone mothers	Single no ch.
Women								
% employed	54.4	71.5	41.5	41.4	36.5	54.3	53.8	48.9
Of these: % full-time	31.4	66.6	39.0	80.0	29.9	53.0	77.2	83.3
Earnings as a % of total household income	12.7	23.1	25.9	16.0	11.0	19.4	40.3	26.8
Men								
% employed	67.7	84.8	—	52.0	93.9	88.6	—	52.7
Of these: % full-time	96.1	96.3	—	91.3	92.8	98.1	—	93.7
Earnings as a % of total household income	36.3	44.1	—	23.4	70.0	57.3	—	30.0

Note: [a] Based on women and men aged less than 60 years for whom
complete information is available on their personal and household
income.

breadwinner but from their own employment in conjunction with this. In Germany the benefits of marriage for women stem to a much greater degree from the access that it (presumably) grants to the breadwinner's income.

Turning to the situation of men – for whom a smaller range of comparisons is made since their marital situation varies less than that of women – we can first see in the last two rows of Table 7.4 evidence that Germany's income model is much more favourable towards husbands and fathers than towards men without primary family responsibilities. The ratio of personal net incomes is nearly 3 to 1, whereas in the UK married men's personal net incomes are no more than 20 per cent higher than those of all other men. Yet it seems that however large are their personal incomes, the toll of being the only or main breadwinner eats into married men's personal incomes to such a degree that they end up with a standard of living that is roughly equivalent to that of non-married men. But, reflecting the higher personal incomes of married women there, the fall effected in men's incomes by having to share them with members of their families is much less severe in the UK. Judged, then, in terms of the comparison between their household income levels and those of other men, the financial costs of marriage to men are much greater in Germany. But then high incomes appear to be a concomitant of marriage for German men and they are unlikely to have such high incomes were they not married.

In the next part of the analysis, I consider the scale of the income risk associated with marriage breakdown and rearing children alone and the likely level of compensation available for such risks in the two national settings.

The Risks Associated with Marriage Breakdown

To the extent that welfare states rely on the family as a source of support for adults and children, their continued operation is threatened by an increase in family breakdown. I have observed that, in terms of individual well-being, one of the greatest financial risks for women in general, but married women in particular, is having to live without access to a male (breadwinner) income. Marriage breakdown is one of the most likely contingencies precipitating such a loss of access to male income. This has led some analysts to suggest that one of the most important criteria for evaluating the 'woman-friendliness' of welfare states is the degree to which they allow women to live autonomously or to maintain independent households (O'Connor 1992; Orloff 1993).

Increasing divorce rates, marital breakdown and lone parenthood are putting women's economic security at great risk. Across the European Union (EU) the divorce rate tripled between 1960 and 1990 (Family Policy Studies Centre 1994: 6–7). Divorce rates in the UK especially soared (increasing sixfold) over the period, so that in 1990 the UK had the highest divorce rate of all member states. The last 30 years also saw an increase in German divorce rates, but this was much more gradual (slightly more than doubling) and German divorce rates still remain around the EU average. The UK is also far ahead of the EU norm on births outside marriage, being second only to Denmark in the proportion that lone-parent families form of households with dependent children (one in six). Germany, in the second highest group of countries (along with France), remains somewhat behind the UK in terms of births outside marriage and lone-parent families as a proportion of all families with dependent children (Roll 1992: 15–16).

Should their marriages break down, 30.1 per cent and 41.7 per cent of married people run the risk of becoming lone parents in the UK and German samples respectively. What are the consequences in each society for the financial well-being of spouses after marriage, and what hypotheses about marital breakdown follow from each welfare state's treatment of marriage? One such hypothesis would be that a strong male breadwinner model such as Germany's would penalize marriage breakdown, allowing likely reductions in living standards to act as a disincentive for people to end their marriage. This might be the case if the perpetuation of marriage and family obligations were the only principle guiding or underlying provision. But if social justice demands that everybody should have some level of income sufficiency, then those experiencing marital breakdown should not be allowed to deviate too much from the customary standard of living. Adding the possibility that a social insurance model as followed in Germany encourages every family to have a breadwinner would suggest a greater role for the market than the state there in the restoration of living standards after divorce or separation.

In the following section I explore the background to marriage breakdown by first identifying what one might call its structural costs – that is, the additional cost of keeping two households instead of one. Following Sørensen (1994), I shall investigate a number of scenarios for post-separation income levels according to different assumptions about likely sources of financial support and their degree. These are, in essence, hypothetical exercises, the aim of which is to identify some possible costs of marriage breakdown for women and men. The divergence between the income levels of currently married women and those of existing divorced or separated women and lone mothers forms the backdrop for my exploration of the likely consequences of marital breakdown. I also seek to identify the different ways in which the family and society in general could apportion the costs involved in marital and family breakdown. For all of the following analyses I restrict the population to those aged under 60 since divorce, separation and lone parenthood are risks mainly experienced by people of working age.

The Costs of Marriage Breakdown and Likely Sources and Levels of Compensation

Two main factors in their current situation determine the standard of living that would be available to married individuals in the event of the break-up of the family or household. The first is the economic consequences of maintaining two households as against one; the second is their existing financial resources, both those available in a personal capacity and through the marital relationship.

Structural Costs Associated with Marriage Breakdown

It is certainly more expensive to maintain two households as against one. Exactly how much more costly we do not know for sure, but the adjustments inherent in equivalence scales may be taken as a gauge of the economies of scale involved in sharing households of various sizes. They therefore provide one estimate of the additional costs incurred when households of particular sizes and composition have to be re-established

Table 7.6 Estimated additional financial costs involved in establishing new households according to the OECD equivalence scale (family size elasticity 0.73)

Pre-break-up household size	Need index	Post-break-up household options	New combined	% increase
2	1.66	1 and 1	2	20.5
3	2.23	1 and 2	2.66	19.3
4	2.75	1 and 3	3.23	17.5
		2 and 2	3.32	20.7
5	3.24	1 and 4	3.75	15.7
		2 and 3	3.89	20.1
6	3.7	1 and 5	4.24	14.6
		2 and 4	4.41	19.2
		3 and 3	4.46	20.5

into two separate households. Table 7.6 demonstrates the additional income needed across a range of new household arrangements on the basis of the adjustments in the OECD equivalence scale.

While the costs vary somewhat according to the size of the original household, the additional expense involved in establishing two households from one is around 19 per cent. In other words, total income needs to increase by about a fifth for a household to be able to maintain the same standard of living after a break-up. The need for additional income varies, however, according to the size of the original household, and also on the basis of the new living arrangements. Given economies of scale, the larger the original household and the more individuals are concentrated together into a new household, the less costly is the break-up (ibid.). This renders a change less expensive, for instance, should one parent take all of the children – a factor that should be an important consideration for how parents decide to organize the living arrangements of their children after the break-up. Note that since the OECD equivalence scale is one that assumes relatively small economies of scale in sharing a household, its estimates of the cost of setting up two households are in turn less than a scale that assumes larger economies from sharing.

Some Scenarios for Compensation for Marriage Breakdown and Lone Motherhood

What if existing households in the two samples were to break up without any change in their financial resources? How many would be forced into poverty by the sole exercise of forming two new households? On

Table 7.7 Proportion of households below the 50% poverty line if current household income were to support two households instead of one (existing poverty rates)[a]

Household type	UK	Germany
Married couples, no dependent children	6.4 (3.7)	4.9 (3.5)
Parents with one child	17.4 (8.6)	11.2 (5.8)
Parents with two children	22.0 (10.2)	20.8 (7.5)
Parents with three or more children	46.1 (25.7)	32.6 (19.1)
All	18.6 (9.6)	12.8 (6.2)

Note: [a] Based on married or cohabiting households with a head aged less than 60 years for which complete information is available on personal and household income.

the basis of the above economies of scale and assuming that equal sharing of total income takes place, Table 7.7 shows the poverty rates for a number of different types of married-couple households were they to split into two households. For comparative purposes the existing poverty rates are presented as well (in brackets).

Almost no family type in either national setting could afford a separation on current income without a significant increase in poverty. The only exception is couples with no dependent children in Germany. Their poverty rate would increase only slightly in contrast to all the other cases where poverty rates would soar, at the minimum doubling, were households to split up. So, if nothing else were to change, the structural costs alone involved in a marriage break-up would lead to a 19 per cent poverty rate in the UK (94 per cent increase) and 13 per cent in Germany (more than double). The poverty risk associated with family breakdown is therefore greater for German households, although in terms of absolute numbers poverty would still be higher in the UK. Families with more than two children, which the existing poverty rates show to be already under pressure, would be especially hard hit, with a poverty rate of around 46 per cent in the UK and a third in Germany.

To go one step further in the exercise of identifying the costs and consequences of marital breakdown, we can incorporate different divisions of new households, along the lines of the different possible combinations outlined in Table 7.6, and identify the consequences for women and men. Assuming that people would have only their current earnings to live on after a separation,[7] Table 7.8 shows how partners' standard of living would change depending on the living arrangements they make for the children.

The financial situation of both spouses would alter dramatically, but women's more so. One of the most striking points from these data is, however, the cross-national contrast in the situation of husbands and fathers. Only in Germany are earnings sufficiently high for these men to allow them, in the event of a break-up, to maintain themselves and their children in another household without any drop in their standard of living. In the UK fathers and husbands' current earnings are simply too low for them not to feel keenly the financial impact of forming a new household. The corresponding data for Germany reveal from another angle men's existing family support obligations there. The income standard of fathers with three children would, for example, double should they choose not to support their wives and children. This finding is repeated across families of different sizes and all post-break-up scenarios. Therefore only German men could be said to have the financial option of initiating a marriage break-up. They can do so secure in the knowledge that their own earnings are sufficient to maintain their current standard of living for both themselves and their children (should they wish to retain the children). The financial welfare and well-being of women would be far more problematic, in its own right and with the additional burden of children.

Now one set of consequences of financial dependence is being revealed. For whichever arrangement women in both national settings adopt, their need for financial support from their husbands is such that the result of a marriage break-up that terminated that support would be a huge drop in their standard of living. Even if they were not to retain the children, mothers' income standard would still fall by a minimum of 44 per cent. Obviously the financial deprivation tends to increase with the number of children. There are two factors at play here. First, each child increases costs and, second, women's own earning potential tends to decrease as the size of their family grows. The contrast in the latter regard with men is noteworthy since married men's earnings tend to be positively associated with family size (up to around a threshold of two children). In all cases the potential drop in income standards is greater for married women in Germany, as is the potential gain for married men.

This obviously would be an unsustainable situation for women. In any case it is a poor indicator of reality in that transfers, from both public as well as private sources, have been excluded and it has been assumed that no increase would take place in married women's labour supply. We can, still following Sørensen, add a further piece to the puzzle by factoring in transfer levels. Here we are, however, faced with something of a dilemma in deciding what level of transfer income to assume. Existing research indicates that after divorce or separation men do not provide anything like the level of financial support they are

Table 7.8 Comparison of existing and estimated gross annual earnings of married spouses and parents were they to live separately with and without their children[a]

	Current situation	If separated with children		If separated without children	
	Adjusted earnings	Adjusted earnings	% risk	Adjusted earnings	% risk
UK (£)					
Couples no dependent children					
Woman	7,875			4,753	−39
Man	7,875			8,776	+11
Couples with 1 child					
Mother	4,737	989	−79	2,631	−44
Father	4,737	3,196	−33	8,502	+79
Couples with 2 children					
Mother	4,241	596	−86	1,955	−54
Father	4,241	2,987	−30	9,785	+130
Couples with 3+ children					
Mother	2,723	312	−89	1,308	−52
Father	2,723	2,028	−26	8,407	+209
All couples with children					
Mother	4,089	671	−84	2,044	−50
Father	4,089	2,860	−30	9,074	+122
Germany (DM)					
Couples no dependent children					
Woman	28,716			16,392	−43
Man	28,716			34,452	+20
Couples with 1 child					
Mother	23,376	7,668	−67	11,520	−51
Father	23,376	27,444	+17	41,172	+76
Couples with 2 children					
Mother	20,160	2,664	−87	5,340	−74
Father	20,160	24,996	+24	49,992	+148
Couples with 3+ children					
Mother	14,880	2,304	−85	5,748	−61
Father	14,880	17,232	+16	43,104	+190
All couples with children					
Mother	20,748	5,232	−75	7,944	−62
Father	20,748	29,664	+43	45,396	+119

Note: [a] Based on married or cohabiting individuals aged less than 60 years for whom complete information is available on personal and household income.

Table 7.9 Ratio of current separated/divorced women and lone mothers' transfer income (from public and private sources) to the current household income levels of wives and married mothers[a]

	UK	Germany
	% risk covered	% risk covered
Wives, no dependent children[b]	18.5	15.5
Mothers, one child	35.3	29.7
Mothers, two children	36.3	29.6
Mothers, three or more children	54.9	41.2
All mothers with children	39.7	30.9

Notes: [a] Based on married or cohabiting women, divorced/separated women and lone mothers aged less than 60 years for whom complete information is available on personal and household income.

[b] The reference group for these women is separated and divorced women without children. For mothers, lone mothers' incomes are the reference point.

presumed to do during marriage. So the most realistic assumption would probably be that existing mothers, in the event of a break-up, could expect to receive a similar level of public and private transfers to those received by current lone mothers. Table 7.9 shows how much of their likely loss of income currently married wives and mothers who keep the children with them can expect to have compensated by transfers were this to be the case.

Clearly, women without children must rely on their own resources or face a huge drop in income should their marriages break up, since the most that either state and/or husband is prepared to compensate for is somewhere between a tenth and a fifth of their income loss. Mothers do rather better in both national settings but especially so in the UK, where they can expect to have about 40 per cent of their income risk covered by transfers in the event of marital breakdown. The vast majority of this compensation comes from the state rather than from private maintenance. In a comparative context, German society provides very unreliable insurance against the loss of income involved for women in marriage breakdown and rearing children alone. In comparison to the UK this can be attributed in large part to a failure of public support policies, since private transfers to existing lone-mother households are about three times in Germany what they are in the UK.

Altering their labour supply may also be a possibility for women. While it is practically impossible to estimate women's labour supply in the event of divorce, we can assume that it would approximate the pattern of existing lone mothers and divorced or separated women

Table 7.10 Ratio of current separated/divorced women and lone mothers' employment income to the current household income levels of wives and married mothers[a]

	UK	Germany
	% income standard replaced	% income standard replaced
Wives, no dependent children[b]	45.3	63.3
Mothers, one child	19.2	32.2
Mothers, two children	21.5	37.3
Mothers, three or more children	33.4	52.2
All mothers with children	22.2	36.3

Notes: [a] Based on married or cohabiting women, divorced/separated women and lone mothers aged less than 60 years for whom complete information is available on personal and household income.

[b] The reference group for these women is separated and divorced women without children. For mothers, lone mothers' incomes are the reference point.

without dependent children.[8] If we attribute existing lone mothers' labour market income to currently married mothers and wives, the following figures (Table 7.10) show how women's wages would approximate their existing standard of living.

Employment is not the positive option for mothers, as is frequently assumed, since it is likely to compensate for only a quarter to a third of their current household standard of living. For women without dependent children there is no doubt that employment is the best option, making it possible for them to replace between a half and two-thirds of their current household income standard. Employment offers a consistently better return in Germany, both in relation to that available from transfers and also the earnings of lone mothers in the UK. Overall, if currently married mothers were to assume the labour supply characteristics of lone mothers in Germany, they could expect paid work to yield an income equivalent to 36 per cent of their current standard of living, whereas in the UK it would come to only 22 per cent. This bodes ill for the Labour Government's current policy response to lone-mother families, which is to encourage, if not push, them into the labour market. Certainly, on the basis of this evidence, in the absence of a broad-ranging set of wage policies the UK labour market has no magic solution to the financial shortages caused by family breakdown. Comparison with income from transfers (Table 7.9) indicates that such women in the UK would be better off claiming through the welfare state, if they are allowed to do so. In Germany employment offers the better return, especially since it is possible there to accumulate benefits with income from employment in a manner which thresholds of hours worked in the basic income support scheme render impossible in the UK.

The Situation of Existing Lone Mothers

In the light of these scenarios, it is not surprising to discover that lone motherhood is quite a different phenomenon in the two national settings. For a start, the extent of lone motherhood is less in the German sample: 2.7 per cent of households, compared with 4.6 per cent in the UK sample, are headed by a woman rearing children aged 16 years and under on her own. As well as the incidence, many of the characteristics of this family form differ across samples. While divorce and separation predominate in both cases as the marital status of the parent, in the UK over a third of the lone mothers are unmarried compared with just 17 per cent in the German case. Among other factors, this renders lone mothers in the UK sample younger than their German counterparts. Lone mothers' attachment to the labour market also varies: only 41 per cent of those in the UK are economically active, compared with 54 per cent in Germany. The higher level of labour market participation among lone mothers compared with married mothers in Germany makes it hard to avoid the conclusion that it is marriage as much as if not more than motherhood that depresses female participation rates there (Table 7.5). In the UK the situation is the reverse. With lone mothers' participation rates a quarter lower than those of married mothers, a kind of opposition appears to exist between lone motherhood and employment. One reason for this may lie in the degree to which cash transfers compensate for non-labour market participation of the household head. In this regard transfers in the UK case offer an income equivalent to 78 per cent of that obtained through employment by the mother/heads who are working, compared with only 38 per cent in Germany. An additional factor may be the relative standard of living obtainable through transfers compared with other claimants. Transfers to British lone-mother families are almost exactly on average, whereas such families in Germany receive transfers that come to only 51 per cent of the average transfer (other than child benefits) received by claimant households. One implication of this is that being on benefit does not disadvantage the UK lone mothers to anything like the same degree that a similar status does in Germany. If one adds the complications and costs of finding child-care facilities along with the disincentives inherent in the British transfer system for employment on the part of lone mothers, labour market participation on their part becomes even more unlikely.

Cross-national differences in labour market participation are reflected in lone mothers' income packages, with cash transfers constituting 47 per cent of lone mother families' income in the UK compared with 25 per cent in Germany. In contrast to Rainwater, Rein and Schwartz's (1986: 108–12) depiction of lone mothers' income packages as complex, there is really no mystique about them in either of the present cases. They are in fact more homogeneous than those of other family types. Notably, transfers from private sources constitute a very small proportion of lone mothers' income, although somewhat more in the German case. These differences in income composition make for another variation between lone-parent households cross-nationally: the gap between their standard of living and that of other households is greater in the UK. As a proportion of mean adjusted household income level, for example, that of lone mothers comes to 54 per cent in the UK and 65 per cent in Germany. So in financial terms lone-mother households are less marginalized in Germany, but this is more a result of their own labour market participation than of transfers from either public or private sources.

Overview

We have seen in this chapter how these two welfare state models coexist with different patterns of dependencies or interdependencies within households. While financial dependence is associated with marriage for women in both national settings, women in Germany must rely on incomes secured by their husbands to a greater degree than is true for the UK. Such issues have a broad-ranging significance, affecting not just the standard of living available to women and men but also the conditions under which they live their lives as members of families and households. We have now an accumulation of evidence that women's place in Germany is in the family and that one of the concomitants is compromised female participation in the labour market.

While we need to be careful about imputing an overall sense of powerlessness to women who are dependent on male incomes, Hirschman's (1970) concepts of exit and voice are relevant here. When applied to the bargaining position of women and men in families, this framework implies the following conditions: 1) the more dependent the weaker the voice; 2) the lower the earnings potential the fewer the exit possibilities; and 3) the fewer the exit possibilities the weaker the voice (Hobson 1990: 238–9). On these conditions women in Germany should have fewer exit options and a weaker voice in making claims within the family than their British counterparts. The first certainly seems to be the case, given divorce or separation patterns. Britons marry more often and divorce more frequently than Germans. Moreover, one in three births in Britain today is to a lone mother compared with less than one in five in Germany. While there is no one-way causal relationship here, it is nevertheless relevant that lone mothers are not marginalized relative to other transfer recipients to the same degree in the UK as they are in Germany. With regard to the strength or weakness of women's voice, I really cannot say but, if there is an association between voice and financial dependence, then German women must speak in whispers. The financial incentives for women to marry and remain married are strong. In Germany married women can obtain a standard of living equivalent to or slightly higher than that available to women in most other marital-status categories without a full-time investment in the labour market on their part. But for German men too, marriage is associated with very high incomes from employment, at least a part of which is due to favourable tax treatment. Voice only becomes important in a situation where people compete for resources, influence and power. In a society such as Germany's, which places more emphasis on the collective unit and less on individual autonomy for men as well as women, it is possible that voice is less important than in the more individualistic-oriented UK. But it is also clear that Germany takes few chances in risking the well-being and survival of a particular form of family relations on which the highly valued societal stability is perceived to hinge. Its preferred manner of protecting families is through a male breadwinner arrangement in which married men earn very high wages and female financial dependence on male wages becomes almost a condition of marriage. Thus Germany's model is underpinned by a very traditional gender order and its welfare state is a mirror in which both the social market economy and civil society can see their own face.

CHAPTER 8

Welfare States and Gender Divisions

The story of gender inequality is a complex one. Rather than repeat the findings of the empirical analyses here, I want to draw on them to reconstruct an account of my general argument and to consider the implications for three sets of issues. These are the impact of the two welfare state models on gender relations, the particular aspects of policies that lead to unequal effects, and gender as a sociological category relevant to welfare state and societal analysis. To reach a better understanding of the impact of existing policy configurations, one must be clear about the criteria whereby welfare states are to be evaluated from a sex and gender perspective. Before presenting the main conclusions about the impact of different policy configurations therefore, I revisit the evaluative parameters that have informed this book. From this it is only a short step to consideration of the mechanisms and processes that render welfare states in general and these two in particular gendered. The policy dynamic of recent years is a necessary part of the backdrop here, along with changing modes of social organization and value systems. Since one of the main objectives of this book has been to develop and apply a gender approach to comparative welfare state analysis, the final word will, accordingly, lie with the meaning and utility of gender as a sociological category.

Welfare State Outcomes: Issues of Equality, Welfare State Policies and Gender

On first impulse, equality appears as the most compelling yardstick for drawing conclusions about the gender dimension of welfare states. One question is then propelled to the foreground: which welfare state model is the more equalizing from a sex and gender perspective? This deceptively simple question forces me to revert to disciplinary type and claim considerable difficulty in answering it. The question itself is problematic in a number of respects: it subsumes different notions of equality; it conflates welfare states' direct and indirect effects; and it presumes a one-way calculus between policies and outcomes (simply put: which gets the plus and which the minus?). Above all the counterfactual is problematic: that equality in benefits and services between women and men is the mark *par excellence* of an ungendered welfare state. Taking on board these kinds of issues is not simply a matter of formal definition but leads to the heart of how welfare states are to be viewed and the approach adopted throughout this book. Is equality relevant in this context, what does it mean and what is its role as a gauge of welfare state outcomes?

The Role of Equality in Appraisals of the Welfare State

Equality is an extremely complex notion. As a concept of abstract universalism, it means applying a uniform standard to different individuals in different situations. In relation to the welfare state, equality can have at least two meanings. The first is akin to equality of access to welfare benefits and services. The second conception relates to outcomes and focuses on the degree of equalization achieved by the welfare state.[1] There is no clear and unproblematic application of either of these interpretations of equality to the situations of women and men. Equality of access implies identical social rights for everybody in a given situation. It is realizable only to the extent that women and men in relatively large numbers experience similar situations. Considerations of gender, which is essentially a concept of difference and diversity, indicate the limits of this view of equality. Simplistic notions of sex equality as parity on the basis of sameness are certainly ruled out. The second notion, equality of outcome, is rendered problematic by virtue of its unspecific and, perhaps unspecifiable, nature. As Jallade (1988: 5) points out in reference to the concept more generally, its final aims are never very clearly described: reduction of inequalities yes, but up to what point and at what cost?

One of the biggest question marks that hangs over gender equality as an evaluative criterion of welfare states derives from the extent to which it is a sought-after objective. For while normative questions are also relevant, any exercise in evaluation must, in part at least, be true to what it is that welfare states set out to do. Nowhere in this book have I taken for granted a commitment towards male–female equality on the part of either the British or the German welfare state. Like it or not, these two welfare states have other business. Some of the main provisions in both

trace their roots to policy objectives that were either indifferent to
male–female inequalities or treated women's inferior economic situation as a concomitant of other policy imperatives. Taking their own
objectives as the point of departure means that the question to be posed
about outcomes becomes more open-ended: how do welfare states
oriented primarily to particular ends – one desirous of income security
(paradigmatically defined around a series of risks specific to the labour
market) and the other oriented to minimum income and poverty reduction – effect changes in women and men's economic relations? Even
when sex and gender equality are not specific goals of welfare states,
however, they could and did find their way onto the policy arena. In
such a light, moves towards equality are seen as forced upon these and
other member states by the EU Directives on equality in wages and cash
transfers or as exigencies arising from welfare states' own need to
'modernize'. Originating from these sources, equality measures have
been grafted on, superimposed according to a kind of 'add women and
don't stir' recipe. The anti-discrimination tenor of the provisions lays
bare their limitations as instruments of equality. At best, contemporary
welfare states should be regarded as aiming at reducing inequalities
between women and men rather than at equality as that term is
normally understood.

The concept of equality should also be subjected to scrutiny for its
capacity to accommodate a notion of social relations. I submit that a
narrow equality perspective, as epitomized by an equal-rights agenda,
tends to strip women and men of their relationships and societal embeddedness.[2] This kind of approach is, furthermore, unrealistic about the
complexity of women's world view and the socio-political context in
which most women live out their lives (Offen 1992). My own approach
embodies a relational view in a number of key respects. Throughout this
book I have worked to an understanding of women and men as engaged
in varied sets of relations in which the situational context of family is
central. Where I have sought to identify the outcomes of welfare states
in my empirical enquiry, the focus has been in some cases on women
and men but more often on male–female (resource-based) relations.
Equally, I have taken pains to identify the kind of dynamic that exists
between welfare states' treatment of individuals and the steps they take
towards supporting families. A relational view also pervades my approach to the welfare state itself. I have treated it as a set of institutional
and normative practices that has its most meaningful expression at the
micro level in 'transfer relations' and at the macro in terms of
the welfare state's interactions with other institutional spheres. In this
light, to adopt a narrow equality perspective would be to short-change
the sociological complexity of both gender relations and welfare state

variations. Rather, one must not only think in terms of trade-offs and compensatory mechanisms but integrate these into an understanding of how outcomes are and can be gendered.

Searching for the roots of the concern with equality leads to the women's movement itself. Perhaps one of the main reasons why equality propels itself to the foreground in considerations of welfare states' sex and gender dimension is that it has been a demand of the women's movement. Feminist politics have indeed come to be almost singularly associated with 'equal-rights' demands, couched in terms of legal, political and economic rights equal to those granted men. Yet historical work, especially that of Lewis (1991), Offen (1992) and Moeller (1993), suggests that another mode of argumentation also prevailed, that the equal-rights type of feminism was primarily an Anglo-American perspective and even in these nations coexisted with quite a different agenda around the 'woman question'. This alternative view, what Offen terms 'relational feminism', is especially relevant to the current comparative exercise because it was pre-eminent in continental European debate. As characterized by Offen, it proffers a gender-based but egalitarian vision of social organization in which the non-hierarchical, male–female couple is the basic unit of society (in contrast to equal-rights arguments that posit the individual, irrespective of sex or gender, as the basic unit). Although relational feminism finds few friends today,[3] it contained both an argument against male privilege and a critique of the hierarchical nature of male–female relations. Equality with men was neither a political objective nor a desired end. Gender relations and roles were viewed as complementary but distinct and, in contrast to the equal-rights approach, relational feminism advanced the claim for a moral equality between the sexes based on an explicit acknowledgement of women and men's differences and complementary responsibilities. Where the two approaches differ most is in their view of desired changes. The equal-rights notions of equality prioritize a very individualized form of personal autonomy as the norm, to the extent that they have been criticized for adopting and promoting a male standard to which women must assimilate. Relational feminism also values self-sovereignty as a goal for women but links such a goal with the more open-ended 'self-realization', which centres on a view of freedom as *freedom to* rather than *freedom from* (Offen 1992: 80). Choice and preference are emphasized in the relational feminist view, in which personal autonomy is but one dimension and, rather than being an end in itself, is a means towards a broader set of goals.

All of the foregoing bears upon the usefulness of equality as a gauge of welfare state outcomes. One of the main merits of the concept is that embedded in it is a reference to processes of social stratification. It therefore allows for the possibility of gender divisions as a dimension of structured social inequality. However, taking into account the ambivalence of both welfare states about equality between women and men as a policy objective, reduction in inequality suggests itself as a better evaluative criterion than equality. But this does not define the full range of sex- and gender-relevant welfare state outcomes. Notions of welfare are also central. This book has thought of the 'welfare-conferring' potential of welfare states in a number of directions: income redistribution, poverty reduction, and increasing the range of incentives offered towards a choice of behaviours on the part of women and men. Not one but three principles have therefore informed its understanding of stratification: income inequality, income insufficiency, and the set of choices around participation and life chances. All three together equip us better to take an overview of how the British and German welfare states affect gender relations.

Reducing Income Inequalities

The first pertinent question to ask here is about the state's activity of allocation, centring on how welfare states distribute their own (that is transfer) income between women and men. In terms of achievements, the British model clearly has the edge. While all transfers there are low in value, there is little evidence of systematic differentiation along sex or gender lines. Male–female gaps in benefit levels are small and there is no strong tendency to privilege men in family roles over women in family roles. Any such effects pale in comparison with the hierarchical nature of German transfer programs. Evidence is abundant that gender is integral to the foundations of this hierarchy. In fact gender serves to separate the two welfare states, with Germany especially marked by a distinct privileging of men in family roles. The upshot is that transfers to women are worth on average only 64 per cent of those to men, whereas in the UK the mean female transfer comes to 79 per cent of the male mean. When the household is the unit of analysis, the sex of the head makes no significant difference as regards transfer access when other factors are controlled for, but in Germany the sex of the head is a factor making for a significant difference in transfer size, independently of other effects. A first fundamental variation between the two welfare states, therefore, is that German transfers are directly unequal on sex and gender grounds.

A second aspect relevant to income inequality is the extent to which welfare states contribute to more equal outcomes by altering sex gaps in income. Two considerations are crucial: first, what we might call the scale of the problem facing the fiscal system in terms of the degree to which it is called on to redress male–female inequalities and, second, how it performs. Here it is even more important to differentiate between the individual and household levels of analysis since the effects of each welfare state vary across units. For individuals the British set of arrangements again performs better. Although confronted with smaller inequalities to begin with, it has the greater positive effect on sex- and gender-based income gaps. Targeting of mothers for the purposes of some transfer receipt and a more favourable treatment of female income by taxation are the mechanisms making this the better system for reducing income inequalities between women and men. Germany's configuration of transfers and taxation effects hardly any improvement at all in the sex- and gender-based inequalities for those aged under 60, even though women's personal income is only about a third of that of men before transfers. Transfers to pensioners are, therefore, the main source of the positive effect, but even this is an indirect effect because of female dominance of the pensioner population.

Conversely, when it comes to households, Germany's set of transfers and taxation makes not only for greater income redistribution overall but also brings the incomes of women and men's households closer together. The contrast with the treatment of women and men as indi- viduals is quite remarkable, so much so that German women fare considerably better from the public transfer arrangements as heads of households than they do as members of households. The analyses clearly indicate that Germany's is a welfare state that is far more tolerant of inequalities between individuals, especially women and men in family roles, than among households. The redistributive division of labour between the state and the family is such that women are as individuals expected to be provided for by the family rather than the state. The position of the British welfare state is more middle-range in two respects. Relative to men, women are also better off as heads of house- holds than as individuals, but the disparity is less there as compared with Germany. Second, the evidence is fairly strong that the British welfare state effects less redistribution overall but is less biased against redistrib- ution between individual women and men.

Reducing Income Poverty

Here again there are two ways of gauging the impact of welfare states: existing levels of poverty and how transfers and taxation act to redis- tribute the poverty burden between women and men and among the households in which they live. As judged by existing poverty rates, Germany's is the better model, with poverty levels less than half those of the UK. The evidence confirms the results of other studies that of the two the UK is the country of higher poverty. Yet this relatively neat cross-national picture is fractured by some important common patterns. In particular, in both national settings women's households outnumber those of men among the poor by a ratio of two to one. Thus while quite different in terms of the overall levels of poverty they are prepared to tolerate, the two welfare models are drawn together by sex differentials in income insufficiency at household level.

When it comes to individual poverty, the vulnerability of women is greater in the UK case. This is not due directly to welfare state effects, however, but rather to the fact that fewer women in this country have access to the (assumed) poverty-reducing effects of sharing a household income. A key element of the cross-national contrast here should not be lost: assuming equal sharing of the collective income, German women have a poverty rate that is less than half that of women in the UK. The fact that their poverty rate is much lower than when they are heads of households also indicates the degree to which women in Germany need financial support from other members of their households or families to stave off poverty.

As we would expect, transfers are hugely important in reducing poverty in both national settings. The effects of transfers and taxation on poverty reduction are consistent with those for income redistribution in the UK, sex differences in poverty for both households and individuals being reduced by the fiscal process. The findings for Germany are more complex. For against a background of greater poverty reduction there overall, the poverty differentials between women and men's households are either unchanged or slightly increased relative to what they would be in the absence of transfers. So while it effects considerable income redistribution between women and men's households, the relatively small group of households left in poverty by the German welfare state is dominated by those headed by a woman. When it comes to individuals, there is evidence again of how German transfers directed primarily at men and male income risks act to disadvantage women. While women have lower poverty rates than men before transfers, their comparative poverty risk is actually higher once transfers have had their effect.

Increasing Choice

As well as having direct financial effects, the welfare state in this book is considered to play a part in affecting the set of opportunities available to women and men. This is a very broad topic. It was rendered manageable by considering the role of marriage, the trade-offs in terms of labour market participation that it appears to involve, and the extent to which women could form autonomous households in the light of existing financial relations between partners and how the welfare state affects such arrangements. The incentive structures are best represented as offering something of a 'Hobson's choice' in both national settings. For German women marriage does, hypothetically at any rate, appear to offer a reasonable standard of living, obviating especially the need for extensive labour market participation on their own part. However, this is a contingent security, subject to two conditions. The first is that married women in Germany must more or less cede their own earning opportunities in order to avail themselves of the (assumed) security of marriage. The second is that they remain dependent on private exchange processes, that is, on their husbands or partners to pass on the income that the German state entrusts to men on behalf of their families. In the UK women are less dependent on family (specifically male) incomes and are more likely to be in the labour market or receiving public transfers than their German counterparts. But it is debatable whether working for relatively low incomes without the benefit of the enabling services that are so important to mothers can be represented as a broadened choice for women.

The well-being of existing lone mothers and divorced or separated women is a litmus test of the range of choices that states and societies make available to women. Once again, the results defy a simple interpretation, especially in terms of which national policy configuration offers women the greater degree of choice. Comparison of the situation of lone mothers indicates that income policies in the UK give women a greater leeway to live apart from the fathers of their children. Or, to be more precise, lone mothers are less marginalized in a minimum-income welfare state model than they are in Germany's hierarchical social insurance model, where no specific provision exists for them and so they have to claim through the stigma-ridden safety-net program. Lone mothers are not specifically targeted in the British welfare state either, but they do receive some extra compensation, and as claimants of the safety-net program they are less marginalized than they would be in Germany because this program is so widely used in the UK. However, lone mothers are actually better off relative to the average in Germany, not because of public transfers but largely through their own labour market participation and a higher yield from private transfers.

An Overview of Outcomes

Taken together, these results tend to confirm certain patterns. At the risk of over-simplifying a complex set of relationships, a flat-rate, low-level benefit model together with a more individualized tax system appears to be more positive from a sex and gender perspective than a high wage replacement, social insurance–based transfer system and a relatively rigid model of joint taxation of married couples. The UK may not be the better society for women but, according to my analysis, its welfare state goes further than the German in reducing male–female income inequalities. In German transfer programs, the privileging of claims originating from the labour market, the close link between wages and benefit levels, a contribution model that prioritizes duration and continuity and a taxation arrangement that favours one-earner couples all act to disadvantage women in personal income terms relative to men. But the cross-national comparison changes considerably if we consider how 'welfare-conferring' are the two sets of arrangements. For judged in terms of overall poverty levels and the income standard attainable by lone mothers, Germany is the better place to live, for women as well as men. Yet, as discussed above, there is a price tag attached: the vast majority of women do not provide for themselves but are supported by male incomes. Ultimately a normative and political issue, only German women and men themselves can say how acceptable this condition is. And German society is the final arbiter of whether the private processes of support so esteemed there are actually superior to more public procedures.

Remaining with the overall comparison, it also has to be said that we have here two welfare states that could not by any standards be held up as models of good practice from a sex and gender perspective. Both rely on an allocational process that differentiates between women and men on the basis of their family status, even though this is less pronounced in the UK. And in many ways they have rather similar outcomes. Women's incomes and their income-related opportunities remain substantially inferior to those of men in both, and any improvements effected by transfers and taxation are matters of degree. At the end of the welfare state day then, women's personal incomes fall short of those of men by between a half and two-thirds, and women's households have double the poverty incidence of those of men in both national settings. What the comparison suggests above all is that neither system has reached any kind of symmetry of welfare between women and men. We should certainly resist the temptation to treat differences in degree as differences in kind. For how significant a difference is it that women's net personal incomes are equivalent to 47 per cent of those of men in one case (the UK) and 37 per cent in the other (Germany)? It would be ill-advised to posit one as unqualifiedly superior to the other.

The overall complexion and impact of the two welfare states offer another ground for caution in choosing between them. For their general outcomes differ fundamentally from their sex and gender effects.

While the British system may be superior to the German in reducing sex- and gender-based income inequalities, it performs more poorly overall. If the British model is chosen, one is then opting for a set of welfare arrangements that effects less income redistribution and less poverty reduction overall, but is less likely to use sex or family status as grounds for different treatment. Transfers are low for everybody, and income insecurity and shortages are a way of life for a sizeable proportion of the population. There are no winners in this system; the degree of stratification among benefit recipients is low. How is this to be weighed against a welfare state model like Germany's which, biased against male–female equalization of income, makes winners of men but yet is the more redistributive overall and the less tolerant of high rates of poverty? If we had to rely on this comparison alone, it would be tempting to assume that a necessary trade-off exists between a model that treats all poorly, whether women or men, and one that undertakes to maintain standards of living and status and privilege over the life course but in a manner that mirrors inequalities and power structures originating elsewhere in the social system. The availability of other welfare state models does, however, temper interpretations of such a trade-off as necessary.

There is, of course, no pure counterfactual case but, in terms of egalitarianism, the Swedish model comes immediately to mind. While no work fully comparable to the present study has been undertaken, there are indications from various sources that this welfare state model is less tolerant of male–female income inequalities. Sørensen (1992), for example, shows that the Swedish taxation system has the effect of not only cutting women's poverty rate in half but of reducing it to a level below the male rate. A high level of wage equalization also exists. Sweden's policy configuration also means that married women are less dependent on men for their income, that women already have a job and access to day-care facilities when they become (lone) mothers and that the poverty rate of lone-mother families is among the lowest in the developed world (Hobson 1994; Sørensen 1994). A number of policy features set this type of welfare state apart (Sainsbury 1996). First, entitlement to many benefits and services is granted on the basis of citizenship or residence rather than need or family status. Second, the establishment of a fairly generous flat-rate grant to all mothers and an extensive system of leaves for parental and other purposes spells a recognition of the principle of care. Work in the home qualifies for (some) entitlement to social benefits in a policy framework that derives, at least in part, from a concern with the accommodation of work and family. Third, the Swedish tax system, especially as reformed in the 1970s, entails neither a single-parent penalty nor a dual-earner marriage penalty. Fourth, the provision of 'collective goods in kind' has been a strong feature of the Swedish welfare model, especially since the 1960s, with economic policies organized around the goal of stimulating the labour supply of married women. All of these measures, as Sainsbury (1994a) points out, weakened the influence of the breadwinner ideology.

Sweden isn't heaven either, though, and there are some trade-offs involved in this model as well. The woman-friendliness of the Swedish model is tempered by sex gaps in hours worked and hence earnings, and a high degree of sex segregation in employment. Yet the male–female income inequalities are generally of a lower order than those characterizing any other welfare state model. While some are critical of the Swedish model for not offering women a real choice between work and family, I would counter-argue that there is a flexibility in the Swedish system that women have been able to exploit. That is, Swedish women have used the generous system of parental and sickness leaves and a general climate of state responsibility for income security to carry out unpaid work during time that is effectively paid. While this model is now experiencing difficulties, its openness towards women's family exigencies and its exploitable flexibilities suggest that the more interventionist the state is in optimizing the conditions for women's labour market participation, the better women's financial situation compares with that of men.

Costs and Conditions Attaching to the Two Policy Models

The different strands of the analysis have served to lay bare the transfer- and tax-specific mechanisms that lead to and perpetuate differences and inequalities between women and men. These bear repetition. In drawing attention to them below, I do not intend to suggest remedies for the problems identified. The exercise of 'policy shopping' is, to say the least, unrealistic. While we may differentiate them for analytic purposes, transfers, taxation and public services come as part of a (societal) package, coexisting with particular legal frameworks, sets of economic incentives and value systems. (However, to digress into comparison for a moment, Germany's is the more neatly packaged arrangement in two senses. First, policies there form a more consistent whole, mutually reinforcing each other and underpinned by a more coherent logic than is the case in Britain; second, of the two, German policies have proved the more resistant to change.[4]) To make a case for detailed changes in welfare state provision while leaving other institutional areas and prevailing ideologies untouched is, therefore, meaningless. The section to follow, accordingly, isolates the key mechanisms that are problematic in these two welfare states, in the light of existing gender relations and in the context of pressures towards change.

Key Shortcomings of Policies from a Gender Perspective

In that both rely on a social insurance model (although the British welfare state less so), their coverage and effectiveness depend not only on income replacement levels but also on the *universe of risks or contingencies covered*. The classic labour market risk universe underlying the social insurance model is these days very leaky. For both the structure of need and the relationship between risk and need have altered – a development that includes but at the same time extends beyond gender issues. In the first place, the occurrence of the classic social risks is no longer an automatic trigger of need since more people now live in two-income households and because people, especially in the UK, make greater recourse to private insurance. In the second place, the classic risk model is flawed by both the growth of social risks that were originally inadequately covered and the emergence of new social risks. Lone motherhood, divorce and what Cantillon (1994: 51) calls the 'new type of worker' are increasing sources of pressure in a framework biased towards risks characterizing the later stages of the life course. Lone motherhood is effectively two risks: having to rear children on one income and having no access to male labour market income. The risks involved in divorce especially jeopardize women's (but not men's) access to the standard of living available to them when married. Women's right to compensation for years spent on unpaid work and their access to social insurance benefits are, in addition, imperilled by divorce, especially in the UK. A third risk, new to the extent that the numbers experiencing it continue to grow, is having to combine paid work with unpaid work. This is also mainly a female risk, the absence of the necessary support services often forcing women to take part-time instead of full-time jobs. All of these lead to a situation whereby the social risks identified for classic social insurance coverage are no longer coterminous with need. In an arrangement like Germany's, additional problems are generated by the relative neglect of status passages in the desire to protect statuses (Voges and Ostner 1995).

A second and related pressure point concerns *care*, both as a need on the part of certain sectors of the population and as an obligation on the part of others. The degree of familization of caring is, according to my model of the gender dimension of welfare states, a key process through which welfare states influence gender relations. Caring in one or another form is being increasingly recognized as a social risk, although to a greater extent in Germany which, since the period in which the present study is set, saw the inauguration of a new branch of social insurance specific to care (in 1995). Apart from the fact that care is either not covered or integrated in a subsidiary way (as outlined in Chapter 3), there is one major problem with welfare states' treatment of it. This is the failure to recognize its dual nature. That is, care is a risk that touches (at least) two people, the person needing care and the one who provides it. When and if caring is drawn into the embrace of the welfare state, giving assistance to one is seen to automatically cover the well-being of the other. A similar kind of fissure characterizes service provision and cash transfers. So, for instance, the provision of payments for care is often taken as a justification for the non-provision or cutting back of relevant services, when in fact both are needed. Finally it is hard to avoid Leira's (1992) conclusion that what is lacking is a recognition of the importance of care to society.

A third problem concerns *benefit levels*. In the UK benefits are low for everybody and too low for most. The nature of the gender disadvantage tends in this system to be indirect in that, since women depend in greater numbers and for longer periods of their life on transfers, lower transfers render them more vulnerable than they do men. Low pensions make women's financial situation especially fragile. The male–female disadvantages inherent in the German high wage replacement model are not only much more pronounced but also more direct. The absence of an effective benefit floor for social insurance purposes contributes in no small way to sex gaps in German benefit levels. Differences in the size of transfers are especially pronounced among women and men of prime age. However, the high numbers of widows among the pensioner population make for a relatively low poverty rate among this age group since the status-based widows' benefits are higher than what most women would obtain on their personal insurance contributions. This is one example of where women directly benefit from a high wage replacement model, but it is a rather lonely instance.

Other Sources of Pressure

In facing their future, both the British and German welfare states share common problems. Existing arrangements are especially problematic because changing economic and social patterns render their fundamental assumptions outmoded (Döring and Hauser 1990). Such assumptions include full-time male employment, stability of the family, a world where people are (supposed to be) organized into male-headed nuclear families living principally from the man's labour market earnings. Economic and demographic changes, which are in the process of delivering us a world marked by insecurity and flexibility across spheres, are eroding the potential of a particularistic social insurance model to provide long-term security. Side by side with these transformations, the old gender order is crumbling, as Nancy Fraser (1997: 22) points out. And social insurance provisions are underpinned by a particular gender order at least as much as they are founded on an economic order.

Since the German welfare state model relies to a far greater degree on social insurance, the nature of its gender settlement and the challenges posed by changing gender relations cast the darker shadow over its future. For this model depends not only on a particular distribution of labour between women and men but on a very specific and increasingly problematic set of arrangements between the state and the family. It first puts its faith in men to pass on their income in sufficient amounts to their wives and children. The counterpart of this is that women will remain content with a role-set in which that of family service provider is predominant. Notwithstanding that German women may still endorse a conception of full-time motherhood,[5] their postponement of child-bearing in favour of growing participation in the labour market, especially among the younger cohorts, indicates that they are voting with their feet and no longer willing to forgo the opportunities, conceived in either self-development or material terms, offered by the labour market. Fertility rates provide telling evidence. German fertility rates are now, at 1.3, among the lowest in Europe, having fallen by a third since 1970 (compared with a decline of a fifth in the UK over the same period). Second, the subsidiarity principle, as a regulator of inter-institutional relations, maintains a certain 'empty space' between the state and the family. This is put under pressure as family vulnerability increases (Kaufmann 1990; Gerlach 1996). A welfare state framework that is grounded in the belief that the proper role of policy is to support the family from a distance has few ways of targeting the losers directly. Gender factors are not alone, though, in securing the continued operation of the German model. Its future also hinges on whether the arduous economic conditions that underpin it can continue to be fulfilled. One such condition is that men continue to obtain and retain over their life course stable jobs with wages high enough to allow them to devote up to half their income to the support of their wives and children. The expensive nature of the German model, which as well as high wages requires high contributions on the part of both employers and employees, leads to very high fixed labour costs. The average proportion of gross wages paid in social contributions in West Germany increased from 12.8 per cent in 1980 to 16.3 per cent in 1995 (Schäfer 1995: 610). The effects of reunification, or rather the use of the social insurance funds to subsidize the cost of reunification, should not be underestimated either. Large transfers from the social insurance funds, for the unemployed, early retirees, ill and elderly people, were a primary means of buying off many of the problems caused by reunification. In fact the use of the funds for political ends transformed the long-standing surplus in the West German social insurance funds into a deficit. Costs are, furthermore, multiplied by forgoing the contributions of the many women who are encouraged not to be employed while receiving health coverage free of charge. It is hard to avoid the conclusion that the German welfare state is in danger of collapsing under its own weight.

The shortcomings of the British system are fairly transparent. Taylor-Gooby (1991) has a convincing claim when he says that the future tensions in this model will be played out primarily on the basis of class issues. Poverty both in and out of employment is the rodent gnawing at the base of this model. While women form a majority of the polarized category, it appears to me that it is exclusion from a decent income associated with satisfactory labour market participation or an adequate income replacement system that defines the main cleavage in Britain rather than the particular order of gender relations per se. Ambivalent from the outset about the place and proper role of social insurance, the adequacy principle has to all intents and purposes been abandoned in Britain. All the indications are that the study period of the present book captured the country in a phase of climbing poverty and marginalization. Britain has the dubious distinction of being home to one in four of the European Union's poor. It is also one of only two European countries where relative poverty rates sharply increased during the 1980s (the other being Ireland): between 1979 and 1988 the proportion of people falling below the 50 per cent poverty line increased from 11 per cent to 19 per cent (van den Bosch 1998). The spectre of low pay looms large: in point of fact one-third of the poor are either employed or self-employed. A model that assumes that poverty is due to short-term interruptions in earnings has few or no mechanisms for dealing with this type of labour market-induced poverty. The remainder of the UK's poor are in receipt of social welfare benefits. Since the reforms implemented over the 1980s redistributed spending within the benefit-claiming population, they led to some change in the fortunes of different groups. Through the strategy of targeting at no net overall cost, families with children were left better off at the expense of the single unemployed and the childless. Bradshaw (1993: 44) sums up the overall tenor of the changes: 'The gap between the living standards of social security claimants and those in work has widened, the number of people living on low incomes has increased and, depending on the poverty threshold used, there has been a sharp increase in the number of people in relative poverty and no evidence that absolute poverty has diminished.'

There appears to be considerable dynamism in the British poverty population, especially among two groups: singles without children (whose numbers doubled as a proportion of the poor over the ten-year period) and pensioner couples whose numbers fell by more than half (from 20 per cent to 6 per cent) (Oppenheim 1993). However, there are no indications that the dynamism around poverty fundamentally challenges the results of the present study on the sex distribution of poverty. If anything, the fiscal changes made after 1985 may have increased women's propensity to be poor. Given that these changes made cash benefits less generous while lowering direct taxes, one of their overall effects was to lower women's income and raise that of men. Modelling the male and female lifetime gains and losses from the welfare state shows that the tax and benefit changes introduced in the 1980s reduced women's net gain by a fifth (Falkingham and Hills 1995: 149). It is estimated that these changes will have the effect of reducing the lifetime income of women by £11,000 while increasing that of men by a similar amount.

In Germany poverty is also on the increase: Hauser (1995) reports 11.5 per cent of persons falling below the 50 per cent of the median income cut-off in the former West Germany in 1993, which represented an increase of around 5 per cent on the 1990 rate. This increase, alarming for Germany, suggests a growing difficulty in simultaneously satisfying income maintenance as a function of insured risks and guaranteed minimum income as a function of need (Cantillon 1994: 47). To put it differently, the old German hierarchy between the three principles of insurance, taking care of (as with civil servants) and social relief is proving increasingly unbalanced. The key question is whether Germany's wise middle way, involving a very particular conception of solidarity and an interpretation of social justice as referring mainly to distribution rather than redistribution, is so wise in contemporary times. Can a system that prioritizes the maintenance of status differentials continue to prevail as the number of 'outsiders' grows?

Adapting to Change

In a context of imperatives for change in the two welfare states, it is interesting to consider, albeit briefly, the broad pathways followed. The essentials of change in German provision can be summed up as 'moderate adjustments'. The thrust of the policy alterations – and there have been many – is to preserve the existing principles while altering some provisions and conditions of entitlement (Nullmeier and Rüb

1993). In attempting to absorb the tensions that arise from a model that tries to balance social stability and social inclusion, the dominant response has been reinforcement of the conservative aspects of its family policy, its incomes and social policy and, more broadly, its gender arrangement. Recent tax reforms, for example, have strengthened support for the one-earner gender arrangement (Ostendorf 1997: 376) and there has been no move away from the traditional German reliance on social insurance. The conditions of receipt are being tightened and the benefits are now less generous. However significant these and other changes may be for the quality of social rights, they do not generally represent a fundamental transformation of the structure or organizational form of Germany's welfare state. This remains a welfare state that prioritizes horizontal over vertical equity and the maintenance of traditional family arrangements and differences of status and occupation. Germany is still a nation of families. While the state may now be prepared to 'purchase' some of women's caring services, this is done in a manner that continues to make women available to the family.

Such has been the volatility of British welfare state provisions that to describe the changes in detail would require many words. I shall therefore limit the discussion to the most important developments in relation to the basic principles.[6] In terms of income-maintenance provisions, Britain has followed a path of strengthening the social assistance principle over that of social insurance. This in tandem with a thrust towards reducing social expenditures has led an assault on both the value of benefits and the conditions under which people can claim them. A quite inventive set of measures has been deployed to reduce the value of benefits: linking of benefit increases to prices rather than earnings (in 1980); the phasing out of the state contribution to the national insurance fund (from 1988); cutting or freezing benefits; removing some benefits from social insurance;[7] encouraging people to move to private provision (as with pensions); removing some of the additional payments that compensated for family support obligations; and replacing special need or hardship grants by loans. A second key change in Britain has centred around the support obligations of the state and the family. In this regard also, elements of the Beveridgean settlement have been further undermined. This is especially visible in regard to young children and young adults and it extends beyond the income maintenance system. The 1980s saw the inauguration of a number of statutes in Britain that had the intention of increasing parental responsibility for children specifically and of extending the duties and support obligations of family members more generally. A 'reprivatization' of support obligations of fathers for their children became official policy in 1992 with the establishment of the Child Support Agency, which had the function of setting, collecting and enforcing maintenance for children from divorced, separated and never-married fathers. This development represents a very significant intervention into family affairs, especially male finances, which had hitherto been treated as more or less private, and it has had the effect of reproducing traditional gender dependence of women on male incomes, even after couples have separated. A third key change in Britain centred on the consensus about the best locus of care for older and disabled people with the emergence of a strong preference for community rather than residential care (Baldwin 1994: 183). This has led to a change in the welfare mix, with greater involvement of both the market and the family as the state has begun to disengage from direct participation in the provision of care services.

While the present government has yet to introduce a full set of policies, its social policy orientation can be gleaned from its 1998 Green Paper on welfare reform and some of the changes already implemented. So far there has been no radical break with the recent Conservative past. Those policy areas where measures have been taken suggest the emergence of a productivist type of welfare state. The 'New Deal', the cornerstone of New Labour's great experiment in social and economic policy, places strong pressures on young unemployed people to either engage in or allow themselves to be prepared for employment. Employers are to be offered hefty subsidies for employing these young people (for limited amounts of time). The policies on lone parents operate in a similar direction and are couched also in a language of encouraging independence and enterprise. The ideology underlying these measures was drawn together and laid bare in the Green Paper released for consultation in March 1998 (DSS 1998). In the British welfare state of the future employment will predominate; for those who cannot work there is but a vague promise of security. In rejecting a very staged set of alternatives, between privatization and a continuation of the status quo, the New Labour government claims to have opted for a third way. Its 'proactive welfare system' is described as one that will prevent poverty by ensuring that people have the right education, training and support and widening the 'exits from dependence by tailor-made help for individuals'. These objectives are to be achieved by creating a welfare system that is flexible, helps and encourages people to work, is friendly towards partnerships with the private sector, and prioritizes the disabled and families with children for benefit and social service purposes. Matters such as low benefit levels and a tax system that favours the better off receive no mention. The subtitling of the Green Paper as a 'new contract for welfare' is telling. In reality in a context within which people and communities are to be given greater initiative, the talk is of less rather than more state and of fewer rights and more responsibilities. It is doubtful if this kind of soil will prove fertile for redressing structural inequalities, including those founded on gender.

It is interesting to ponder for a moment the dilemmas surrounding the inclusion of women. It certainly seems that Germany's set of privileges cannot or will not be universalized. Since the model would then lose a crucial differentiating function, provisions for women and caring have had to be implemented on an alternative basis, for example flat-rate benefits, funded and organized at federal level and therefore outside the normal channels of interest mediation. Categorical benefits now make their appearance in a system that has long avoided them. A relatively less differentiated and low-paying benefit system like Britain's has a greater capacity to integrate women. People tend to be treated more as individuals, and public policy has never been strongly supportive of the family. In recent years, however, Britain has rediscovered the family as a potential sharer of the welfare and care burden and I predict that not only will this new partnership between the state and the family prove increasingly attractive in Britain but it will bear especially heavily on women.

The Significance of Gender as a Sociological Phenomenon

Gender as a category of analysis requires discussion at two levels: as a general sociological category and in relation to the study of welfare states.

Gender in Stratification Theory

As Siltanen (1986: 97) points out, there is in the literature on gender and social stratification a tension between attempts to develop an explanation of aggregate-level inequalities between women and men and the recognition that neither group is homogeneous. Women and men do not constitute two social categories with identical characteristics. Sex is therefore flawed as a theoretical category with general validity. Nor can gender relations be assumed to be invariant social properties or universally salient bases of differentiation. These are primary reasons why studies such as the present one are situated within the objective of investigating the variability of gender relations. I have operationalized gender in a manner that attempts to transcend a simplistic sex divide, and I have furthermore sought to encompass similarities and differences of a gendered character by placing women and men in their familial and social contexts.

But operationalized in this way, gender is a characteristic of individuals. It therefore begs questions about, and leaves me open to criticism were I not to specify, the societal processes that are animated by and result in gendered divisions. The underlying reference is to stratification mechanisms more broadly, and in particular to how systematic inequalities between women and men are related to processes that generate (other) social divisions. In this work I have concentrated mainly on one institutional sphere, the welfare state, which admittedly forms just one set of the determinants of gendered relations. While gender is undoubtedly a wider societal phenomenon, I believe that a reasonable claim can be made on the basis of this study that the welfare state is involved in either redressing or compounding gender inequalities. Gov-erning as it does access to material and other types of resources as well as opportunities for participation, the welfare state is a vital part of the hierarchical social structure in which social, political and economic differences are superimposed on the biological (Connell 1987). To put it somewhat differently, the set of relations, processes and practices involved in gender inequality is vitally influenced by the form and operation of the welfare state (and vice versa). The question of how gender divisions in the welfare state are related to structured social inequalities more broadly is another crucial one.

Much ink has been spilled on this question, but it is still not clear where we should look for a conclusive explanation. The feminist response to conventional analysts' fixation with class (at a macro-theoretical level at any rate) has been to posit patriarchy as a system of male power existing either independently of class (Walby 1990) or along with capitalist relations as two separate and interrelated systems (Hartmann 1979). Without entering into the finer points of the ensuing debate,[8] it does not appear to me that a satisfactory case has been made for patriarchy as a structure of social action comparable to those within the range of class polarization or status group consolidation. For patriarchy to meet the necessary theoretical preconditions, one would have to accept men's oppression of women as a universal practice and as deriving its life-blood from forces independent of capitalism. An alternative set of conditions would stipulate that for men and women to be considered as two classes they would have to be separated by such a conflict of interest that it would provide the basis for oppositional political mobilization. This condition is also difficult to meet, although women's political engagement around suffrage and the reactivated women's movement of the 1960s and 1970s were centred on sex-specific conflicts of interest. The theoretical preconditions for positing women and men as two distinct status groups, although not as arduous, are also difficult to fulfil. While there is evidence for status differentiations on the basis of sex,[9] I think that the argument of sex and/or gender as a distinct *and* significant basis of status hierarchy cannot be theoretically sustained (especially the condition that this source of status differentiation should supersede others).

But it might also be said that class analysts do not always meet the preconditions which they set up, rather highmindedly, for those making claims for new concepts. They are especially vulnerable to the criticism that their focus on the production system, true of both neo-Marxist and neo-Weberian perspectives, gives too little space to redistributive processes and institutions.[10] Approaches that focus only on production have no means of dealing with three facts. The first is that however resources are distributed to individuals in society, people organize themselves (for example in families and households) to redistribute them (Curtis 1986). Second, as a response to market forces, social groups have felt the need to inaugurate and continue to support structures for societal redistribution, and these make a huge impact on individual well-being and life chances. Third, women's financial well-being is constituted in quite a different manner to that of men.

Wherever one may choose to lay the blame for the theoretical impasse that exists today and for the languor about readdressing some of the big questions, the fact remains that we need a theory of the distribution of income and opportunities to people that can explain sex and gender divisions where they occur. This must also, *contra* much feminist work, be a theory that can account for those aspects of social processes that yield similar outcomes for women and men (Siltanen 1986: 102). In this regard I tend to agree with Crompton's (1993: 207) conclusion that what is required is not so much new theories or methodologies but rather a flexible approach that recognizes the connectedness of the different aspects of the complex area of stratification as a whole. Although the latter observation does not obviate the need to consider or provide an answer to the question of the relationship between gender differentiations/inequalities and other axes of division, it does allow me some respite in moving to a lower level of exposition. As the study of structured social inequality, the raw material of stratification is people's – as individuals and members of collectivities – relations to hierarchical social system(s). Such social stratification is governed by both productive and redistributive processes. How can we conceptualize relations to these structures or systems of distribution in a manner sensitive to gender? For this purpose the interactive model of state–family–market outlined in the Introduction is indispensable. We are now in a position to specify in greater detail a number of different dimensions to these interrelations, as in Figure 8.1.

For a start, one can think of the interrelations between the three institutions in terms of how they govern processes of participation and allocation. Here, an important aspect of stratification processes more broadly is the conditions or rules that the market, the family and the

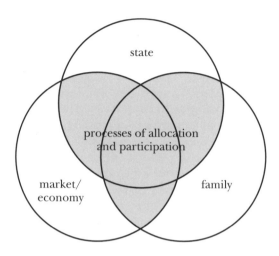

Principles: age/generation; family background; occupational capital/position; race/ethnic origin; sex/gender

Figure 8.1   A model of stratification

state set up for their participatory and allocative processes. It is possible also to identify axes or principles of inclusion/exclusion on which these hinge. Some such principles readily suggest themselves: age, sex/ gender, family background, occupational status, capital and seniority (e.g. skills, education/training, 'career'), race, ethnic/immigrant origin. Obviously these are not independent of each other and vary in their significance across the three institutional spheres. Obviously also, following Giddens (1984), these factors become part of the interaction itself and can therefore be changed by it. The second dimension is types of relations to both systems of production and redistribution. The idea of relations invokes the social embeddedness of individuals. It also invokes agency, individuals negotiating and bargaining against a context of institutional structures and norms. One may think of this interaction process in terms of claims-making whereby individuals or collectivities attempt to establish a right or practice to participation in key activities and to gain access to the distributive processes involved. Again, this bargaining process takes place within the three spheres but varies in the extent to which it is individualized. This way of thinking about stratification is, I suggest, more sensitive to gender as one of a number of social divisions.

Gender in the Study of the Welfare State

A principal objective of this study has been to understand more precisely the nature of welfare state effects on gender relations. Picturing it graphically as in Figure 8.1, I sought to make concrete the processes and practices that inhabit the conjuncture between state, family and market and to specify the relationships between welfare state forms and particular outcomes. The evidence makes it clear that we cannot accept sex differentiations in welfare state provision as an invariant feature of welfare states. Even with a two-country framework, a considerable degree of variation in welfare state patterning along gender lines is evident. Moreover, on a number of occasions in the analysis I found that gender was not the decisive factor underlying the patterns identified. In any case, claims about universal sex differences also lack precise and concrete meaning.

I have in this work advanced a conceptual framework for the relation between gender and the welfare state. Viewing gender as integral to welfare states, I made the claim that the relation is expressed in the structure or content of relevant policies, the processes to which policies give rise, and the outcomes that are effected by policies. The scope and nature of welfare institutions and the normative design inherent in social policies pertain to what one might call the structure and content of the welfare state. Institutions – embodied in the range and type of welfare state activities, especially income transfer, taxation and public service arrangements – matter. But the ideologies and normative imprint that pattern and colour welfare states' programmatic provision also matter. Taking an integrated institutional and normative perspective, I wish to suggest that three features of welfare states best capture how they might be gendered in content: the universe of covered risks, the construction of entitlement, and the treatment of different family types. My claim is that an examination of how welfare states organize the coverage and location of 'female' as well as 'male' risks, whether they use an individual or collective unit of eligibility, and the degree to which and how they differentiate among family types will serve to reveal how their policies are gendered in content.

In regard to how they generate new and affect existing gendered processes, welfare states' activities should be considered along one central axis: the extent to which state policies situate intra-familial (productive and redistributive) relations on a continuum from private to public. This I identify as a process of (de)familization and it has two dimensions. The first, intra-familial production, essentially refers to care-giving, which can be defined as activities oriented to the care of the young, the ill and the elderly as well as the maintenance of those of prime age. All welfare states contain at their core a position about caring: where it should be located, who should do it, how it should be supported. If such work is not located within the home, it is most likely that the welfare state has undertaken either to provide caring services directly or to subsidize them in the market or semi-public sphere. Whichever position welfare states adopt, their effects have a long reach. We may also associate with the welfare state an effect on redistributive processes that take place within and outside the family. Through the conditions attaching to its benefits and services, the welfare state sets up and/or influences other circuits of redistribution between women and men. Here one may attribute to the welfare state a more general, if more covert, effect in shaping gender roles and power relations.

Consideration of the gender-relevant outcomes moves me on to the third dimension of my framework: the welfare state as an agent of social structure. The welfare state is in this regard conceived primarily as a motor of stratification. To establish stratificational effects, I draw attention first to the impact of welfare state programs on financial relations, visible through their effect on male–female income inequalities and poverty risks. There is a second element to stratification also that centres on the broader set of opportunities that are (made) available for women as well as men. As we now know from existing work, the extent to which welfare states liberate individuals or groups from the rigours of the market has been widely trumpeted as one of their most significant activities and sources of variation. I suggest that this understanding of welfare states' significance needs to be considerably extended. In particular, for women the welfare state may have greater significance in 'freeing' them or not from the family, in the sense of both altering dependence on male incomes and affecting opportunities to participate or not in paid employment. I therefore suggest a broad view of the stratificational potential of welfare states, especially the extent to which they are associated with an expansion or delimiting of opportunities in relation to both the labour market and the family for women and men.

My framework avoids positing fixed processes and outcomes. For if one were to study the British and German welfare states separately, one would be justified in concluding that each is gendered. Two quite different welfare states are each implicated in skewing the distribution of income, and income-related opportunities, between different groups of women and men. But they do this through rather different means and to a differential degree. Studying these two welfare states simultaneously, therefore, begs a more complex understanding of how welfare states in themselves (that is, through their own practice) lead to systematic inequalities between women and men and how they react to inequalities arising elsewhere in the social system. The British system could be said to be gendered not so much in its direct effects but rather in its failure to sufficiently counteract women's financial disadvantage. The German system reinforces male–female income inequalities both directly and indirectly but more among individuals than households. To a considerable extent, Wilensky's (1975: 40) old insight, which seems new only in the light of the current fashion for 'typologizing', is apposite: practices in rich countries fit a mixed model.

But a sole focus on gender also has limitations. For the results of the present study suggest a general 'lack of fit' between the gender dimension of these two welfare states and their general outcomes. That is, the model that performs better on gender performs less well overall. Two insights and one question flow from this. First, it seems clear that gender divisions cut across welfare state features, defying a unidimensional characterization or monocausal interpretation. Second, being critical of my own approach, redistribution on the basis of gender is not an adequate statement of the general impact of welfare states. Of course, the corollary of this is equally true: if gender does not predict other outcomes then neither do approaches focusing solely on redistribution between economic interest groups predict gender outcomes. Neither can be the whole story. The question then is how to maximize the strengths of the two sets of approaches.

My response is the following. As well as elaborating gender at a conceptual and empirical level, I have followed a particular approach for studying the welfare state and gender together. Two exercises are involved. The first is to claim an analytic place for the family as a locus of welfare activities and of important redistributive processes and practices. This is to make the claim that what happens within the family and the relative positions and relations across family types as they are influenced by welfare state policies are crucial. The second exercise is to bring the experience and life situations of women to the centre alongside those of men and to examine how these are affected by welfare state provisions and the kinds of accommodations that exist between state, family and market at macro level. Existing approaches and concepts have to be rethought from both vantage points.

APPENDIX I

The Data Sources and
Some Necessary Modifications

The two data sources are as follows: for the UK, the Family Expenditure Survey, and for Germany one wave of the German Socio-economic Panel.

Details on the Data Sets

The Family Expenditure Survey

The Family Expenditure Survey is a continuous survey of income, expenditure and other aspects of household finances in the UK that has been carried out annually since 1957 in Britain and since 1968 in Northern Ireland. Its origins lie in a recommendation of the Cost of Living Advisory Committee and since 1962 information from it has been used for the annual reweighting of the General Index of Retail Prices (Department of Employment 1987: i). Although its name may suggest otherwise, the sampling unit is private households. A stratified random sampling method is used with private households as the sampling unit. The sample is stratified according to postal sector (or ward size), region, area type and by two census variables: proportion of owner-occupiers and proportion of renters. The sample in 1986 was based on 672 postal sectors in Britain and in Northern Ireland on a random sample from Rating and Valuation Lists. In Britain 7,045 households (69 per cent of the effective sample) agreed to co-operate, as did 62 per cent in Northern Ireland. Out of the 751 households in the latter area, 133 were selected at random to form part of the UK FES report, giving a total UK sample of 7,178 households. Among these households are represented some 18,330 individuals, aged 15 years and over. The sampling design is intended to be self-weighting and no additional weights are provided.

Information is obtained by three instruments. The first is a house-hold schedule that collects information on the household mainly from the household head or the 'housewife'. As well as background informa-tion on the characteristics of the household and its individual members, the questions are mainly about expenses of a recurrent nature, including both household and individual expenditure. The second instrument is an individual income schedule. This primarily focuses on income from all sources, national insurance contributions and income tax. Infor-mation is also obtained on employment status and recent absences from work. Third, there is a set of diary records which, completed by each member of the household aged 16 and over, keep a record of all expenditure of that individual over a fourteen-day period. For the present research exercise, only the household and income schedules are used.

German Socio-economic Panel

The German Socio-economic Panel comprises panel data on households and individuals gathered annually since 1984. As a longitudinal data set, all household members of 16 years and over are (re)interviewed annu-ally in about 6,000 households. The Panel consists of three separate samples: A, B and C. Samples A and B have existed since the inaugura-tion of the Panel in 1984 and Sample C was initiated in 1990 when the Panel was extended to cover the territory of the former German Democratic Republic. Sample A consists of a random sample[1] of private households living in the Federal Republic whose head of household is either German or of another nationality apart from Turkish, (former) Yugoslavian, Greek, Italian or Spanish. Sample B consists of five random samples of households with heads of any of the latter five nationalities – essentially the former guestworker-recruiting countries. Since the sampling method varied for Samples A and B and there is some evidence of over-sampling for the latter, I use only those households and individ-uals in Sample A. The valid population n for this sample is 3,962 house-holds and 8,009 individuals. All retrievals from the Panel were performed using the RZOO 1.2 program as developed by Rohwer (1992). Access to the Panel data was gained in connection with the 'Household Dynamics and Social Inequality' Project at the European University Institute (1989–1992).

Respondents who move continue to take part in the Panel as long as their new location is within the area covered by it. One household member, typically the household head (most usually nominated by the householders themselves), provides details on the household by com-pleting the household questionnaire. This person also usually provides information on all 'children' in the household (defined as those under 16). The data include information on the dwelling, the neighbourhood, family care patterns and residential moves, as well as receipt of various types of transfer income (at an aggregate level) and the composition of aggregate income. Much of the latter type of information is also available for individuals and is collected in a separate questionnaire; in addition to income data, this also collects information on time use and leisure patterns, period-related information on fertility, marital and cohabitation events, other biographical information, employment events involving actual or planned changes of occupational position, unemployment and periods out of the labour force. Attitudinal information is also available on general satisfaction levels with life, human capital assets and some plans for the future.

While there are considerable differences between the two databases in terms of structure, content and level of use, both contain the following common sets of information which are important for the present purpose:

Data for Individuals
Sources and amounts of income
Taxes and other deductions from income
Detailed patterns of receipt of social security and social assistance
Employee status and some information on work history
Financial constraints and commitments
Demographic data
Racial/ethnic origins

Data for Households
Household composition
Demographic details on household members
Characteristics and costs of housing
Details on household income
Situation of children

The UK sample is the larger one in terms of its size relative to the population base. In all, 7,178 households and 18,330 individual members of these households were personally interviewed. For comparative purposes just one wave of the German panel data will be used, the relevant wave being Wave 3 for the year 1986. As outlined above, in this wave there were 3,962 households and 8,009 adults.

Missing Cases

Income was the most problematic variable, in the sense of leading to the highest number of missing cases, in both samples.

Income data in each case is generally constructed on both an individual and household basis. However the two databases differ fundamentally on the derivation of household income. The German Socio-economic Panel gathers data on net household income for the last month through the household questionnaire. More detailed information on individual members' income, on both a gross and net basis, is gathered through the individual questionnaire. In the UK study, much of the income information is compiled for the household on the basis of information on individual incomes. Of the original 18,330 individual respondents, full information on personal income was available for 15,335, that is 83.7 per cent. The German completion rate was lower. The numbers of individuals for whom full information is available on their personal and household incomes is in the German case 6,284 (that is, 78.5 per cent of the total sample). Of all the 3,962 households in Sample A of Wave 3 of the German Socio-economic Panel, complete income data was available for 3,077, that is 77.7 per cent.

Income Data and Some Necessary Modifications to the German Data

Some synchronization of the income data with regard to timing was required in the German case. Since the fieldwork for the German survey takes about eight months to complete, it is important to closely match the periods for which the income data are valid. This survey contains both current income data (on either a weekly or monthly basis) as well as income for the previous year (income other than for the current month is gathered by a successive wave of interviews). For the German sample, all of the fieldwork for Wave 3 was completed in 1986. The valid date for the household income varies from February to October (with April as the mean) of the current year, whereas that for the individual income data is the previous year. In order to synchronize the time periods, therefore, the information on household income for Germany was taken from the second wave of the Panel, whereas all other information is taken from the third wave. In both cases then the income information refers to the 1985/86 period.

One of the most difficult problems encountered before analysing incomes related to the calculation of personal net incomes for individual respondents in the German survey. Three sources of difficulty existed. First, no net personal incomes are gathered apart from those from paid work; only gross personal income figures are gathered (from employment and transfers for each month of the last year and the

monthly average for each for the last year as a whole). A second problem is that the information necessary to calculate net incomes, for
example taxes paid, is collected in subsequent waves of the Panel. Fairly
detailed matching of information across waves is therefore necessary,
entailing some attrition. In the case of taxation information, for instance, data has to be matched over two waves since the taxes paid in
any particular year are only ascertained two years later.[2] Third, the
manner in which the taxation information is gathered leads to two
particular difficulties in regard to distributing the tax burden. The first
distributive task pertains to the redistribution of taxes within married
couples. This is necessary because only the total income taxes paid by
individuals, regardless of whether they paid taxes as individuals or as
members of joint tax-paying units, are collected. There is therefore no
way of ascertaining from the data set how the tax burden breaks down
between those husbands and wives – the majority – who chose to pay
taxes as a joint unit. Moreover, this particular distribution of the tax
burden is complicated in cases where one member of the couple
reports paying no tax while the other classified him/her self as part of a
joint tax-paying unit. Both may, of course, be factually correct in that
the spouse or partner may have had no taxable income which, given the
bias in the German tax system towards one-earner married couples,
makes it attractive for the main earner to pay tax on behalf of the
couple. How, given the general nature of the figures available, should
the tax burden be distributed between partners? Sharing it equally
within couples would lead to large negative incomes, especially on the
part of women. Therefore it was decided to distribute the tax burden
proportional to each spouse's share of the joint income. One consequence should be carefully noted: this method may overestimate the
taxes paid by the second partner in that the major income-earner gets
the main benefit of any tax allowances or exemptions. Where the
second partner's income was untraceable, as happened in 700 cases, the
tax burden of the respondent individual was made equal to the average
share of the tax paid by individual members of joint tax-paying couples
(i.e. 67 per cent for men, 33 per cent for women).

The second redistributive task related to how some sources of
income are to be treated for tax purposes. It too arises from the fact that
the information collected on taxes paid is an overall figure that does not
discriminate as regards the make-up of income sources. There were two
particular problems here. First, two types of income are available only
on a household basis in the German Panel. These are some cash transfers, typically those paid on behalf of the collective unit such as
Kindergeld and monies paid as part of the means-tested safety net
scheme – *Sozialhilfe*. Note 5 in Chapter 4 describes how income from

these sources was allocated among household members. Second, income from investments and property necessitated a similar decision about redistribution among individuals since it too was available only on a household basis. In the end it was decided to distribute such incomes equally among the adult members of the household. But first the gross income (the only form in which this income was available) from these sources was adjusted in the following manner. To take income from rentals and property first, the 9.6 per cent of households that declared an income from this source in the year in question contained just over 1,000 adults. Net income from this source was computed on the basis of deducting tax from the gross amount less declared costs. As regards income from interest and dividends, just over 1,000 households containing some 2,100 adult members declared a known amount of income from this source for the year in question, the remainder providing an estimate only. Again it was decided to divide income from this source equally among the adult members of the household, even though it is unlikely to be so divided in real life. Here it should be noted that female incomes are especially likely to be overestimated by these data.

APPENDIX II

Issues of Poverty Measurement

A major issue in poverty measurement is how to take account of different dimensions of poverty and, indirectly, the desirable properties of a good summary index of poverty. In recent years the utility of the most common measure of poverty – the head count – has been increasingly queried. A key property of the head-count measure is its sensitivity to the relative number of poor. But, it has nothing to say about the depth of poverty and for that reason is best accompanied by a measure of the poverty gap, which is based on the income shortfall of those below the poverty line. This measure has the merits of sensitivity to the mean level of income of the poor relative to the poverty line. These two measures of poverty – head counts and poverty gaps – are therefore used in this study.

On their own, however, head counts and poverty gaps are limited. As Phipps (1993: 166) reminds us, the head-count measure will show no increase in poverty even if the incomes of all currently poor households fall. Nor will it register a change if a poor household transfers income to a non-poor household. The shortcomings of the poverty gap measure, on the other hand, are that it pays no attention to the number of poor households in the society and that it registers no increase in poverty if a poor household transfers income to a less poor household. Furthermore, given the focus of the present study, it is vital that the poverty measure used be decomposable, facilitating the distribution of poverty into male and female shares. One class of measures that is decomposable is that proposed by Foster, Greer and Thorbecke (1984) and operationalized by Wright (1992, 1993) and Phipps (1993). This FGT index $P(a)$ may be defined as

$$P(a) = (1/n)\sum_{i=1}^{q}\left[\left(\frac{y^*-y_i}{y^*}\right)\right]^a$$

where y^* is the poverty line, y_i is the unit income, q is the number of poor units in the population (i.e. $y_i < y^*$), and n is the total number of units in the population; a is a parameter that takes on a value greater than or equal to zero. As a gets larger the index becomes more sensitive to the income circumstances of the 'poorest poor'. This index is bound by the unit interval with a value of '0' representing the situation of no poverty and the value of '1' representing the situation of 'total poverty'.

The FGT index incorporates both the head-count and poverty gap measures. If $a = 0$ the index is equivalent to a head count ratio calculated as follows:

$H=q/n$.

When $a = 1$ it is the product of a head-count ratio and a normalized poverty gap (that is, the gap divided by the poverty line) and reduces to

$H \bullet I$

where $I = (y^* - \bar{y}_p)/y^*$

and $\bar{y}_p$ is the average income of the poor.

However, for higher values of a, raising each unit's normalized deficit to the power of a means that poor households are weighted more heavily in the calculation of the poverty index. In deciding which value of a to use, we are led by Wright (1992, 1993), who suggests a value of 2 to capture the relative deprivation of the poor. $P(2)$ therefore reduces to

$$H \bullet \left[I^2+(1-I)^2 \bullet C_q^2\right]$$

where C_q is the coefficient of variation of income among the poor.

As mentioned above, a key advantage of the FGT index in the present context is that it allows for the decomposition of poverty by subgroup weights. More specifically with respect to male and female poverty, the total or overall poverty rate may be written as follows:

$$P(a) = (n_f/n) \bullet P(a)_f + (n_m/n) \bullet P(a)_m$$

where the subscripts 'f' and 'm' denote male and female respectively. The ratios n_f/n and n_m/n are the relative population shares of females and males (n_f/n and $n_m/n = 1$), $P(a)_m$ are the FGT poverty indices for a given value of (a) calculated separately for females and males.

Because $P(a)$ is additively decomposable with population share weights, the female and male shares $S(a)_k$ of this total are:

$$S(a)_f = (n_f/n) \bullet P(a)_f/P(a) \text{ and } S(a)_m = (n_m/n) \bullet P(a)_m/P(a)$$

If poverty is shared equally, then each group's relative poverty share should equal its relative population share $S(a)_f = n_f/n$ and $S(a)_m = n_m/n$. Therefore a description of how overrepresented women or men are among the poor is simply how much their poverty share exceeds their population share. A convenient way of summarising the magnitude of this advantage or disadvantage is the ratio of the subgroup's share to its population share:

Ratio f = $S(a)_f/ (n_f/n)$

If $Ratio_f >1$ then women are overrepresented amongst the poor. Conversely, if $Ratio_f >1$ then women are underrepresented amongst the poor. If the $Ratio_f =1$ poverty is shared equally between women and men.

Notes

Introduction

1 The referent for theoretical and policy purposes throughout this book is Britain, although the empirical data refer to the United Kingdom (UK), which includes Northern Ireland. It is customary, even when referring to the UK, to speak of the British welfare state. This is not completely correct, though, for there are some differences between social security provision in Northern Ireland and that prevailing in Britain. Historically, the politically sensitive nature of developments in Northern Ireland made for differences in particular programs and the general level of social security spending there as compared with Britain. In addition, welfare tended to be delivered more often by intermediate bodies than was true of Britain. Since the 1970s, though, social policy and provision in Northern Ireland have been closer to that in Britain. Nevertheless it should be borne in mind that there are differences between the two units. In the case of Germany the reference unit is West Germany, the then and now former *Bundesrepublik Deutschland*.

2 This is not to imply that sexuality is purely biologically determined or to claim that the welfare state has no effect on the construction of sexuality. Indeed, it is acknowledged that sex is also a social category, which means that it is neither purely objective nor fixed in meaning.

3 Orloff (1994) also underlines the need for an analytical distinction between gender-based difference and inequality.

1 Theory on the Welfare State

1 'Feminist' is somewhat of a problematic label, either because it is forced to embrace work with increasingly different orientations or because in popular parlance it has become a politically loaded term. As a consequence of either or both, some scholars are slow to apply the epithet to their work, just as others are very deliberate about doing so. The term 'feminist' is used in this book to apply to work that has focused centrally upon the position of women, has developed a critique of existing work (referred to throughout this book as 'conventional' scholarship) from the perspective of its capacity to countenance or explain the position

of women and/or has treated gender as a structuring mechanism of contemporary societies.

2   This listing is explained by the fact that we limit our attention here to theoretical approaches which have centrally focused upon the welfare state. This narrowing of the focus excludes in large part theories and theoretical developments oriented to explaining the nature of the state writ large. In particular, rational and public choice theories and those which have been developed under the new institutionalism rubric (for example March and Olsen 1984) are not considered in their own right (although of course their importance for a comprehensive under-standing of agency by and in relation to the state is fully acknowledged). Needless to say, the literature considered is not all-inclusive but rather serves to demonstrate the main features of alternative approaches to the welfare state.

3   This has also been referred to as a 'labourist' interpretation or as the 'social democratic model'.

4   A number of versions of this approach exists. The 'simple democracy' thesis, for example, regards political democracy as a sufficient explanation for the rise of the welfare state: it represents the outcome of the demo-cratic class struggle (Myles 1989). See Shalev (1983) for an outline of the main themes and the development of scholarship within the social demo-cratic paradigm.

5   The 'anomalous cases' of Australia and New Zealand also demonstrate that working-class mobilization does not necessarily lead to social demo-cratic power and from there to welfare statism (Castles 1985). Van Kers-bergen (1991) shows how christian democracy has a distinct logic in relation both to working class mobilization and the welfare state form that it fosters.

6   Pedersen (1993) is especially interesting here, showing how the campaigns by British feminists around family policy in the early decades of the century helped to make powerful male organizations more conscious of their members' identities and claims as husbands and fathers. She argues against an approach that identifies key groups – trade unions, employers, feminists, civil servants – as the bearers of transparent class interests, preferring instead to uncover the more complex identities and loyalties that motivated their struggles.

7   Labels are always problematic. For a classification of feminist approaches to the welfare state, see Williams (1989: 41–86).

8   For a taste of this work see the collections by Glendinning and Millar (1987), Showstack Sassoon (1987), Jones and Jónasdóttir (1988) and Sainsbury (1994b). In reference to the overall thrust of women's scholar-ship on the welfare state, Gordon (1990a) identifies three phases of activity since feminism was (re)born in the late 1960s. The first comprised work that demonstrated the discriminatory character of welfare programs; in its second stage feminism generated a structured critique of welfare. Comprising the main bulk of feminist work on the welfare state, scholar-ship here has attempted to illustrate how state welfare's purpose and end effect is to keep women economically dependent on men and men depen-dent on the wage and personally dependent on women. The third stage as outlined by Gordon documents women's political activism and influence on the shaping of welfare states.

9   However, Birgit Pfau-Effinger (1996) has developed it in relation to
      Germany, Finland and the Netherlands, and Duncan (1995) has sought
      to use it for an analysis of social policy variations in Europe as a whole.
      But these are by and large empirical applications and it remains the case
      that the theoretical constructs, and in particular the relations between
      them, are not only underspecified but derive ultimately from the Swedish
      case.

10   The state steps in, according to McIntosh, because the family is not the
      ideal form for the reproduction of labour power for two reasons. First the
      ratio of earners to dependants varies widely in families; secondly, families,
      if left to themselves, do not necessarily bear the correct number of chil-
      dren to meet capitalist requirements. Hence the state through its income
      support policies shores up family structures and through its population
      policies ensures the maintenance of population numbers.

11   Three elements of classical independence on which citizenship was
      founded were the capacity to bear arms, the capacity to own property and
      the capacity for self-government (Pateman 1988: 238).

2   The Gender Dimension of Welfare States

1   For other gender-sensitive typologies see Siaroff (1994), Mósesdóttir
      (1995) and Daly (1996).

2   Esping-Andersen's work has been criticized also for other omissions, apart
      from those that are gender-related. Also absent from his conceptual frame-
      work are non-worker groups and non-state actors as well as non-standard
      and non-state forms of welfare provision. See Kvist and Torfing (1996: 8–12).

3   Ragin's (1994) re-examination of Esping-Andersen's regime clusters from
      the point of view of pension systems also reinforces the point of some
      countries' lack of fit in the typology. Using some of the very same criteria
      applied by Esping-Andersen himself, Ragin finds the following six anom-
      alous cases which form a separate cluster: Germany, Ireland, Japan,
      Netherlands, New Zealand and UK. He comments: 'The three-world
      scheme does not capture existing diversity adequately, even when
      measures reported in Esping-Andersen (1990) are used, and some cluster
      assignments contradict the ad hoc assignments made by Esping-Andersen'
      (1994: 336).

4   A centrally co-ordinated database which, drawing on national microdata,
      presents information on national income patterns in a common frame-
      work. The data are derived from three main sources: surveys of tax files,
      specifically designed income or consumption surveys and general popula-
      tion surveys.

5   In any case, the construction of welfare as uniformly oppressive of women
      allows women no agency, representing them as passive victims of oppres-
      sive actors, be it men or the state. In addition, such a static view of the
      welfare state obscures the gains that have been made by women and, more-
      over, represents any gains as an inevitable epiphenomenon of moderniza-
      tion rather than as the result of political activism (Gordon 1990a: 186).

6   For a discussion of the different legal bases underlying rights in social
      insurance and social assistance see Holtmaat (1992). For strong argumen-
      tation that the former is male in character and the latter female see
      Gordon (1988) and Fraser (1989).

7   See Graham (1991, 1993) and Thomas (1993) for an overview of how the
    concept of care has developed and a critique of its application. Leira
    (1992) provides a detailed outline of the features of care work and how it
    is treated by welfare states in Scandinavia.

3   British and German Welfare States

1   No clear and established definition of family policy and its instruments
    exists. Family policy tends to be defined by default – as the residue of social
    policies outside the mainstream that relate in some central way to the wel-
    fare of children (see Kamerman and Kahn 1978). The definition provided
    by Skrede (1993: 1) is among the best: 'family policy [is] ... public policy
    measures affecting the economic situation of parents and dealing with the
    regulation of the responsibility and sharing of costs and social reproduc-
    tion between the private and the public sphere, or more specifically,
    between the *state* and the *family*' (original emphases).

2   Concern about national efficiency was heightened by declining industrial
    competitiveness and the implications of Boer War defeat. Hence Wilson
    (1977: 100) tells us that the poor and the unemployed were seen in rela-
    tion to imperial effectiveness and the strength of the nation rather than in
    terms of their potential for national disorder and unrest.

3   The changes made to cash transfer programs during the 1980s had,
    according to Clarke and Langan (1993: 57), three objectives: to reduce
    the disincentive and dependency creating effects of transfers; to create a
    more 'efficient' benefit system by targeting benefits at the most needy;
    and to encourage moves away from the state as the primary agent of social
    insurance.

4   Tax allowances for children have a longer tradition in Germany than cash
    allowances, having been introduced in 1920. Surviving subsequent poli-
    tical upheavals, they were abolished by the Social Democrats in 1975, on
    the grounds that they benefited higher earners disproportionately, to be
    reintroduced and considerably extended in 1983 by the Christian Demo-
    crat/Free Democrat coalition (Bundesministerium für Familie und
    Senioren 1993; Bahle 1995). In Britain, tax allowances for children were
    abolished by the Labour government in the 1970s as part of the upgrading
    of child cash allowances They have not been reintroduced.

5   The others are Italy, Luxembourg, Spain and the USA.

6   Initially this benefit consisted of a flat payment of DM600 per month for
    the first six months, thereafter being means-tested. It is now means-tested
    for its entire duration for children born in 1994 and subsequently. It is
    independent of the former employment status of the recipient parent but
    can be received only if the said parent is engaged in employment for no
    more than 19 hours a week.

7   Ostner (1994: 40–3) is perceptive about the philosophical underpinnings
    of this component of the Basic Law. She says that West German marriage
    and family policies have been strongly influenced by romantic anti-
    contractual and social Catholic ideas which, while stressing the dignity of
    institutions and the intrinsic value of human relations, have been
    tempered by the modern idea of the independent individual. Each adult
    is guaranteed individual protection in marriage, which extends also in
    cases of divorce, and individuals are regarded as being continuously

engaged in vertical and horizontal relations along both gender and generational lines.

8   Note in this regard that family support obligations are more widespread
     in Germany in that they extend in both directions between parents and
     children, whereas in Britain the obligation of children to support their
     parents was abolished in 1948. Married people are also of course legally
     obliged to support each other and there has been some extension of this
     obligation to cohabiting couples, but only in social welfare law. German
     children have personal rights (for example, to orphan's pensions, study
     loans) and after 14 years of age an individual entitlement to *Sozialhilfe*.
     Moreover, the right to child support as enshrined in family law is also an
     individual right of the child. In Britain children and young persons below
     the age of majority have no personal claim to welfare benefits: child-
     related benefits and supplements are bestowed in the person of the
     parent or guardian.

9   Apart from the Child Support Agency, which is a more recent develop-
     ment, two long-standing provisions affect this expectation, both of which
     set these families apart from others. The first is the 'liable relative' rule
     which, uniquely applied within the national context to lone-parent fami-
     lies, manifests the view that someone outside the household (a husband or
     the father of the child(ren)) is expected to provide support. The second is
     the 'cohabitation rule' through which members of a couple deemed to be
     living together as man and wife are treated as if they were married. Their
     resources are aggregated and they are treated as one unit for claimant
     purposes rather than two.

10   It therefore instituted in 1979 a program of Advanced Maintenance Pay-
     ments whereby a public advance on maintenance is granted in cases where
     an absent parent fails to fulfil his or her child support obligations. Based
     on the minimum child support amounts for children, these payments are
     available for all children with an absent, non-supporting parent, regardless
     of whether the parents are unmarried, separated or divorced. The
     maximum duration of receipt is 72 months.

4   Sex, Gender and Cash Transfer Systems

1   This is not to claim that the gender roles assumed in the active years do not
     affect well-being, and especially access to financial resources, in the later
     stages of the life course. Clearly they do, as attested to by women's lower
     access to pensions in their own right, for instance. However, since the avail-
     able information does not allow me to trace the effects of economic activity
     patterns pursued over the life course and since inclusion of those aged 60
     and over biases the gender comparison, it seems best for analytic purposes
     to operationalize gender as a characteristic of people of prime age.

2   A household 'head' was already available in both data sets. In the German
     case the head was typically the chief income-earner or the person knowing
     most about the household and was usually designated by the household.
     For the Family Expenditure Survey, the household head is designated by
     the researchers according to members' status vis-à-vis housing – the person
     designated as the head either owns the property or has chief responsibility
     for renting it. Where there are two or more individuals with equal claim to
     this status, the head is by default the oldest male. Each individual aged 16

or over completes a separate expenditure schedule, but only when married are 16–18 year-olds counted as adults in the income schedule.

3 The condition of requiring full information on individual as well as household income took its toll on the population number. In the German Panel incomplete income information led to the exclusion of 21.5 per cent of the total individual sample and to 22.3 per cent of the household sample. In the UK case, full information on personal incomes was not available for 16.3 per cent of the individual population but complete income information existed for the entire household file. Appendix I gives details of samples and missing cases.

4 Note that in this chapter I consider only public transfers, excluding occupational benefits. The latter, almost exclusively retirement pensions, are far more important for the UK population. They will be included in later analyses – especially in those sections which consider the impact of benefits and taxes – but are excluded from this chapter because its aim is to explore the public transfer apparatus.

5 The data collection process was in both cases organized so that all transfer data, with three exceptions in the German case, was obtained from individual respondents and then aggregated for households. However, receipt of *Kindergeld*, *Sozialhilfe* and assistance with housing costs is known in the German Socio-economic Panel only at the household level. Therefore for the purpose of the individual analyses a decision was required on how to distribute these three types of transfer among individual members of households. This was done by differentiating between transfers oriented to income supplementation and those directed towards income maintenance (measured on the basis of the size of transfers). Those deemed to be of the former type, *Kindergeld* and assistance with housing costs, were attributed as income to the household head since they are normally paid to a representative of the household and are designed to assist with basic household costs. *Sozialhilfe* was distributed equally between the adult members of the household in that it is needs-driven and is intended for the purpose of income maintenance. All in all, however, these are very minor sources of income, accounting for 3.1 per cent of total individual net income and 3.3 per cent of household net income.

6 It is a source of some analytical handicap that neither data set differentiates between benefits secured oneself and those secured through a spouse's contribution. The latter is likely to be the case for quite large numbers of women. However, there are no firm indications that the two transfer systems differ significantly here in that married women in both are likely to have a heavy reliance on transfers obtained by their husbands.

7 In Chapter 2 three female-specific risks were identified: loss of male income through widowhood, divorce or separation, loss of income through maternity, loss of income through having to care for others. Because of either too few cases or multicollinearity between the different indicators, it was necessary to either modify these risks for the purposes of the regression analyses or to exclude them. The first risk – loss of a male breadwinner income – will be interpreted as the risk of lone motherhood. There are too few cases to isolate out maternity as a specific risk – only about 1 per cent in both samples. Maternity is therefore excluded. The third risk, that of caring, should be picked up by the family status/low-income variable.

8   Empirically this variable is operationalized by differentiating between parents, spouses and 'others'. Parents are defined as those with children aged 16 or under. Spouses as defined here are married men and women who either have no children or whose children are 17 years of age or over. 'Others' includes women and men who are neither parents nor spouses so defined. Since there is quite a high correlation between mothers with low-incomes and lone parents, low-income mothers had to be omitted from the logistic regression analyses.

9   The marginal distribution on the dependent variable is in the region of 15:85 per cent.

10   In the latter regard I calculated the marginal impact of each variable choosing a probability value as close as possible to the mean. Working with logit the marginal impact at p is calculated as follows: where k is the index of the variables. $\frac{dp}{dxk} = p(1 - p)xk$

Note that this calculation probably overstates the degree of impact since the marginal impact is calculated on the tangent and not on the cumulative distribution $F(X)$ itself.

11   The measure used is McFadden's pseudo r^2 which is computed as follows:

$$1 - \frac{(-2\log \text{ likelihood of the unconstrained model})}{(-2\log \text{ likelihood of the constrained model})}$$

12   For the purposes of these calculations, each recipient was only allowed one claim, the program yielding the highest income being taken as the reference program for those receiving two or more benefits simultaneously.

13   The marginal distribution on the dependent variable is in the region of 25:75 per cent.

5   Income Inequality and Resource-based Relations

1   Although the family is the unit I use conceptually, for empirical purposes I am forced to rely on the household, mainly because the data do not allow me to differentiate between the two in all cases. Family and household are similar to the extent that both are units of redistribution based on personal relations. However, as Acker (1988) points out, personal distribution in the family takes place between related individuals usually in contexts that include love, commitment or friendship. To the extent that we are interested in how these relations constitute elements in the underlying social structure – not least of which being the degree to which the welfare state links into and helps to define ties of obligations and support within families – it is important to bear in mind that different principles may underlie redistribution in households as distinct from families.

2   The place of occupational transfers is not unambiguous. Some studies treat them as market income while others follow the procedure that I use here and place them alongside public transfers. The rationale for this placing is twofold. First, occupational transfers are not strictly equivalent to market income since they are transfers deriving on the basis of a (social) insurance principle. Second, they are closely influenced by state policies and provision and may even be, as was the case in the UK before the most recent change of government, encouraged by them.

3   Note that services are therefore considered as an indirect effect. See Smeeding et al. (1992) for an international comparison of the distribution of education, health care and imputed rental income from home ownership.

4   Overall, there were considerable problems in matching information on sources of income in the two data sets. The UK study was by far the better in two respects: itemizing income from all possible sources and gathering all income information with the individual as the unit of analysis. In the latter regard, the German Socio-economic Panel gathers income from interest and dividends and some cash transfers only at the household level. The user of the data is therefore left with the decision of how best to allocate these sources of income among the adult members of the collectivity. See the following note for how the interest and dividend income were allocated among individuals and note 5 in Chapter 4 for how the household-based transfer income was distributed. See also Appendix 1 for details about the two samples, especially with regard to missing information on incomes and in the case of the German data the transformation of gross into net income.

5   The German data posed considerable problems in regard to these sources of income. Since information on income from interest and dividends as well as income from property was collected only on a household basis, a decision was required on how this income should be distributed among the individual adults in the household. In effect, it was decided to distribute both sources equally among household members. Given this, it should be noted that female income from these sources is likely to be over-estimated.

6   These are defined as married women either with no children or children aged 17 and over. They are so defined in order to differentiate them from mothers. Husbands are differentiated from fathers in the same manner. Note 8 in Chapter 4 explains the procedure.

6   Sex, Gender and Poverty

1   All the poverty estimates in this chapter are based on income before housing costs. This is mainly for cross-national comparability purposes since housing patterns and therefore housing costs vary considerably between the UK and Germany. See Johnson and Webb (1990: 57–60) for a discussion of the implications for poverty measurement of including and excluding housing costs.

2   Note, therefore, that I adopt a relative approach to poverty. The main shortcoming of this method is that the proportion of poor in the population, being tied to the shape of the income distribution rather than real income, responds only to changes in the income distribution.

3   The marginal distribution on the dependent variable is in the region of 10:90 per cent.

4   Note that for this analysis, the income base is net income minus net public transfers received. Therefore, the effects of income taxation are not included here. Note also that occupational pensions, which are quite significant for the UK sample, are not treated as 'public transfers' for the purposes of the analysis here but are included as 'pre-transfer' income.

5   The sequence used is the one that approximates most closely the logic of how both transfer systems are organized. That is, family benefits tend to be near universal in both systems and therefore come first. Second, short-term and long-term exit programs, although contingency-related, are

rights-based and therefore available to those who have earned them. Minimum income or poverty programs logically come last since as means-tested programs they are forthcoming only when other resources are demonstrably not available.

6   The marginal distribution on the dependent variable is in the region of 10:90 per cent.

7   Marriage, Financial Relations and Women's Economic Risks

1   This is really Curtis's point (1986: 179). To develop the nature of the trade in traditional marriage a little further, he asks what did the husband trade? Little or nothing, it seems, because through the vow of obedience he got to retain control over, and in some cases ownership of, her share of the collective income and also over any property she acquired during the marriage.

2   Henceforth I shall refer to both married and cohabiting women and men as married. Note that both are included in all references to married couples in this chapter and that the vast majority of respondents are married.

3   Note that all of the calculations that are based on married or cohabiting couples pertain only to spouses or partners and their dependent children (16 years and under). That is, where households consist of other adults apart from the married couple and dependent children, only the income of the couple is included in these calculations. The underlying rationale is that the assumption of the spouse's full and equal claim is tenable only as regards the income of the other spouse and that spouses bear the full costs of their dependent children. Where I refer to household income for married couples with and without children, therefore, it is the joint income of the spouses that is the point of reference. For an analysis that assumes that all members of households fully pool and share equally their income see Sørensen and McLanahan (1989).

4   It should be noted that all of the calculations of support provided are based on the proportion of one's own income that is transferred, whereas the degree of dependence is based on the proportion of one's household share that is received as a transfer from the other spouse.

5   In calculating support obligations I proceeded as follows. I began with the child aged 16 years or under. In order to estimate the costs involved in rearing children I used the adjustments inherent in the OECD equivalence scale. Thus, in a two-parent and one-child household, 23 per cent of the total income is calculated as for the support of the child, in a two-child household the proportion is 37 per cent, in a three-child household it is 47 per cent and in a four-child household 54 per cent. Having identified the proportion of the collective income that can be assumed to be absorbed by children's needs, I then made two particular assumptions about the significance and division of these costs among parents. The first was that parents share equally the costs of supporting children, equality here meaning that each contributes to the cost of children, proportionate to her or his share of the total income. So if the wife's personal income is equal to 30 per cent of the total, she bears 30 per cent of the costs of children and her husband 70 per cent. Of course if one partner has no income then the other bears the full cost of the support of the children. The second assumption is that parents give priority to

the support needs of their children. This was interpreted to mean that the necessary monies for children's needs should first be subtracted before the support obligations of spouses towards each other were calculated. The degree of spouses' support obligations towards each other was then calculated by distributing the income that remains (both personal and collective), and comparing personal income to household share.

6   This is undoubtedly related to the relative absence, or certainly low provision, of public child care services in both countries. Research suggests a significant link between the availability of public child care and mothers' capacity for labour market participation (Davies and Joshi 1990).

7   And here we rely on gross earnings since it is practically impossible to estimate what the tax burdens of households would be following a break-up.

8   Note that the labour market participation of women in the UK is thereby assumed to fall considerably while that of German women increases.

8   Welfare States and Gender Divisions

1   Equity has a different meaning: that each individual should get back from the welfare state the equivalent value of what s/he contributed to it.

2   Nancy Fraser's (1997) recent attempt to break away from the assumption that gender equity can be identified with or reduced to any single value or norm is an important contribution. Even though Fraser's overall perspective retains traces of an equal-rights approach, she has sought to develop gender equity as a complex concept comprising a plurality of five distinct normative principles. The first is an anti-poverty principle, in which she specifically refers to welfare states' commitment to reducing poverty among women. Fraser's second principle is anti-exploitation. This is set in a context where need and lack of alternatives renders people exploitable, and her policy prescriptions in this regard draw upon the availability of an alternative source of income through the state as a matter of right (thereby countering exploitation at the hands of individual family members, state officials or employers). The third principle, equality, is seen by Fraser to involve three distinct conceptions: income equality, leisure time equality and equality of status and respect. Her fourth principle emphasizes anti-marginalization, which Fraser interprets to embrace women's full participation on a par with men in all areas of social life. Her final principle is that of anti-androcentrism, and here her concern is to counter the tendency to represent male life patterns as the norm to which women must assimilate. It is Fraser's view that no welfare state can realize gender equity unless it satisfies all five principles, albeit that some of the principles are potentially in conflict. While offering much potential for a research and policy agenda on welfare states' gender-related outcomes, Fraser's conclusion – that gender equity requires the dismantling of gender differences – suggests that her framework cannot deal with difference. In addition, while it is sensitive to family roles and obligations, it remains within an individualist idiom.

3   However some of the ideas have reappeared in work that offers a pluralist participatory vision of society (Phillips 1991, for instance). Here the ideal is to create a pluralist and differentiated society in which women and men have multiple political and other roles, including parenthood. Maternalist

thinking, which was often an underlying ideological current in relational feminism, is rejected in this view, which gives priority to the need to democratize the family as well as public life. There is an echo also of the concerns of relational feminism in the emerging literature on citizenship in postmodern societies. Although he does not specifically address gender differences, Donati (1995) touches on relevant dilemmas in his writings about the opposition between a universal concept of citizenship and growing plurality and social polarization.

4   Schmidt (1989) provides an excellent account of the institutional and political factors that make for policy rigidity in Germany. Read together with its sister paper for Britain (Dunleavy 1989), a convincing case is made that institutional and political factors go a considerable distance in explaining differences in the policy process in the two countries. See also Borchert (1995) for an outstanding study of how four conservative governments – in Canada, Germany, Great Britain and the USA – managed and packaged their welfare state retrenchment policies during the 1980s.

5   In a recent study of value systems across nine European countries, German women and men emerge as among the most conservative in relation to the family. For example, only 22 per cent support planned lone parenthood and 62 per cent of the German respondents – double the European average – believe that working mothers would fail to maintain an equally warm relationship with their children as women who stayed at home (Ashford and Timms 1992). These conservative values with regard to the family co-exist with relatively liberal values on some issues (34 per cent support complete sexual freedom and 30 per cent approve of abortion on demand).

6   Much has been written on the Thatcher years in Britain. See Jessop (1992) for a general overview and the collections by Loney et al. (1991), Cochrane and Clarke (1993) and Hills (1995) for changes in welfare state policies in general. Lister (1992) remains one of the best examinations of the effects of the changes on women.

7   This is a very significant change. For illness, accident and maternity transfers, eligibility through social insurance contributions has been replaced by a combination of earnings thresholds and stipulations about the nature of the employment contract. Only unemployment and old-age pensions retain a link with the insurance contribution record. But all insurance programs retain the link with labour market participation.

8   See Crompton and Mann (1986) for an excellent collection of responses and counter-responses from a range of conventional and feminist scholars.

9   In that, following Weber, women and men are differentially evaluated or socially estimated. Women's lower status or men's higher status is sustained by men's monopolisation of 'ideal goods and opportunities', of which material monopolies are the most effective means of closure or exclusion, and such monopolization is guaranteed by conventional legal or religious sanctions. See Lockwood (1986).

10 Apart from theoretical considerations, conventional approaches should not be spared criticism for the empirical paths they have followed in seeking to validate the empirical existence and nature of class. Their general failure to deal with the unit of analysis issue, either by accepting the family or household as the unit or by studying individuals stripped of their household context, is especially problematic for its (in)capacity to

countenance satisfactorily the position of women. Accepting the family as the most appropriate unit in practice means a derived status for all except the household head/main breadwinner. Not only is equality within the collective unit assumed but the contribution that other family members make to a household's class or status position is largely disregarded. In the case of women it is assumed, as Stanworth (1984) points out, that they are 'declassed' upon marriage. In effect, since married women are assigned a conjugal class whereas everyone else gets an occupational class, such women are integrated into the analysis by abandoning the rules governing the concept of social stratification (Delphy 1981).

Appendix I

1   For households headed by Germans or those not of the five other nation-alities prioritized as 'foreign' households, a random selection method with a proportional household probability was used to draw 584 sample loca-tions. To select sample location households, a 'Random-Route Procedure' was then used. Each interviewer, using a starting address and following fixed rules, selected every seventh household. To sample the households classified as 'foreign', the first step taken was to identify representative geographical locations for each sample using the central register. Then a random selection process with proportional probabilities was again used. Through address records provided by the authorities, the respondent households were chosen either randomly or on the basis of every seventh address. Response rates for the population in question, that is Sample A of Wave C of 1986, were 87.5 per cent for households and 79.1 per cent for individuals.

2   The response rates are, therefore, also affected by attrition. Between waves 2 and 3 the rate of attrition for the existing household and individual samples (that is, not counting new entrants to the Panel) was 4.3 per cent. See also Wagner et al. (1991).

References

Acker, J. 1989, 'The problem with patriarchy', *Sociology* 23(2): 235–40.

Adams, J. 1998, 'Feminist theory as fifth columnist or discursive vanguard? Some contested uses of gender analysis in historical sociology', *Social Politics* 5(1): 1–16.

Alber, J. 1986, 'Germany' in Flora *Growth to Limits* vol. 2, pp. 1–154.

Alber, J. 1988, 'Continuities and changes in the idea of the welfare state', *Politics and Society* 16(4): 451–68.

Alber, J. 1989, *Der Sozialstaat in der Bundesrepublik 1950–1983*, Frankfurt a.M.: Campus.

Anderson, C. D. 1996, 'Understanding the inequality problematic: From scholarly rhetoric to theoretical reconstruction', *Gender and Society* 10(6): 729–46.

Anttonen, A., and Sipila, J. 1996, 'European social care services: Is it possible to identify models?', *Journal of European Social Policy* 5(2): 87–100.

Arber, S., and Ginn, J. 1991, *Gender and Later Life. A Sociological Analysis of Resources and Constraints*, London: Sage.

Ashford, D. 1986, *The Emergence of the Welfare States*, Oxford: Blackwell.

Ashford, S., and Timms, N. 1992, *What Europe Thinks: A study of Western European values*, Aldershot, Hants: Dartmouth.

Bahle, T. 1995, *Familienpolitik in Westeuropa*, Frankfurt a.M.: Campus.

Baldwin, P. 1990, *The Politics of Social Solidarity: Class bases of the European welfare states 1875–1975*, Cambridge: Cambridge University Press.

Baldwin, S. 1994, 'The need for care in later life: Social protection for older people and family caregivers', in Baldwin and Falkingham, pp. 180–97.

Baldwin, S., and Falkingham, J. (eds) 1994, *Social Security and Social Change: New challenges to the Beveridge model*, Hemel Hempstead, Herts: Harvester Wheatsheaf.

Becht, M. 1995, Tenure Choice, Housing Demand and Residential Mobility in Germany. Thesis submitted with a view to obtaining the Degree of Doctor of the European University Institute, Florence, May.

Benería, L., and Roldán, M. 1987, *The Crossroads of Class and Gender*, Chicago: University of Chicago Press.

Bock, G., and Thane, P. (eds) 1991, *Maternity and Gender Policies: Women and the rise of the European welfare states, 1880s–1950s*, London: Routledge.

255

Borchert, J. 1995, *Die konservative Transformation des Wohlfahrtsstaates*, Frankfurt a.M.: Campus.

Bradley, H. 1989, *Men's Work, Women's Work: A sociological history of the sexual division of labour in employment*, Cambridge: Polity Press.

Bradshaw, J. 1993, 'Developments in social security policy', in C. Jones (ed.), *New Perspectives on the Welfare State in Europe*, London: Routledge, pp. 43–63.

Bradshaw, J. et al. 1993, *Support for Children: A comparison of arrangements in fifteen countries*, London: HMSO, Department of Social Security, Research Report No. 21.

Buhmann, B. et al. 1988, 'Equivalence scales, well-being, inequality and poverty', *Review of Income and Wealth* 34 (June): 115–42.

Buhr, P. 1995, *Dynamik von Armut: Dauer und biographische Bedeutung von Sozialhilfebezug*, Opladen: Westdeutscher Verlag.

Bundesministerium für Familie und Senioren 1993, *Zwölf Wege der Familienpolitik in der europäischen Gemeinschaft*, Schriftenreihe Band 22.1, Stuttgart: Kohlhammer.

Bussemaker, J., and van Kersbergen, K. 1994, 'Gender and welfare states: Some theoretical reflections', in Sainsbury, *Gendering Welfare States*, pp. 8–24.

Cameron, D. 1978, 'The expansion of the public economy', *American Political Science Review* 72: 1243–60.

Cantillon, B. 1994, 'Family, work and social security', in Baldwin and Falkingham, *Social Security and Social Change*, pp. 45–61.

Casper, L. et al. 1994, *The Gender Poverty Gap: What can we learn from other countries?* Luxembourg: Luxembourg Income Study, Working Paper No. 112.

Cass, B., and Whiteford, P. 1989, 'Income support, the labour market and the household', in D. Ironmonger (ed.), *Households Work: Productive activities, women and income in the household economy*, Sydney: Allen & Unwin, pp. 140–69.

Castles, F. G. 1978, *The Social Democratic Image of Society. A Study of the Achievements and Origins of Scandinavian Social Democracy in Comparative Perspective*, London: Routledge & Kegan Paul.

Castles, F. G. (ed.) 1982, *The Impact of Parties*, Beverly Hills, Calif.: Sage.

Castles, F. G. (ed.) 1989, *The Comparative History of Public Policy*, Cambridge: Polity Press.

Castles, F. G., and Mitchell, D. 1990, *Three Worlds of Welfare Capitalism or Four?* Canberra: Australian National University Public Policy Programme, Discussion Paper No. 21.

Clarke, J., and Langan, M. 1993, 'Restructuring welfare: The British welfare regime in the 1980s', in Cochrane and Clarke, *Comparing Welfare States*, pp. 49–76.

Cochrane, A., and Clarke, J. (eds) 1993, *Comparing Welfare States: Britain in International Context*, London: Open University/Sage.

Connell, R. W. 1987, *Gender and Power: Society, the person and sexual politics*, Stanford: Stanford University Press.

Cook, J., and Watt, S. 1992, 'Racism, women and poverty', in C. Glendinning and J. Millar (eds), *Women and Poverty in Britain The 1990s*, Hemel Hempstead, Herts: Harvester Wheatsheaf, pp. 11–23.

Crompton, R. 1993, *Class and Stratification: An introduction to current debates*, Cambridge: Polity Press.

Crompton, R., and Mann, M. (eds) 1986, *Gender and Stratification*, Cambridge: Polity Press.

Curtis, R. F. 1986, 'Household and family in theory on inequality', *American Sociological Review* 51 (April): 168–83.

Dahlerup, D. 1987, 'Confusing concepts – confusing reality: A theoretical discussion of the patriarchal state', in Showstack Sassoon, *Women and the State*, pp. 93–127.

Dahrendorf, R. 1979, *Life Chances Approaches to Social and Political Theory*, London: Weidenfeld & Nicolson.

Daly, M. 1994, 'Comparing welfare states: Towards a gender friendly approach', in Sainsbury, *Gendering Welfare States*, pp. 101–17.

Daly, M. 1996, *Social Security, Gender and Equality in the European Union*, Brussels: Commission of the European Communities.

Daly, M. 1997, 'Welfare states under pressure: Cash benefits in European welfare states over the last ten years', *Journal of European Social Policy* 7 (2): 129–46.

Daly, M. 1999, 'The functioning family: Catholicism and social policy in Germany and Ireland', *Comparative Social Research* 18: 105–33.

Daly, M., and Lewis, J. 1998, 'Conceptualising social care in the context of welfare state restructuring', in J. Lewis (ed.), *Gender, Social Care and Welfare State Restructuring in Europe*, Aldershot, Hants: Ashgate, pp. 1–24.

Davies, H., and Joshi, H. 1990, *The Foregone Earnings of Europe's Mothers*, London: Birkbeck College, Discussion Paper in Economics 24/90.

Davies, H., and Joshi, H. 1992, *Sex, Sharing and the Distribution of Income*, London: Birkbeck College, Discussion Paper in Economics, 9/92.

Davis Hill, D., and Tigges, L. M. 1995, 'Gendering welfare state theory: A cross-national study of women's public pension quality', *Gender and Society* 9 (1): 99–119.

Delphy, C. 1981, 'Women in stratification studies', in H. Roberts (ed.), *Doing Feminist Research*, London: Routledge & Kegan Paul, pp. 114–28.

Delphy, C. 1984, *Close to Home: A materialist analysis of women's oppression*, London: Hutchinson.

Delphy, C., and Leonard, D. 1992, *Familiar Exploitation: A new analysis of marriage in contemporary western societies*, Cambridge: Polity Press.

Department of Employment 1987, *Family Expenditure Survey 1986*, London: HMSO.

Department of Employment 1989, *Family Expenditure Survey 1986*, [SN: 2556] Colchester, Essex: The Data Archive [distributor], 13 January 1989.

Dey, I. 1996, *The Poverty of Feminisation*, Edinburgh: Department of Social Policy, University of Edinburgh, New Waverley Papers, Social Policy Series No. 10.

DHSS 1986, *Social Security Statistics 1986*, London: HMSO.

DHSS 1989, *Social Security Statistics 1988*, London: HMSO.

Donati, P. 1995, 'Identity and solidarity in the complex of citizenship: the relational approach', *Innovation* 8 (2): 155–73.

Döring, D., and Hauser, R., (eds) 1990, *Sozial Sicherheit in Gefahr*, Frankfurt a.M.: Suhrkamp.

Döring, D., et al., (eds) 1990, *Armut im Wohlstand*, Frankfurt a.M.: Suhrkamp.

Douglas, G. 1990, 'Family law under the Thatcher government', *Journal of Law and Society* 17 (4): 411–26.

DSS 1990, *Households Below Average Income: A statistical analysis 1981–87*, London: Government Statistical Service.

DSS 1998, *New Ambitions for our Country: a New Contract for Welfare*, London: Stationery Office.

Duncan, S. S. 1994, 'Theorising differences in patriarchy', *Environment and Planning A* 26(8): 1177–94.

Duncan, S. S. 1995, 'Theorising European gender systems', *Journal of European Social Policy* 5(4): 263–84.

Dunleavy, P. 1989, 'The United Kingdom Paradoxes of an ungrounded statism', in Castles, *The Comparative History of Public Policy*, pp. 242–91.

Esping-Andersen, G. 1985, *Politics against Markets: The social democratic road to power*, Princeton: Princeton University Press.

Esping-Andersen, G. 1990, *The Three Worlds of Welfare Capitalism*, Cambridge: Polity Press.

Esping-Andersen, G. 1994, 'Welfare states and the economy', in N. J. Smelser, and R. Swedberg, (eds), *The Handbook of Economic Sociology*, Princeton: Princeton University Press, pp. 711–32.

Falkingham, J. and Hills, J. 1995, 'Redistribution between people or across the life cycle?', in J. Falkingham and J. Hills (eds), *The Dynamic of Welfare: The welfare state and the life cycle*, London: Harvester Wheatsheaf, pp. 137–49.

Family Policy Studies Centre 1994, *Families in the European Union*, London: Family Policy Studies Centre.

Ferge, Z., and Kolberg, J. E. (eds), 1992 *Social Policy in a Changing Europe*, Frankfurt a.M./Boulder: Campus Verlag/Westview Press.

Flora, P., (ed.) 1986, *Growth to Limits: The Western European Welfare States since World War II*, 4 vols, Berlin: De Gruyter.

Flora, P., and Alber, J. 1981, 'Modernization, democratization, and the development of welfare states in Western Europe', in Flora and Heidenheimer, *The Development of Welfare States*, pp. 37–80.

Flora, P., and Heidenheimer, A. (eds) 1981, *The Development of Welfare States in Europe and America*, New Brunswick and London: Transaction Books.

Foster, J., Greer, J., and Thorbecke, E. 1984, 'A class of decomposable poverty measures', *Econometrica* 52(3): 761–66.

Fraser, N. 1989, *Unruly Practices: Power, discourse and gender in contemporary social theory*, Cambridge: Polity Press.

Fraser, N. 1997, 'After the family wage: A postindustrial thought experiment', in B. Hobson, and A. M. Berggren, (eds), *Crossing Borders: Gender and citizenship in transition*, Stockholm: Swedish Council for Planning and Coordination of Research, pp. 21–55.

Fraser, N., and Gordon, L. 1994, 'Dependency demystified: Inscriptions of power in a keyword of the welfare state', *Social Politics* 1(1): 4–31.

Freeman, R., and Clasen, J. 1994, 'The German social state: An introduction', in J. Clasen and R. Freeman (eds), *Social Policy in Germany*, Hemel Hempstead, Herts: Harvester Wheatsheaf, pp. 1–17.

Furniss, N., and Tilton, T. 1977, *The Case for the Welfare State: From social security to social equality*, Bloomington, Ind.: Indiana University Press.

Gauthier, A. H. 1991, *Family Policies in Comparative Perspective*, Oxford: Centre for European Studies, Nuffield College, Discussion Paper No. 5.

Gerlach, I. 1996, *Familie und staatliches Handeln*, Opladen: Leske und Budrich.

Giddens, A. 1984, *The Constitution of Society: Outline of the theory of structuration*, Cambridge: Polity Press.

Ginsburg, N. 1979, *Class, Capital and Social Policy*, London: Macmillan.

Ginsburg, N. 1992, *Divisions of Welfare: A critical introduction to comparative social policy*, London: Sage.

Glendinning, C. 1992, '"Community care": The financial consequences for women', in Glendinning and Millar, *Women and Poverty in Britain*, pp. 162–75.

Glendinning, C., and McLaughlin, E. 1993, *Paying for Care – Lessons from Europe*, London: HMSO.

Glendinning, C., and Millar, J. (eds) 1987, *Women and Poverty in Britain*, Brighton: Wheatsheaf.

Glendinning, C. and Millar, J. (eds) 1992, *Women and Poverty in Britain The 1990s*, Hemel Hempstead, Herts: Harvester Wheatsheaf.

Gordon, L. 1988, 'What does welfare regulate?', *Social Research* 55(4): 609–30.

Gordon, L. 1990a, 'The welfare state: Towards a socialist-feminist perspective', *Socialist Register* 27: 171–200.

Gordon, L. (ed.) 1990b, *Women, the State, and Welfare*, Madison: University of Wisconsin Press.

Gough, I. 1979, *The Political Economy of the Welfare State*, London: Macmillan.

Graham, H. 1991, 'The concept of caring in feminist research: The case of domestic service', *Sociology* 25(1): 61–78.

Graham, H. 1993, 'Social divisions in caring', *Women's Studies International Forum* 16(5): 461–70.

Hantrais, L., and Mangan, S. (eds) 1994, *Family Policy and the Welfare of Women*, Loughborough: Cross-National Research Group, European Research Centre, Cross-National Research Papers, Third Series.

Hartmann, H. 1979, 'The unhappy marriage of marxism and feminism: Towards a more progressive union', *Capital and Class* Summer: 1–33.

Hauser, R. 1995, 'Das empirische Bild der Armut in der Bundesrepublik Deutschland – ein Überblick', *Aus Politik und Zeitgeschichte* B31-32: 3–13.

Heclo, H. 1974, *Modern Social Politics in Britain and Sweden: From relief to income maintenance*, New Haven: Yale University Press.

Hills, J. 1995, *The State of Welfare: The welfare state in Britain since 1974*, Oxford: Clarendon Press.

Hirdman, Y. 1994, *Women – from Possibility to Problem? Gender Conflict in the Welfare State – the Swedish Model*, Stockholm: the Swedish Center for Working Life, Research Report Series 3.

Hirschman, O. 1970, *Exit, Voice and Loyalty: Responses to decline in firms*, Cambridge: Cambridge University Press.

Hobson, B. 1990, 'No exit, no voice: Women's economic dependency and the welfare state', *Acta Sociologica* 33(3): 235–50.

Hobson, B. 1994, 'Solo mothers, social policy regimes and the logics of gender', in Sainsbury, *Gendering Welfare States*, pp. 170–87.

Holtmaat, R. 1992, *Met Zorg een Recht?*, Amsterdam: W.E.J Tjeenk Willink-Zwolle.

Jallade, J. P (ed.) 1988, *The Crisis of Distribution in European Welfare States*, London: Trentham Books.

Jallade, J. P. 1992, 'Is the crisis behind us? Issues facing social security systems in Western Europe', in Ferge and Kolberg, *Social Policy in a Changing Europe*, pp. 37–56.

Jenkins, S. P. 1990, *Poverty Measurement and the Within-household Distribution: Agenda for action*, Frankfurt: Sonderforschungsbereich 3, J.W. Goethe-Universität Frankfurt und Universität Mannheim, Working Paper No. 331.

Jenson, J. 1997, 'Who cares? Gender and welfare regimes', *Social Politics* 4(2): 182–87.

Jessop, B. 1992, 'From social democracy to Thatcherism: Twenty-five years of British politics', in N. Abercrombie, and A. Warde, (eds), *Social Change in Contemporary Britain*, Cambridge: Polity Press, pp. 14–39.

Johnson, P., and Webb, S. 1990, *Poverty in Official Statistics: Two Reports*, London: Institute of Fiscal Studies, Commentary No. 24.

Johnson, P., and Webb, S. 1991, *UK Poverty Statistics: A comparative study*, London: Institute of Fiscal Studies.

Jones, C. 1985, 'Types of welfare capitalism', *Government and Opposition* 20(3): 328–42.

Jones, K. B., and Jónasdóttir, A. G., (eds) 1988, *The Political Interests of Gender: Developing theory and research with a feminist face*, London: Sage.

Kakwani, N. 1986, *Analyzing Redistribution Policies: A study using Australian data*, Cambridge: Cambridge University Press.

Kamerman, S. B., and Kahn, A. J. 1978, *Family Policy: Government and families in fourteen countries*, New York: Columbia University Press.

Kamerman, S. B., and Kahn, A. J. 1981, *Child Care, Family Benefits and Working Parents*, New York: Columbia University Press.

Kaufmann, F. X. 1990, *Zukunft der Familie: Stabilität, Stabilitätsrisiken und politischen Bedingungen*, Beck: München.

Kerr, C., et al. 1973, *Industrialism and Industrial Man. The Problems of Labour and Management in Economic Growth*, 2nd edn, Harmondsworth: Penguin.

Knijn, T., and Kremer, M. 1997, 'Gender and the caring dimension of welfare states: Towards inclusive citizenship', *Social Politics* 4(3): 328–61.

Kolberg, J. E. 1991, 'The gender dimension of the welfare state', *International Journal of Sociology* 21(2): 119–48.

Kolberg, J. E., and Uusitalo, H. 1992, 'The interface between the economy and the welfare state: A sociological account', in Ferge and Kolberg, *Social Policy in a Changing Europe*, pp. 77–93.

Korpi, W. 1980, 'Social policy and distributional conflict in the capitalist democracies. A preliminary comparative framework', *West European Politics* 3(3): 296–316.

Korpi, W. 1985, 'Power resources approach vs action and conflict: On causal and intentional explanations in the study of power', *Sociological Theory* 3: 31–45.

Korpi, W. 1989, 'Power politics, and state autonomy in the development of social citizenship: Social rights during sickness in eighteen OECD countries since 1930', *American Sociological Review* 54(3): 309–28.

Korpi, W., and Palme, J. 1998, *The Paradox of Redistribution and Strategies of Equality: Welfare State Institutions, Inequality and Poverty in the Western Countries*, Luxembourg: Luxembourg Income Study, Working Paper No. 174.

Koven, S., and Michel, S. 1990, 'Womanly duties: Maternalist policies and the origins of welfare states in France, Germany, Britain, and the United States, 1880–1920', *American Historical Review* 95(4): 1076–108.

Krause, P. 1992, 'Einkommensarmut in der Bundesrepublik Deutschland', *Aus Politik und Zeitgeschichte* B49/92, 28(November): 3–18.

Kulawik, T. 1994, 'Wie solidarisch ist der sozialdemokratische Universalismus? Wohlfahrtsstaatstheorie und soziale Staatsbürgerschaft in Schweden', in E. Biester et al. (eds), *Das unsichtbare Geschlecht der Europa: der europäische Einigungsprozes aus feministischer Sicht*, Frankfurt a.M: Campus, pp. 62–84

Kulawik, T., and Sauer, S., (eds) 1996, *Der halbierte Staat Grundlagen feministischer Politikwissenschaft*, Frankfurt a.M.: Campus.

Kvist, J., and Torfing, J. 1996, *Changing Welfare State Models*, Copenhagen: Centre for Welfare State Research, Working Paper 5.

Land, H. 1978, 'Who cares for the family?', *Journal of Social Policy* 7(3): 257–84.

Land, H. 1989, 'The construction of dependency', in M. Bulmer, J. Lewis and D. Piachaud (eds), *The Goals of Social Policy*, London: Unwin Hyman, pp. 141–59.

Land, H. 1993, 'The 'public' and the 'domestic' – changing boundaries or changing meanings?', paper presented at conference 'Comparative Research on Welfare States in Transition', Oxford, 9–12 September.

Lee, P., and Raban, C. 1988, *Welfare Theory and Social Policy*, London: Sage.

Leibfried, S. 1990, 'Income transfers and poverty in EC perspective: On Europe's slipping into Anglo-American welfare models', paper presented at EC seminar 'Poverty, Marginalisation and Social Exclusion in the Europe of the '90s', Alghero, Italy, 23–25 April.

Leibfried, S., et al. 1995, *Zeit der Armut Lebensläufe im Sozialstaat*, Frankfurt a.M.: Suhrkamp.

Leira, A. 1992, *Welfare States and Working Mothers*, Cambridge: Cambridge University Press.

Leisering, L., and Walker, R., (eds) 1998, *The Dynamics of Modern Society Poverty, policy and welfare*, Bristol: Policy Press.

Lenhardt, G., and Offe, C. 1984, 'Social policy and the theory of the state', in Offe, *Contradictions of the Welfare State*, pp. 88–117.

Lewis, J. 1991, 'Models of equality for women: The case of state support for children in twentieth century Britain', in Bock and Thane, *Maternity and Gender Policies*, pp. 73–92.

Lewis, J. 1992, 'Gender and the development of welfare regimes', *Journal of European Social Policy* 2(3): 159–73.

Lewis, J. 1994, 'Gender, the family and women's agency in the building of 'welfare states': The British case', *Social History* 19(1): 37–55.

Lewis, J., and Ostner, I. 1991, 'Gender and the evolution of European social policies', paper presented at workshop on 'Emergent Supranational Social Policy: The EC's Social Dimension in Comparative Perspective', Center for European Studies, Harvard University, 15–17 November.

Lister, R. 1990, 'Women, economic dependency and citizenship', *Journal of Social Policy* 19(4): 445–67.

Lister, R. 1992, *Women's Economic Dependency and Social Security*, Manchester: Equal Opportunities Commission, Research Discussion Series No. 2.

Lister, R. 1994, '"She has other duties" – Women, citizenship and social security', in Baldwin and Falkingham, *Social Security and Social Change*, pp. 31–44.

Lister, R. 1997a, 'Dilemmas in engendering citizenship', in B. Hobson, and A. M. Berggren, (eds), *Crossing Borders: Gender and citizenship in transition*, Stockholm: Swedish Council for Planning and Coordination of Research, pp. 57–114.

Lister, R. 1997b, *Citizenship Feminist Perspectives*, Basingstoke, Hants: Macmillan.

Lockwood, D. 1986, 'Class, status and gender', in Crompton and Mann, *Gender and Stratification*, pp. 11–22.

Loney, M., et al., (eds) 1991, *The State or the Market: Politics and welfare in contemporary Britain*, London: Sage.

March, J., and Olsen, J. P. 1984, 'The new institutionalism: Organisational factors in political life', *American Political Science Review* 78: 734–48.

Marklund, S. 1990, 'Structures of modern poverty', *Acta Sociologica* 33(2): 125–40.

Marsh, C., and Arber, S., (eds) 1992, *Families and Households: Divisions and change*, Basingstoke, Hants: Macmillan.

Marshall, T. H. 1964, *Class, Citizenship and Social Development*, Chicago and London: University of Chicago Press.

McIntosh, M. 1978, 'The state and the oppression of women', in A. Kuhn and R. M. Wolpe (eds), *Feminism and Materialism*, London: Routledge & Kegan Paul, pp. 254–89.

McLaughlin, E., and Glendinning, C. 1994, 'Paying for care in Europe: Is there a feminist approach?', in Hantrais and Mangan, *Family Policy and the Welfare of Women*, pp. 52–69.

Mink, G. 1990, 'The lady and the tramp: Gender, race and the origins of the American welfare state', in Gordon, *Women, the State, and Welfare*, pp. 92–122.

Mishra, R. 1993, 'Typologies of the welfare state and comparative analysis: The "Liberal" welfare state', paper presented at conference 'Comparative Research on Welfare States in Transition', Oxford, 9–12 September.

Mitchell, D. 1991, *Income Transfers in Ten Welfare States*, Aldershot, Hants: Avebury.

Moeller, R. G. 1993, *Protecting Motherhood Women and Family in the Politics of Postwar West Germany*, Berkeley: University of California Press.

Morris, L. 1990, *The Workings of the Household. A US–UK Comparison*, Cambridge: Polity Press.

Mósesdóttir, L. 1995, 'The state and the egalitarian, ecclesiastical and liberal regimes of gender relations', *British Journal of Sociology* 46(4): 623–42.

Moss, P. 1990, 'Childcare in the European Communities 1985–1990', Supplement No. 31, *Women of Europe*, Brussels: Commission of the European Communities.

Myles, J. 1989, *Old Age in the Welfare State: The political economy of public pensions*, rev. edn, Lawrence, Kansas: Kansas University Press.

Myles, J. 1990, 'States, labour markets and life cycles', in R. Friedland and A. F. Robertson (eds), *Beyond the Marketplace: Rethinking economy and society*, New York: de Gruyter, pp. 271–98.

Nullmeier, F., and Rüb, F. 1993, *Die Transformation der Sozialpolitik vom Sozialstaat zum Sicherungsstaat*, Frankfurt a.M.: Campus.

O'Connor, J. 1973, *The Fiscal Crisis of the State*, New York: St Martin's Press.

O'Connor, J. S. 1992, 'Citizenship, class, gender and the labour market: Issues of de-commodification and personal autonomy', paper presented at conference 'Comparative Studies of Welfare State Development: Quantitative and Qualitative Dimensions', University of Bremen, 3–6 September.

O'Connor, J. S. 1996, 'From women in the welfare state to gendering welfare state regimes', *Current Sociology* 44(2): 1–125.

OECD 1988, *The Tax/Benefit Position of Production Workers 1984–1987*, Paris: OECD.

Offe, C. 1984, *Contradictions of the Welfare State*, London: Hutchinson Education.

Offe, C. 1985, *Disorganised Capitalism*, Cambridge: Polity Press.

Offen, K. 1992, 'Defining feminism: A comparative historical approach', in G. Bock and S. James (eds), *Beyond Equality and Difference Citizenship, feminist politics and female subjectivity*, London: Routledge, pp. 69–88.

Ogus, A. I., et al. 1988, *The Law of Social Security*, 3rd edn, London: Butterworths.

O'Higgins, M. 1988, 'Inequality, social policy and income distribution in the United Kingdom', in Jallade, *The Crisis of Distribution in European Welfare States*, pp. 27–72.

O'Higgins, M., and Jenkins, S. 1989, 'Poverty in Europe: Estimates for 1975, 1980 and 1985', paper presented at EUROSTAT Conference at Noordwijk, the Netherlands.

O'Higgins, M., et al. 1990, 'Income distribution and redistribution: A microdata analysis for seven countries', in Smeeding, et al., *Poverty, Inequality and Income Distribution*, pp. 20–56.

Orloff, A. 1993, 'Gender and the social rights of citizenship: The comparative analysis of gender relations and welfare states', *American Sociological Review* 58(3): 303–28.

Orloff, A. 1994, 'Restructuring welfare: Gender, work, and inequality in Australia, Canada, the United Kingdom and the United States', paper presented at conference 'Crossing Borders', Stockholm, 27–29 May.

Orloff, A., and Skocpol, T. 1984, 'Why not equal protection? Explaining the politics of public social spending in Britain 1900–1911, and the United States, 1880s–1920', *American Sociological Review* 49(6): 726–50.

Oppenheim, C. 1993, *Poverty: The Facts*, London: Child Poverty Action Group.

Ostendorf, H. 1997, '"Liberalisierung" der sozialen Sicherung und steuerliche "Edukation" der Ehefrau – Wie zusammenpaßt, was nicht zusammengehört', *Zeitschrift für Sozialreform* 43(5): 365–96.

Ostner, I. 1994, 'The women and welfare debate', in Hantrais, and Mangan, *Family Policy and the Welfare of Women*, pp. 35–51.

Ostner, I. 1995, 'Sozialstaatsmodelle und die Situation der Frauen', in W. Fricke (ed.), *1995 Jahrbuch Arbeit und Technik Zukunft des Sozialstaats*, Bonn: Dietz, pp. 57–67.

Pampel, F. C., and Williamson, J. B. 1989, *Age, Class, Politics and the Welfare State*, Cambridge: Cambridge University Press.

Pateman, C. 1988, 'The patriarchal welfare state', in A. Gutman (ed.), *Democracy and the Welfare State*, Princeton: Princeton University Press, pp. 231–60.

Pedersen, S. 1990, 'Gender, welfare and citizenship in Britain during the Great War', *American Historical Review* 95(4): 983–1006.

Pedersen, S. 1993, *Family, Dependence and the Origins of the Welfare State Britain and France 1914–1945*, Cambridge: Cambridge University Press.

Pfaff, A. 1992, 'Feminisierung der Armut durch den Sozialstaat', in S. Leibfried and W. Voges (eds), *Armut im modernen Wohlfahrtsstaat Kölner Zeitschrift für Soziologie und Sozialpsychologie*, Sonderheft 32 Opladen: Westdeutscher Verlag, pp. 421–45.

Pfau-Effinger, B. 1996, 'Analyse internationaler Differenzen in der Erwerbsbeteiligung von Frauen', *Kölner Zeitschrift für Soziologie und Sozialpsychologie* 48(3): 462–92.

Phillips, A. 1991, *Engendering Democracy*, Cambridge: Polity Press.

Phipps, S. 1993, 'Measuring poverty among Canadian households: Sensitivity to choice of measure and scale', *Journal of Human Resources* 28(1): 162–84.

Pierson, C. 1991, *Beyond the Welfare State? The New Political Economy of Welfare*, Cambridge: Polity Press.

Pollert, A. 1996, 'Gender and class revisited; or, the poverty of "patriarchy"', *Sociology* 30(4): 639–59.

Quadagno, J. 1987, 'Theories of the welfare state', *Annual Review of Sociology* 13: 109–28.

Ragin, C. 1994, 'Comparative analysis of pension systems', in T. Janoski and A. Hicks (eds), *The Comparative Political Economy of the Welfare State*, Cambridge: Cambridge University Press, pp. 320–45.

Rainwater, L. 1988, *Inequalities in the Economic Well-being of Children and Adults in Ten Nations*, Luxembourg, Income Study Working Paper No. 19.

Rainwater, L., Rein, M., and Schwartz, J. 1986, *Income Packaging in the Welfare State: A Comparative Study of Family Income*, Oxford: Clarendon Press.

Rein, M. 1985, *Women in the Social Welfare Labour Market*, Berlin: Wissenschaftszentrum, Discussion Paper No. 85-18.

Rein, M., et al., (eds) 1987, *Stagnation and Renewal in Social Policy: The Rise and Fall of Policy Regimes*, Armonk, New York: M. E. Sharpe.

Rimlinger, G. 1971, *Welfare Policy and Industrialisation in Europe, America and Russia*, New York: Wiley.

Ringen, S. 1991, 'Do welfare states come in types?', in P. Saunders and D. Encel (eds), *Social Policy in Australia: Options for the 1990s*, Sydney: University of New South Wales Social Policy Research Centre Reports and Proceedings No. 96.

Ringen, S., and Uusitalo, H. 1992, 'Income distribution and redistribution in the Nordic welfare states', in J. E. Kolberg (ed.), *The Study of Welfare State Regimes*, Armonk, New York: M.E. Sharpe, pp. 69–91.

Ritakallio, V. M. 1994, *Finnish Poverty: A cross-national comparison*, Luxembourg, Luxembourg Income Study, Working Paper No. 119.

Rohwer, G. 1992, *RZOO: Efficient storage and retrieval of social science data*, Florence: European University Institute Working Paper in Political and Social Sciences, SPS 92/19.

Roll, J. 1991, *What is a Family? Benefit models and social realities*, London: Family Policy Studies Centre, Occasional Paper No. 13.

Roll, J. 1992, *Lone Parent Families in the European Community*, Brussels: Commission of the European Communities.

Rosenhaft, E. 1994, 'Social welfare in Germany – past and present', in J. Clasen and R. Freeman (eds), *Social Policy in Germany*, Hemel Hempstead, Herts: Harvester Wheatsheaf, pp. 21–41.

Ruspini, E. 1997, *Gender and the Dynamics of Poverty: The cases of (West) Germany and Great Britain*, Essex: ESRC Research Centre on Micro-social Change, Paper no. 97-24.

Sainsbury, D. 1991, 'Analysing welfare state variations: The merits and limitations of models based on the residual-institutional distinction', *Scandinavian Political Studies* 14(1): 1–30.

Sainsbury, D. 1993, 'Dual welfare and sex segregation of access to social benefits: Income maintenance policies in the UK, the US, the Netherlands and Sweden', *Journal of Social Policy* 22(1): 69–98.

Sainsbury, D. 1994a, 'Women's and men's social rights: Gendering dimensions of welfare states?', in Sainsbury, *Gendering Welfare States*, pp. 150–69.

Sainsbury, D. 1994b, *Gendering Welfare States*, London: Sage.

Sainsbury, D. 1996, *Gender, Equality and Welfare States*, Cambridge: Cambridge University Press.

Sapiro, V. 1986, 'The gender basis of American social policy', *Political Science Quarterly* 101(2): 221–38.

Schäfer, C. 1995, 'Soziale Polarisierung bei Einkommen und Vermögen – zur Entwicklung der Verteilung 1994', *WSI Mitteilungen* 48(10): 605–33.

Scheiwe, K. 1994, 'Labour market, welfare state and family institutions: The links to mothers' poverty risks', *Journal of European Social Policy* 4(3): 201–24.

Scheiwe, K. 1995, 'Family obligations in Germany', in J. Millar and A. Warman (eds), *Defining Family Obligations in Europe*, University of Bath: Bath Social Policy Papers No. 23, pp. 107–28.

Schmidt, M. G. 1982, *Wohlfahrtsstaatliche Politik unter bürgerlichen und sozialdemokratischen Regierungen: Ein internationaler Vergleich*, Frankfurt a.M.: Campus.

Schmidt, M. G. 1989, 'Learning from catastrophes West Germany's public policy', in Castles, *The Comparative History of Public Policy*, pp. 56–99.

Shalev, M. 1983, 'The social democratic model and beyond: Two "generations" of comparative research on the welfare state', *Comparative Social Research* 6: 315–51.

Shanahan, S. E., and Tuma, N. B. 1994, 'The sociology of distribution and redistribution', in N.J. Smelser and R. Swedberg, *The Handbook of Economic Sociology*, Princeton: Princeton University Press, pp. 733–65.

Shaver, S. 1990, *Gender, Social Policy Regimes and the Welfare State*, Sydney: Social Policy Research Centre, University of New South Wales, Discussion Paper No. 26.

Shaver, S. 1991, 'Gender, class and the welfare state: The case of income security in Australia', in M. Adler et al., (eds), *The Sociology of Social Security*, Edinburgh: Edinburgh University Press, pp. 145–63.

Shaver, S., and Bradshaw, J. 1993, *The Recognition of Wifely Labour by Welfare States*, Sydney: Social Policy Research Centre, University of New South Wales, Discussion Paper No. 44.

Showstack Sassoon, A., (ed.) 1987, *Women and the State: The shifting boundaries of public and private*, London: Hutchinson.

Siaroff, A. 1994, 'Work, welfare and gender equality: A new typology', in Sainsbury, *Gendering Welfare States*, pp. 82–100.

Siltanen, J. 1986, 'Domestic responsibilities and the structuring of employment', in Crompton and Mann, *Gender and Stratification*, pp. 97–118.

Skocpol, T. 1980, 'Political response to capitalist crisis: Neo-Marxist theories of the state and the case of the New Deal', *Politics and Society* 10(2): 155–201.

Skocpol, T. 1992, *Protecting Soldiers and Mothers: The Political Origins of Social Policy in the United States*, Cambridge Mass.: The Belknap Press of Harvard University Press.

Skocpol, T., and Ritter, G. 1991, 'Gender and the origins of modern social policies in Britain and the United States', *Studies in American Political Development* 5(1): 36–93.

Skrede, K. 1993, 'Family policy and the costs of reproduction: Distributional strategies and conflicting priorities', paper presented at conference 'Comparative Research on Welfare States in Transition', Oxford, 9–12 September.

Smart, C. 1991, 'Securing the family? Rhetoric and policy in the field of social security', in Loney et al., *The State or the Market*, pp. 153–68.

Smeeding, T. et al. 1990, 'Income poverty in seven countries: Initial estimates from the LIS database', in T. Smeeding et al., (eds), *Poverty, Inequality and Income Distribution in Comparative Perspective: The Luxembourg Income Study*, Hemel Hempstead, Herts: Harvester Wheatsheaf, pp. 57–76.

Smeeding, T. et al. 1992, *Noncash Income, Living Standards and Inequality: Evidence from the Luxembourg Income Study*, Luxembourg: LIS Working Paper No. 79.

Sørensen, A. 1992, 'Zur geschlechtsspezifischen Struktur von Armut', in Leibfried, S.. and Voges, W.. (eds), *Armut im modernen Wohlfahrtsstaat, Kölner Zeitschrift für Soziologie und Sozialpsychologie*, Sonderheft 32: 345–66.

Sørensen, A. 1994, 'Women's economic risk and the economic position of single mothers', *European Sociological Review* 10(2): 173–88.

Sørensen, A., and McLanahan, S. 1987, 'Married women's economic dependency, 1940–1980', *American Journal of Sociology* 93(3): 659–87.

Sørensen, A., and McLanahan, S. 1989, 'Women's economic dependency and men's support obligations: Economic relations within households', paper presented at Colloquium 'Gender and Class', University of Antwerp, 18–20 September.

Stanworth, M. 1984, 'Women and class analysis: A reply to John Goldthorpe', *Sociology* 18(2): 159–70.

Statistisches Bundesamt, *Statistisches Jahrbuch für die Bundesrepublik Deutschland*, 1988, 1990 and 1991, Wiesbaden: Statistisches Bundesamt.

Stephens, J. 1979, *The Transition from Capitalism to Socialism*, London: Macmillan.

Sullivan, M. 1987, *Sociology and Social Welfare*, London: Allen & Unwin.

Taylor-Gooby, P. 1991, 'Welfare state regimes and welfare citizenship', *Journal of European Social Policy* 1(2): 93–105.

Thomas, C. 1993, 'De-constructing concepts of care', *Sociology* 27(4): 649–69.

Titmuss, R.M. 1974, *Social Policy An Introduction*, London: Unwin Hyman.

Tomasson, R. F., (ed.) 1983, *Comparative Social Research: The welfare state 1883–1983*, vol. 6, Greenwich, Connecticut: JAI Press.

Trifiletti, R. 1995 'The gendered "rationalization" of Italian social policies in the nineties', paper presented at the Second European Sociological Association Conference 'European Societies: Fusion or Fission', Budapest, Hungary, 30 August – 2 September.

Ungerson, C. (ed.), 1990, *Gender and Caring: Work and Welfare in Britain and Scandinavia*, Hemel Hempstead, Herts: Harvester Wheatshseaf.

Ungerson, C. 1997, 'Social politics and the commodification of care', *Social Politics* 4(3): 362–82.

Uusitalo, H. 1985, 'Redistribution and equality in the welfare state: An effort to interpret the major findings of research on the redistributive effects of the welfare state', *European Sociological Review* 1(2): 163–76.

van den Bosch, K. 1998, 'The evolution of financial poverty in western Europe', in M. Rhodes, and Y. Meny, (eds), *The Future of European Welfare: A new social contract?*, Basingstoke, Hants: Macmillan, pp. 97–124.

van Kersbergen, K. 1990, 'The welfare state: A (re) evaluation of the literature', paper presented at seminar 'State and Economy – Structural changes in contemporary capitalism', European University Institute, Florence, October.

van Kersbergen, K. 1991, Social Capitalism. A Study of Christian Democracy and the Post-War Settlement of the Welfare State, thesis submitted with a view to obtaining the Degree of Doctor of the European University Institute, Florence, December.

Vermeulen, H. et al. 1995, *Tax Systems and Married Women's Labour Force Participation: A seven country comparison*, Essex: ESRC Research Centre on Micro-social Change, Paper No. 95–8.

Voges, W., and Ostner, I. 1995, 'Wie arm sind alleinerziehende Frauen?', in K. J. Bieback and H. Milz (eds), *Neue Armut*, Frankfurt a. M.: Campus, pp. 122–47.

Vogler, C. 1989, *Labour Market Change and Patterns of Financial Allocation within Households*, Nuffield College Oxford: ESRC/SCELI Working Paper No. 12.

Wagner, G., et al. 1991, *The Socio-Economic Panel (SOEP) for Germany: Methods of Production and Management of Longitudinal Data*, Berlin: Deutsches Institut für Wirtschaftsforschung, Discussion Paper No. 31a.

Walby, S. 1986, *Patriarchy at Work*, Oxford: Polity Press.

Walby, S. 1990, *Theorising Patriarchy*, Oxford: Basil Blackwell.

Wilensky, H. 1975, *The Welfare State and Equality: Structural and ideological roots of public expenditure*, Berkeley, Calif.: University of California Press.

Wilensky, H., and Lebaux, C. L. 1965, *Industrial Society and Social Welfare*, New York: Free Press.

Williams, F. 1989, *Social Policy: A critical introduction*, Oxford: Polity Press.

Wilson, E. 1977, *Women and the Welfare State*, London: Tavistock.

Wright, R. 1992, *Gender, Poverty and Intra-household Distribution of Resources*, Luxembourg: Luxembourg Income Study, Working Paper No. 83.

Wright, R. 1993, *Women and Poverty in Industrialised Countries*, Luxembourg: Luxembourg Income Study, Working Paper No. 96.

Zaretsky, E. 1982, 'The place of the family in the origin of the welfare state', in B. Thorne, and M. Yalom (eds), *Rethinking the Family*, New York: Longman, pp. 188–224.

Index

Acker, Joan 6, 32, 249 n.1
Alber, Jens 21, 22, 26, 47, 74
Australia, welfare state type 49, 53–4, 61, 244 n.5
Autonomy *see* Dependence/independence

Baldwin, Peter 25, 26
Bases of entitlement *see* Cash transfers, access to
Benefits *see* Cash transfers; Social assistance; Social insurance
Benería, Lourdes 7
Beveridgean welfare state 1–2, 11, 76, 77, 225
Bismarckian welfare state 1–2, 11, 75; *see also* German welfare state
Borchert, Jens 253 n.4
Bradshaw, Jonathan 59, 80, 91, 223
Breadwinner model *see* Male breadwinner model
British welfare state
  characteristics of 10–12, 75–7, 78, 93–7, 168, 187, 211, 217–8, 223–4
  historical overview 75–8
  and family and caring policies 78–86
  pressures on 219–24
  reform of 1–2, 77, 224–7; *see also* New Deal
  type of 10–11, 49, 53, 54, 61;
    see also Liberal welfare state; Beveridgean welfare state

Canada, welfare state type 49, 54, 61, 253 n.4
Cantillon, Bea 222, 224

Care
  defined 68, 231–2
  theoretical scholarship on 38–9, 58, 60, 246 n.7
  policies towards 78–86, 87, 220–1, 226, 246 n.6
  process of and welfare state 64, 67–8, 85, 231–2
Cash transfers
  access to 66–7, 99–100, 102–9, 116–20
  conditions of entitlement 66–7, 88–90
  different types of claim to 109–11, 120–3
  for caring for the ill and elderly 82–6
  for families with children 78–82, 84–86, 78–82, 100–1, 103;
    see also British welfare state and familiy and caring policies; German welfare state and family and caring policies
  and income redistribution 139–47, 213–4
  levels of 111–16, 120–3, 161, 221
  and the reduction of poverty 164–71, 175–80, 181–3, 214–15, 250 n.4
Castles, Francis G. 25, 53, 54, 60, 61
Catholicism and German welfare state 77, 84–5, 187, 246 n.7
Child support, estimates of 189–93, 201–2
Christian democracy and welfare state 244 n.5; *see also* Continental European welfare state
Citizenship 40–3, 61, 245 n.10; *see also* Social rights